Central Notions of Smithian Liberalism

The chapters derive mostly from substantial articles previously published in scholarly journals, though revised. Chapters expound Smith's tri-layered justice, liberty, jural dualism, Humean conventionalist political theory, and Smithian liberalism. A chapter written with Erik Matson, "Convention without Convening," explains natural convention, transcending "nature" and "convention" and attesting to the place of Hume and Smith in natural law traditions and enlarging our understanding of those traditions. Another chapter asks and answers, "Is It Just to Pursue Honest Income?" Another exposits the conservative liberalism of Hume, Smith, and Burke. Another identifies four sets of nonconflicting rules, namely (1) government law, (2) commutative justice, (3) ethics writ large, and (4) just government law. Other chapters relate Smithian liberalism to: Iain McGilchrist's concept of the divided brain; being grateful *for* without being grateful *to*; and the Export-Import Bank. The final chapter considers the fortunes of liberalism in relation to prevailing attitudes toward allegory and God.

About the author:

Daniel Klein is professor of economics and JIN Chair at the Mercatus Center at George Mason University, where, with Erik Matson and Don Boudreaux, he leads a program in Adam Smith. He is also research fellow at the Ratio Institute (Stockholm) and chief editor of *Econ Journal Watch*. With Matson, he is also codirector of CL Press and the Adam Smith Works/Liberty Fund monthly feature Just Sentiments.

Eight Testimonials for Dan Klein scholarship on Adam Smith

Richard Whatmore, Professor and Chair of Modern History, University of St. Andrews, editor of *History of European Ideas*, and Co-direct of St. Andrews Institute of Intellectual History:

> "In 2023 Adam Smith will be 300 years old. There will be a very large number of ill-informed books about him being published in this special year. Smith—now that we are recovering the actual historical Smith—still has a great deal to say to us. Dan Klein knows this, understands Smith as well as any scholar and has a gift for communicating (understatement). Everything he publishes is accessible and significant. It is also worth saying that his public presence is remarkable and remarkably wide-ranging. He reaches audiences fellow academics simply cannot reach."

Deirdre Nansen McCloskey, Distinguished Professor Emerita of Economics and of History, and Professor Emerita of English and of Communication, adjunct in classics and philosophy, at the University of Illinois at Chicago:

> "Klein is the rare economist who listens to what others say. In this he follows Smith, and with these volumes emerges as the sage's leading listener. He writes beautifully and with purpose, to bring us away from the Smith of left or right coercion and towards the Smith of what he calls "spiral," a vein of the Scottish enlightenment, and still therapeutic for our own troubled times."

Knud Haakonssen, Long-term Fellow at the Max Weber Centre for Advanced Cultural and Social Studies, University of Erfurt, Professor of Intellectual History, University of St. Andrews and Co-direct of St. Andrews Institute of Intellectual History, and General Editor of the Liberty Fund book series Natural Law and Enlightenment Classics.

> "Dan Klein's collection of papers represents an imposing body of work on Smith as an historical figure and as thinker of lasting relevance. The papers have an impressive range, which is

what Smith's many-sided work requires. At the same time, there is a keen engagement with the scholarly and critical literature. Klein's writing is clear and direct. It is a pleasure to recommend the collection."

Vernon Smith, Nobel laureate in Economics and Professor, Smith Institute for Political Economy and Philosophy, Chapman University:

"Three centuries after his birth, Adam Smith was never more relevant and inspiring. Dan Klein's essays convey that inspiration in an accessible style reinforcing the relevance of this greatest of 18th century scholars."

Thomas W. Merrill, Associate Professor, Department of Government, American University, Director of Special Programs at the Political Theory Institute, American University:

"Dan Klein has long been constructing a portrait of Adam Smith in his complexity—moving back and forth in a deepening spiral between Smith's policy recommendations, his rich phenomenology of ethical life, and even his reflections on our place in the cosmos. With this collection we can now see the richness of Klein's reading of Smith in synoptic view, both in the specificity of its parts and in the vision that animates the whole. Klein is a spirited and skilled advocate for liberalism in its original political sense. He sheds light on the presumption of liberty, the structure of justice, the spiraling complexity of ethical life, the subtlety of Smith's rhetoric, and Smith's religion. This work will be helpful to readers just coming to know Smith for the first time, and it certainly deserves the attention of scholars of Smith and of the history of liberalism. It enriches our sense of Smith even as we argue with it. It is an achievement worth celebrating."

Douglas Den Uyl, Vice President of Educational Programs, Liberty Fund:

> "Dan Klein is one of the most distinctive and thorough interpreters of Adam Smith working today. His insights into Smith are both instructive and compelling. It is of immense value to have many of these insights collected together, especially because so many of them are accessible to the scholar and general intelligent reader alike."

Peter Minowitz, Professor of Political Science, Santa Clara University and author of *Profits, Priests, and Princes: Adam Smith's Emancipation of Economics from Politics and Religion*:

> "An economist with abiding interests in public policy, Klein has developed an acute appreciation of how carefully Adam Smith wrote—and of how comprehensively he thought. Klein manifests a rare combination of virtues, and they are especially valuable in our world, which struggles to balance economic and non-economic goods. The precision and efficiency of Klein's prose, furthermore, provide a fitting tribute to Smith. More importantly, they should inspire—and even equip—us to counteract the literary degradations associated with tweeting and partisan hyperbole."

James Otteson, Professor of Business Ethics, University of Notre Dame, and author of *Adam Smith's Marketplace of Life* (Cambridge, 2002), *Actual Ethics* (Cambridge, 2006), *Adam Smith* (Bloomsbury, 2013), *The End of Socialism* (Cambridge, 2014), *Honorable Business: A Framework for Business in a Just and Humane Society* (Oxford, 2019):

> "Adam Smith is one of the most widely cited and least read great figures in the West. He is often pressed into the service of contemporary authors' ends without sufficient regard for the breadth, depth, subtlety, and sophistication of his work. Daniel Klein's essays provide an important corrective. Klein combines

close reading of Smith with a critical yet charitable eye, helping us understand both the details in Smith's work and its larger aims, and, in the process, showing why Smith deserves a place in the pantheon of great philosophers. Those new to Smith may be astonished at the range and penetration of Smith's insights revealed by Klein's essays. Even Smith scholars will find much that is new, enlightening, and challenging. This collection provides a rich resource for philosophers, economists, historians, and anyone else interested in one of the great observers of human behavior."

Central Notions of Smithian Liberalism

Daniel B. Klein

CL Press

Published by CL PRESS
A project of the Fraser Institute
1770 Burrard Street, 4th Floor
Vancouver, BC V6J 3G7 Canada
www.clpress.net

Central Notions of Smithian Liberalism
Daniel B. Klein

© 2023 by CL Press

Corrected August 2023

ISBN: 978-1-957698-03-8

Cover design by John Stephens
Interior layout by Joanna Andreasson

Contents

Preface

This book is one of three by me published during Smith's tercentenary (God willing).

1. *Central Notions of Smithian Liberalism*: The present book treats Adam Smith and the liberalism he shared with David Hume and Edmund Burke. It explores notions jural, political, and economic, though other things as well. It uses Smith and others in developing classical liberalism.

2. *Contemplating with Adam Smith* treats notions central to Smith's allego-theistic moral approach—the dialectics of virtue, propriety, beneficialness, sentiment, sympathy, and "impartial spectator." In its chapters, classical liberalism plays a less conspicuous role.

    Poor Richard (Franklin 1914, 13) said, "An empty bag cannot stand upright."

    This book, *Central Notions of Smithian Liberalism*, treats things that make Smithian thought stand upright. It treats things *inside the bag*.

    Contemplating with Adam Smith is more about the bag itself. There is the bag's fabric—it matters whether the bag is of silk, burlap, suede, or toughened leather, or some combination. And there is the design of the bag itself, which will affect the ordering it lends to things inside of it. Montaigne said that "ill-matched objects, put in a bag without order, find of themselves a way to unite and fall into place, often better than they could have been arranged by art" (1960, 730). But it depends on the bag—not all bags are alike. *Contemplating with Adam Smith* delves into allegory, organonic formulations, nonfoundationalism, and Smith's esotericism.

2

Its motif is "spiral"—the emblem of nonfoundationalism.

3. *Smithian Morals*: Whereas *Central Notions of Smithian Liberalism* and *Contemplating with Adam Smith* contain substantial pieces deriving from scholarly articles, *Smithian Morals* contains shorter pieces, deriving from essays in media such as Liberty Fund's Adam Smith Works. Many of its 28 chapters are suitable for beginners.

Contemplating is the most contemplative, *Smithian Morals* the least. The present book is in-between. Chapter abstracts appear before Chapter 1.

Acknowledgments

I thank coauthors on four of the chapters, Erik Matson, Mark Bonica, and Jonathon Diesel. I thank Iain McGilchrist for his support with Chapter 13 including the Foreword reproduced here with that chapter. I am very grateful to Jane Shaw Stroup who copy-edited the final manuscript and Jon Murphy for proof-reading. I thank Jacob Hall for helping to put this book together. I thank Joanna Andreasson for layout and typesetting the interior, and John Stephens for designing the cover.

Of the 14 chapters here, 12 derive from a piece in a scholarly journal or edited volume:

1. Chapter 1 derives from: "Commutative, Distributive, and Estimative Justice in Adam Smith," *Adam Smith Review* 12, 2021: 82-102. The publisher of *Adam Smith Review* is Routledge.

2. Chapter 2, "The Presumption of Liberty in Adam Smith," is not based on something previously published.

3. Chapter 3 derives from: "Mere-Liberty in David Hume," with Erik W. Matson. *A Companion to David Hume.* Edited by Moris Polanco, Universidad Francisco Marroquin, 2020: 125–160.

4. Chapter 4 derives from: "Convention without Convening," with Erik W. Matson, *Constitutional Political Economy* 33(1), 2022: 1–24. The publisher of *Constitutional Political Economy* is Springer Nature.

5. Chapter 5 derives from: "Conservative Liberalism: Hume, Smith, and Burke as Policy Liberals and Polity Conservatives," *Journal of Economic Behavior and Organization* 183,

2021: 861–873. The publisher of *Journal of Economic Behavior and Organization* is Elsevier.

6. Chapter 6 derives from: "Adam Smith on Reputation, Commutative Justice, and Defamation Laws," with Mark J. Bonica, *Journal of Economic Behavior and Organization* 184, 2021: 788–803. The publisher of *Journal of Economic Behavior and Organization* is Elsevier.

7. Chapter 7 derives from: "Instilling Duties above Instilling Rights: Two Features of Adam Smith's Talk of Justice and Liberty," *The Independent Review*, forthcoming. The publisher of *The Independent Review* is The Independent Institute.

8. Chapter 8 derives from: "A Call to Embrace Jural Dualism," with Jonathon Diesel, *Economic Affairs* 41, 2021: 442–457. The publisher of *Economic Affairs* is Wiley.

9. Chapter 9, "Four Sets of Nonconflicting Rules," is not based on something previously published.

10. Chapter 10 derives from: "Is It Just to Pursue Honest Income?" *Economic Affairs* 39, 2019: 400–409. The publisher of *Economic Affairs* is Wiley.

11. Chapter 11 derives from: "Gratefulness, Resentfulness, and Some Modern Slogans," *Economic Affairs 42, 2022: 135–143*. The publisher of *Economic Affairs* is Wiley.

12. Chapter 12 derives from: "Of Its Own Accord: Adam Smith on the Export-Import Bank," *Econ Journal Watch* 12(3), 2015: 379–387.

13. Chapter 13 derives from: "Think Spiral: The Divided Brain and Classical Liberalism," *Society* 57, 2020: 614–26. The publisher of *Society* is Springer Nature.

14. Chapter 14 derives from: "Liberalism and Allegory: A Tragedy," *Laissez-Faire* No. 48–49, September 2018: 58–67. The publisher of Laissez-Faire is Universidad Francisco Marroquin.

I am grateful to the editors, referees, journals, and publishers listed above for their assistance in the development of these ideas by coauthors and myself. Many of the articles from which chapters here derive contain acknowledgments to individuals who aided with that article, and, without naming them here, I once again thank them.

Citing Works by Adam Smith and David Hume

Adam Smith's works:

TMS 263.5 means page 263, paragraph 5 of *The Theory of Moral Sentiments*. Citations to Smith's works are to the Glasgow Edition, published by Oxford University Press and republished by Liberty Fund. The abbreviations are as follows:

TMS—*The Theory of Moral Sentiments*
WN—*The Wealth of Nations*
EPS—*Essays on Philosophical Subjects*
LJ—*Lectures on Jurisprudence*
LRBL—*Lectures on Rhetoric and Belles Lettres*
Corr.—*The Correspondence of Adam Smith*

David Hume's works:

T—*A Treatise of Human Nature* (Hume 2007a [1739–1740]), followed by book, part, section, and paragraph number.
DP—*A Dissertation on the Passions* (Hume 2007b [1757]), followed by chapter and paragraph.
EHU—*An Enquiry Concerning Human Understanding* (Hume 2000 [1748]), followed by section, part, and paragraph number.
EPM—*An Enquiry Concerning the Principles of Morals* (Hume 1998 [1751]), followed by section, part, and paragraph number. Sections without parts in EHU and EPM are referred to by section and paragraph.
EMPL—*Essays, Moral, Political, and Literary* (Hume 1994), followed by page number.
H—*The History of England* (Hume 1983), followed by volume (in roman numerals) and page number.

Chapter Abstracts

Chapter 1: Commutative, Distributive, and Estimative Justice in Adam Smith

In Smith there is something of a contrariety, or double doctrine, on justice: much of Smith's writing leaves us with the impression that we should use *justice* and its cognates to mean commutative justice, and only that. But much also authorizes the conclusion that we should embrace and talk of three different senses of justice. I exposit the three senses of justice, but leave aside Smith's intentions in leaving such diverging signs. In *The Theory of Moral Sentiments*, he distinguishes and describes commutative justice, distributive justice, and a third justice, a name for which he does not give but is here called *estimative*. Smith showed that commutative justice is very special, yet he affirmed and abundantly practiced justice talk beyond commutative justice. According to my tri-layered interpretation, estimative justice looms large in matters determined by the jural "superior," that is, the governor. I believe that Smith denominates such matters not in terms of distributive justice, but rather in terms of estimative justice (as well as commutative justice).

Chapter 2: The Presumption of Liberty in Adam Smith

This chapter gathers many of the quotations showing Smith's propounding of the presumption of liberty and identifying several Smith scholars who affirm such reading of Smith. Exceptions do not destroy the liberty principle's principlehood. Exceptions should be regarded as exceptional; they should provoke careful scrutiny and reflection.

Chapter 3: Mere-Liberty in David Hume
Coauthor: Erik W. Matson

Erik Matson and I ask: What does Hume mean by liberty? Though it is clearly important to him, Hume never clarifies the matter explicitly. In his texts, liberty often seems to be a matter of government rules being certain, general, regular, etc., and often a matter of political form or constitution—the place of parliament or republicanism, checks to power, and so on. Many scholars have highlighted such elements in Hume's idea of liberty. We argue more fundamentally that liberty in Hume bears a central meaning: liberty is a flipside of (commutative) justice. The injunction or precept of (commutative) justice is to not mess with other people's stuff. The flipside is: *others not messing with one's stuff.* And it is especially in relation to government (as opposed to, say, a robber) that that flipside concept is what Hume often signifies with the word *liberty.* Because *liberty* is polysemous in Hume's writings, we call that meaning "mere-liberty." Hume sees the achievement of a high degree of mere-liberty as dependent on authority, which itself depends on contraventions of mere-liberty. We advance mere-liberty not against the other meanings, but with them, with mere-liberty central to Hume's political outlook.

Chapter 4: Convention without Convening
Coauthor: Erik W. Matson

David K. Lewis published his brilliant PhD dissertation in 1969, *Convention; A Philosophical Study.* With a lag, scholarship on David Hume has come to elaborate the similitude between Lewis and Hume on convention. Reading Hume along the lines of Lewis gives us a vocabulary with which we can better appreciate and articulate the innovativeness of Hume's theory of convention. This chapter, coauthored with Erik Matson, contributes to that appreciation and rearticulates Hume's innovative analytical

framework for thinking about the unformalized duties and obligations—sometimes glossed as *institutions* or *culture*—underlying
social interaction and economic behavior. After summarizing
Lewis, we treat Hume's account of the emergence of the conventions of language, justice, and political authority in broadly Lewisian terms. Another purpose is to draw on Hume to develop a
concept of "natural convention." A natural convention is a social
practice whose concrete form in time and place is conventional in a Lewisian sense, but whose generalized form is necessary,
and hence natural, for more advanced social organization. In the
final section of the paper, we consider the semantic originality
of Hume's convention talk. Drawing from a large-scale textual
search, we find scant evidence that the English word "convention" was used in a Lewisian sense—that is, in a sense that did not
entail a literal convening—prior to Hume.

Chapter 5: Conservative Liberalism: Smith, Hume, and Burke as Policy Liberals and Polity Conservatives

On regular issues of policy reform—presupposing a stable integrated polity—Hume, Smith, and Burke were liberal in the original political meaning of "liberal." Thus, on *policy reform*, although
they accorded the status quo a certain presumption (as any reasonable person must), the more distinctive feature is that they
maintained (even propounded, most plainly in Smith's case) a
presumption of liberty in matters of policy reform. But we need
another conceptualization that treats their attitudes about establishing, reforming, and securing the wider structure of political
institutions, political procedure, and political culture and character—matters of *polity reformation*. On polity reformation, they
showed sensibilities for which "conservative" is apt (though such
conservatism was not otherwise purely neutral). Hume, Smith,
and Burke were basically in agreement on the matters treated
here. They are polity conservatives. The article develops the two

conceptualizations—policy reform and polity reformation—, an understanding of "liberal" applicable to policy reform, and an understanding of "conservative" (namely, a heavy presumption of the status quo) that may be applied to policy reform and to polity reformation. If we code the three thinkers as PLPC (policy liberals and polity conservatives), we may put the matter this way: It would be *wrong* to code them instead PCPC (policy conservatives and polity conservatives). I call their outlook conservative liberalism. Here I deal disproportionately with Burke, to tussle with two sets of imagined interlocutors, one on Burke as liberal, and the other on Burkean insight on polity reformation.

Chapter 6: Adam Smith on Reputation, Commutative Justice, and Defamation Laws
Coauthor: Mark J. Bonica

Mark Bonica and I interpret Adam Smith on reputation, commutative justice, and defamation laws. We address two major questions. The first question concerns whether Smith thought that "one's own" as covered by commutative justice included one's reputation. Several passages point to the affirmative. But reputation is left out of Smith's "most sacred laws" description of commutative justice. Most importantly, so much of reputation —e.g., "Steve's work stinks"—does not fit Smith's description of commutative justice's rules (precise and accurate). Our reading makes use of older terminology from Pufendorf, Carmichael, and Hutcheson distinguishing "simple" and "intensive" reputation. We suggest that the "reputation" that sometimes appears in Smith's characterizations of "one's own" is of a simple variety ("Steve steals horses") that potentially incites invasion of commutative justice's three staples—person, property, promises due. On that reading the "reputation" that comes under commutative justice, though not a staple, belongs to the penumbra around the three staples, just as incitement and endangerment belong to that penumbra. We also recruit Hume, who nowhere even hinted at reputation being a constituent of commutative justice.

The second question is: Did Smith favor defamation laws (libel, slander) that reached beyond simple reputation, so as to cover some intensive-reputation detraction? Were Smith to favor intensive-reputation defamation laws (against, say, "Steve's work stinks"), we would have to count that as another exception made to the liberty principle. Smith's remarks are mixed, but we think he was rather inclined against aggressive or extensive laws of such kind. (Also, we draw a parallel to patent and copyright.)

We also suggest that if Smith thought that wantonly telling malicious lies like "Steve's work stinks" was not in violation of commutative justice and, moreover, is best left perfectly legal, those are judgments that the liberal project's great prophet would hardly want to make plain, because indifferent readers would misunderstand them and adversaries would misrepresent them.

Chapter 7: Instilling Duties above Instilling Rights: Two Features of Adam Smith's Talk of Justice and Liberty

People are keener to assert rights than to fulfill duties, and more trouble can come from the asserting of supposed rights than fulfilling duties. Did those differences affect how Adam Smith talked "justice" and "liberty"? Yes, I argue. Smith's discourse shows two features that instill duties above rights. The first has to do with his manner of talking "justice"; I distinguish between calling loudly and proffering coolly. The other has to do with not using the word "liberty" for the loose or imperfect sort of rights. In modern, complex society, we must assume and promote duties which do not clearly correlate to distinct rights of other people. We have duties to truth, to importance, to right, to good, to God. The two features in Smith's discourse arise, I suggest, from the danger of neglecting such duties and of unleashing claims of "rights," "freedom," and "liberty." That danger stems in part from

knowledge problems, which grow more dire the further we get
from the primeval band.

Chapter 8: A Call to Embrace Jural Dualism
Coauthor: Jonathon Diesel

This chapter, coauthored with Jonathon Diesel, explores concepts under a rubric termed "jural," the meaning of which is
differentiated from "legal." Within the conceptualization of the
modern nation-state, there are two categories of jural relationships. In the first, both parties have equal jural standing (equal-
equal), as between neighbors. In the second jural relationship
(superior-inferior), one party has standing as a special jural player, essentially, the governor. The jural superior wields the coercive powers of government. Human beings, we argue, are pre-
disposed to folding this jural superior back into the equal-equal
relationship, thus notionally collapsing two relationships back
to one, or collapsing from jural dualism into jural monism. Two
varieties of the tendency stand out, namely, collectivist thinking
that sees government as a set of rules and arrangements arrived
at voluntarily, and Rothbardian libertarianism, which sees government as a criminal organization and proposes its elimination.
Those two varieties of the tendency are sometimes explicit, but
sometimes implicit, perhaps not thought-through. In this chapter, we call for a conscious embrace of jural dualism.

Chapter 9: Four Sets of Nonconflicting Rules

This chapter exposits four sets of nonconflicting rules: (1) The
actual current governmental law—in other words, legal rules or
"positive" law. (2) The grammar-like rules of commutative justice. (3) All laws (both precise and accurate, and loose, vague,
and indeterminate) that delineate the rightness of any decision,

made by anyone; ethics writ large. (4) The would-be laws of government conformant to the previous set; just government law, in the full sense of justice. The chapter might aid a resuscitation of natural jurisprudence as the study of rules and laws that duly recognizes commutative justice as one of the important sets of rules.

Chapter 10: Is It Just to Pursue Honest Income?

Is it just to pursue honest income? Certainly, it's commutatively just. But is it a becoming use of one's own? Is it distributively just? Presumptively, yes. The burden of proof should be on the one who denies that someone's pursuit of honest income is distributively just. Drawing closely on Adam Smith, I argue for that presumption. I treat focal points and price signals: If you think prices are imperfect signals for universal benevolence, just think how imperfect the *other* signals are! Virtues are swallowed up by self-interest as rivers are lost in the sea, said La Rochefoucauld. We come to the commercial humanism Smith constructed, including his *invisible* parable of the poor man's son, producing the Great Enrichment. Cameos are made by Humphrey Bogart and caveats to our maxim that it is presumptively just to pursue honest income.

Chapter 11: Gratefulness, Resentfulness, and Some Modern Slogans

Scholars distinguish between gratitude and gratefulness. Both sentiments involve an appreciation of the benefits that one enjoys. Gratitude, however, also involves a positive feeling directed to the benefactor. Gratefulness does not necessarily involve any benefactor, much less a feeling towards one ("I am grateful for the warm sunshine"). I suggest a parallel distinction between resentment and resentfulness. I suggest that in the primeval band resentfulness would be provoked by inequality and by non-inclusiveness and give rise to proper resentment. But we are not in the band anymore. Now, resentfulness is bad, and it should be deemed an atavism. Gratefulness is, rather, a virtue, and should be encouraged. This article suggests that the propagandistic power of the modern slogans of "inclusiveness" and "equity" is atavistic.

Chapter 12: Of Its Own Accord: Adam Smith on the Export-Import Bank

This chapter assembles quotations by Adam Smith regarding bounties—subsidies paid to producers for their productions, usually for export. The quotations presented here suggest, perhaps, what Adam Smith would say today about the Export-Import Bank of the United States. The export subsidies that Smith treated were bounties paid directly to exporters, whereas those of the Export-Import Bank principally take the form of subsidized credit. But the form does not much affect most of Smith's analysis of export subsidization.

Chapter 13: The Divided Brain and Classical Liberalism
Foreword: Iain McGilchrist

Iain McGilchrist richly explains the right and left hemispheres of the brain, how each functions and what each tends to do. This chapter serves, firstly, as a primer to McGilchrist's fascinating exposition. Second, it offers a formulation that uses a spiral to structure the iterative and layered relationship. Third, it presents McGilchrist's concerns about how modernity has enfeebled the right hemisphere, and how the left hemisphere is, at it were, running amok. Fourth, it considers some of McGilchrist's political overtones. Sharing McGilchrist's concerns, finally, I elaborate on why they might lead us to look to classical liberalism as the best way to avoid the traps of the left hemisphere, to invigorate the health of the right hemisphere, and to cope with modernity.

Chapter 14: Liberalism and Allegory

Adam Smith was allegorical, knowingly and profoundly, but after him things went downhill, or even dropped off a cliff. From science anxieties, many liberals spurned allegory, touting foundations, facts, science, etc. But we see in their discourse, notably on the economic system as cooperation, and later on the price system as communication, the poetry they pretended to have cast out. Liberals turned away from allegory, and the world turned away from liberalism. The present chapter explains some of the reasons why it is good to embrace allegory, and why it is good to be open about doing so.

CHAPTER 1
Commutative, Distributive, and Estimative Justice in Adam Smith

T his chapter interprets Adam Smith on justice. It treats the justices beyond commutative justice—namely, distributive justice and a third justice, a name for which he does not give but is here called *estimative*.

Consider two possible doctrines on the matter of how to talk "justice":

- Doctrine 1: We should not talk justice beyond commutative justice.

- Doctrine 2: We should embrace and talk all three senses of justice.

Smith's chief indication of Doctrine 1 in *The Theory of Moral Sentiments* (TMS) is how he discourses about commutative justice as "justice" *simpliciter*, withholding until Part VII the exposition of the three senses of justice (269–270.10).[1] If Smith *wanted to make obvious* a preference for Doctrine 2 over Doctrine 1, he would have much earlier clarified *and endorsed* the polysemy of *justice*, and introduced "commutative."

Scholars have suggested variously that (1) Smith confined his justice talk to commutative justice,[2] (2) he talked both commutative and distrib-

---

1. Other indications of doctrine 1 include Smith's unpublished words: "which can alone properly be called Justice" (Frag, TMS 390) and "not in a proper but a metaphoricall sense" (LJ 9).

2. Works that seem to explicitly portray Smith as confining justice to commutative justice include Cropsey 2001, 35, 126–127; Campbell 1971, 187–189; Winch 1978, 99, 174; Buchanan 1979, 121; Winch 1992, 110; Salter 1994, 301; Brown 1994, 113, 211; Young 2005, 98; Ross 2010, 117; Forman-Barzilai 2010, 227.

utive justice,[3] and (3) he recognized and embraced the three senses of justice (e.g., Minowitz 1993, 49–50; Griswold 1999, 232; see also Mitchell 1987, 417). I contend that Smith's works affirm talking all three senses of justice, even while providing plenty of sentences that would seem to support Doctrine 1, and while clearly emphasizing the special nature and the special importance of commutative justice. I show with copious citations that Smith abundantly practiced distributive and estimative justice talk. Here I confine myself to expositing the three justices in Smith and leave to future consideration why he would generate such a contrariety, that is, why he would leave us with a paradoxical presentation of seemingly contrary doctrines on justice.

I employ the following abbreviations:

CJ = commutative justice

DJ = distributive justice

EJ = estimative justice

Commutative justice: Not messing with other people's stuff

In TMS, commutative justice is one of those virtues you should practice. You practice it by "abstaining from what is another's" (269.10, 297.11). I prefer to formulate it as *not messing with other people's stuff.* The formulation[4] has within it factors specific to the moment in time and place, factors that play

---

3. Works that seem to portray Smith as recognizing and embracing commutative and distributive justice but give no notice to estimative justice include Young and Gordon 1996; Witztum 1997.

4. I see several advantages to "not messing with other people's stuff" over "abstaining from what is another's": (1) "stuff" affords us a term to correspond to the Latin *suum*; also, the colloquial quality of "stuff" allows us to include as stuff not only one's own person and property but promises due one by voluntary consent or contract; (2) it is useful to separate questions of "stuff" from "other people's" or questions of whose stuff it is; (3) it is useful to be able to remove the "not" so that we can focus on "messing with." Think how weak the flipside would otherwise sound: *Others abstaining from one's stuff.* One would thus be said to "abstain" from a restaurant even though one partakes of it!—provided that the partaking is voluntary. The vagueness of "abstain" misses the definite misdeed of "messing with." And again I think well of the colloquial quality, for notions of "messing with" bubble up not only from formal legal authorities but also, even primarily, from norms, practice, and experience of ordinary life and sentiment. The colloquial quality of "stuff" and "messing" is in the spirit of Lon Fuller's *The Morality of Law* (1969). In sum, the preferred formulation more neatly frames the three important historicistic questions about CJ: What counts as stuff? What makes the stuff one person's rather than another's (or no one's)? What counts as messing with it?

a role in delineating, in that moment, "stuff," "other people's," and "messing with." Whether the plot of land is property, whether it is Jim's, whether picking its flowers is stealing, whether certain terms are implicit in an agreement—all depend on factors specific to the moment. Here we have uniformity amidst variety—uniformity in the broad formulation, and variety in the specifics of "stuff," "other people's," and "messing with."

But the veins of variety, of historicity, matter within elements of the general formulation, and matter only within limits. For example, in all moments in time and place, a soul owns the person it animates and comes with; one's hand is one's hand. The soul of Frederick Douglass owned, even in slavery to 1838, the person it animated and came with; the fact of Douglass's slavery is the fact that other people messed with Douglass's stuff. CJ "is neither free from historicity nor reducible to it" (Griswold 2006, 185; see likewise Haakonssen 1981, 43–44).

The guts of CJ are most fully described in TMS as follows:

> The *most sacred laws* of justice, therefore, those whose violation
> seems to call loudest for vengeance and punishment, are the laws
> which guard the life and person of our neighbour; the next are
> those which guard his property and possessions; and last of all
> come those which guard what are called his personal rights, or
> what is due to him from the promises of others. (84.2, italics added)

The "most sacred laws" description does not include reputation (nor does 339.32), but elsewhere Smith does include reputation as something that is covered by CJ. Perhaps Smith's inclusions were less than whole-hearted. Besides the inconstancy, there is the more important point that, short of inciting arrest or assault by tarnishing another's "simple esteem" (Pufendorf 2009, 94), reputation does not fit what Smith says about CJ (Bonica 2013, and ch. 6 here). I downgrade the standing of reputation as part of CJ.

The "most sacred laws" description communicates the idea that the chief concern in CJ is the precept or injunction against initiating any messing with someone else's stuff. What CJ says about just response to messing (or just sanction) is secondary and is not treated in the present paper.

The equal-equal jural relationship (E-E) and the superior-inferior jural relationship (S-i)

The concept of CJ affords us the distinction between two kinds of jural relationships. The word *jural* is not familiar today. In *Black's Law Dictionary* (1983) the first definition is: "Pertaining to natural or positive right, or to the doctrines of rights and obligations," as in "jural relations."[5] In the present book, Chapter 8, Jonathon Diesel and I expound a more elaborate definition of jural rules (as opposed to non-jural rules), the gist of which is that jural rules aspire to be (or pretend to aspire to be) precise and accurate and that force is potentially involved in sanctions for violating the rule's precept. By "jural relationships," we mean uncloaked, publicly displayed, conventional relations in which the physical force (or threat thereof) is potentially exercised. As Diesel and I say in Chapter 8, "jural" subsumes both legal rules and CJ rules.

Following especially Hume,[6] Smith insisted on accepting two fundamental and distinct kinds of jural relationships:

1. The equal-equal jural relationship, which I denote as E-E.
2. The superior-inferior jural relationship, which I denote as S-i.

In expositing CJ, Smith signals E-E by saying "among equals" or "for equals" or "from equals" (notably at TMS 80–82.7–9). Here, "equals" means *jural equals*. Within E-E, all are equal as regards CJ. Each is expected to practice the virtue of not messing with others' stuff, and each expects it from fellow equals. The criminal acts of ordinary criminals also occur in

---

5. Although Hume and Smith do not use the term, William Whewell (1845, 1853) wrote significantly of "jural," as did Wesley N. Hohfeld in expositing jural relations in the *Yale Law Journal* (1913, 1917).

6. It was common in natural jurisprudence (e.g., Grotius and Pufendorf) to speak of government authority as a "superior" and to imply jural dualism (E-E and S-i) (Diesel 2020). What is special about Hume, however, is that, in developing a notion of convention *broader than* consent, he explicitly rejects the notion of jural superiority being based on a lineage of political consent or contract. In his view, allegiance to the established government (and to the principles of CJ) are matters of convention, not consent. Hume's conventionalist interpretation of the jural superior and political authority is discussed by Hardin (2007), Sabl (2012), and ch. 4 here.

E-E. In robbing or burglarizing, the ordinary criminal does not step outside of E-E. Acting within E-E, he simply fails in the duty of CJ.

Amid his exposition of CJ in the context of E-E, Smith pauses to turn out from E-E. He averts the reader from any misapprehension that what he says about conduct within E-E also goes for conduct within S-i. The paragraph begins: "A superior may, indeed, sometimes, with universal approbation, oblige those under his jurisdiction to behave...with a certain degree of propriety to one another" (81.8). Smith signifies the meaning of "a superior" by methodically varying terms throughout the paragraph, starting with "A superior" and then substituting in turn "The laws," "The civil magistrate," "the sovereign," and "a law-giver." Smith apprehends a special player, a jural superior, one who is special in regard to jural relationships, as opposed to someone who happens, within E-E, to be a merely comparative superior. Sir Isaac Newton was a comparative superior but not a jural superior (Diesel 2020).

A jural superior is a player whose actions may *overtly* traverse the lines of CJ, as well as affect the locations of those lines in the historical context. A superior faces limits on his behavior, of course, but the point here is that he is not bound by the rules of CJ in the same way that people in E-E are. Another way to put S-i would be the governor-governed relationship. The distinction between E-E and S-i allows us to formulate a principle that perhaps illuminates why the historicity inside of "stuff," "other people's," and "messing with" does not render CJ amorphous and thoroughly malleable: We understand our formulations such that the following holds: An action (taken by the jural superior) is a CJ violation in S-i if and only if such an action (taken by a jural equal) is a CJ violation in E-E.

The specialness of commutative justice

Smith speaks of "that remarkable distinction" between CJ and all the other virtues.[7] CJ's specialness may be enumerated in six points:

---

7. Smith speaks of "that remarkable distinction" at 80.5; he also points out CJ's specialness at 79.5, 175.10 (juxtapose the opening of that paragraph with the opening of 174.9), 175.11, 327.1, 329.7. Smith is less direct when it comes to the crucial role of CJ in many of the book's important ideas.

1. Unlike the rules of all the other virtues, the rules of CJ are "precise and accurate" (TMS 327.1).

Items (2) through (6) depend on (or are co-extensive with) the "precise and accurate" feature, and therefore are, also, among the virtues unique to CJ.

2. The "messing" actions it treats are most aptly seen as ones we *are not to do*; as a corollary, doing nothing (passiveness) is often sufficient to fulfill CJ (TMS 82.9).

3. Feedback on one's performance of CJ is only negative (or neutral); one does not receive positive feedback on fulfilling CJ (TMS 82.9, 330.8).

4. In E-E, an observance of the rules of CJ is "indispensable," in that otherwise society stagnates or degenerates (TMS 175.11, 86.4, 211.16).

5. In E-E, we feel a stricter obligation (and a higher presumption) to observe CJ than we do for other virtues; violations provoke resentment, and the duties associated with CJ's rules may even be forced (TMS 79-80.5, 175.10, 269.10).[8]

6. CJ is neatly invertible: Its precise and accurate duties designate precise and accurate claims or rights. You practice CJ by not messing with other people's stuff. The flipside is others not messing with your stuff. That flipside is by Smith usually signified by either of two names: in E-E, "security," and in S-i, "liberty" (sometimes "natural liberty").

The Justices table (Figure 1.1)

Smith's major paragraph on justice (TMS 269-270.10) I call *the Justices Paragraph*. In it Smith distinguishes and describes the three senses of justice. In all of its senses, justice pertains to an action, but the "action" may be

---

8. On points 2 and 3, see Weinstein 2001, 83–85; on points 1 through 5 see Forman-Barzilai 2010, 221–37.

non-muscular, such as an act of deciding to do something, and even quite notional or hypothetical, such as an act of maintaining a certain attitude or sentiment in regard to some object. An action implies an actor.

Next I introduce a figure that the reader will not find to be readily comprehensible. Much of the remainder of the present paper is devoted to explaining its scheme and different cells. The figure is Figure 1.1, which I call "The Justices Table."

Figure 1.1 has columns CJ, DJ, and EJ. But what it is that is categorized by, for example, the CJ column is *matters of* CJ. Using the word *jurisprudence* playfully, we may understand the columns as: commutative jurisprudence, distributive jurisprudence, and estimative jurisprudence. Indeed, the abbreviations CJ, DJ, and EJ are often best understood with those significations.

The rows correspond to different types of actors. The first row speaks of the ordinary, non-government person, an "equal," acting in E-E. The second row also speaks of an equal, and again acting in a sort of E-E, but a special sort, namely, as an employee, officer, or owner of a governmental organization, such as a school, a facility, a department, or an agency. The third row is an actor *qua* superior, the capital S in S-i. The fourth row represents the actor *qua* inferior, the little i in S-i. Such inferiority would seem to be primarily or even exclusively passive.

FIGURE 1.1: THE JUSTICES TABLE

JUSTICES CHARACTERIZED IN TERMS OF A PERSON'S OWN.			
The actor acts as...	Commutative Justice	"Beyond-CJ"	
		Distributive Justice	Estimative Justice
An Equal	(A1) Other's Own: **Grammar-like stuff** (However, Smith frequently included reputation.)	(B1) Actor's Own: **Social resources** available for distributing. Includes: grammar-like stuff; social capital; approbation; assistance; etc.	(C) Actor's Own: **Estimations** (esteem, valuations, regard, appreciation, etc.) of: 1. Objects *external* to his/her self 2. Objects *internal* to his/her self: one's own judgments, habits, sentiments, purposes, estimations, intentions, and interests. EJ recursivity: The estimation of an object can be treated as another object of estimation.
Government actor as a sort of Equal, **not** *qua* Superior	(A2) Other's Own: *Grammar-like stuff*	(B2) Actor's Own: *Social resources* (as above in B1)	
A Superior	(A3) Inferior's Own: *Grammar-like stuff*	(B3) Not applicable	
An inferior	(A4) Not applicable	(B4) Actor's Own: **Social resources** (as above in B1)	

Commutative justice among equals (cell A1)

In the Justices Paragraph, Smith writes: "The first sense of the word coincides with what Aristotle and the Schoolmen call commutative justice, and with what Grotius calls the *justitia expletrix*, which consists in abstaining from what is another's, and in doing voluntarily whatever we can with propriety be forced to do" (269.10). Of this sense of justice, Smith, in the same paragraph, says: "This is that justice which I have treated of above...," meaning especially in Part II, Section II, "Of Justice and Beneficence" (78–92).

Distributive justice among equals (cell B1)

In Smith's famous parable, the now-rich poor man's son trades and contracts for "his luxury and caprice." In paying for them, he inevitably renders benefits upon those who "would in vain have expected it from his humanity and his justice" (184.10). Benefits flow from CJ-abiding transactions, but could not have been expected from "his justice." That is, from his *distributive* justice (DJ).

Smith says that DJ consists "in the becoming use of what is our own" (270.10). In the Justices Paragraph, Smith writes that DJ

> consists in proper beneficence, in the becoming use of what is our own, and in the applying it to those purposes either of charity or generosity, to which it is most suitable, in our situation, that it should be applied. In this sense justice comprehends all the social virtues. (269-270.10)

The elaboration that Smith gives to the noun "use" helps to authorize us, when talking of DJ, to think of the use in question as a sort of *distributing*. We have "what is our own," that is, a set of resources, and, Smith says, we are to *apply it* to purposes that are most suitable, in our situation. Your conformance to DJ consists in how you *distribute* your resources.

As for "what is our own," as perceived through the lens of DJ, we step toward the loose, vague, and indeterminate, and toward the metaphorical. Whereas the "stuff" of CJ consists in the tangibles of property, person, and promises due, the stuff of our own of DJ includes that stuff, but also other resources, such as our energy, attention, assistance, approbation, love, privacy, influence, and so on, so long as we understand them to include a performative social element, a distributing of social resources. These things could be rendered in terms of "stuff" in the CJ sense of "stuff," since one's tongue and one's hands are used in rendering assistance, approbation, and so on. But it is more natural to allow approbation, etc. to be a species of "one's own" when talking DJ, rather than rephrasing them in terms of tongues and hands.

DJ, Smith says, "comprehends all the social virtues." DJ tends to view your act of distributing as an act that is social in that you are distributing resources to people (or their interests). It might be the case that you fall short in DJ when you fail to serve, assist, or applaud some praiseworthy person, or when you fail to shun, reprimand, or blame some blameworthy person. The personalization of the ones to whom DJ is done often becomes vague and indeterminate. But the tendency of DJ is to see DJ as something done to a person or persons (including, possibly, to the actor himself or herself).

Here is another passage, from the Justices Paragraph, describing DJ:

In another sense we are said not to do justice to our neighbour unless we conceive for him all that love, respect, and esteem, which his character, his situation, and his connexion with ourselves, render suitable and proper for us to feel, *and unless we act accordingly.* It is in this sense that we are said to do injustice to a man of merit who is connected with us, though we abstain from hurting him in every respect, if we do not *exert ourselves* to serve him and to place him in that situation in which the impartial spectator would be pleased to see him. (269.10, italics added)

I italicize "and unless we act accordingly" and "exert ourselves" to emphasize that DJ entails acting and is done to persons.

The justice that is due is due not upon any grammar-like rules, but upon the rules of what is pleasing to the impartial spectator. Such rules for what is due, or duties, are aesthetic: The rules for what is pleasing to the impartial spectator are like rules for what is beautiful. Fulfilling such duties is becoming. And the adjective *becoming* itself suggests personal development confirmed in the reaction of others, confirmed in sympathy. Becoming is a social affair. Figure 1.2 indicates 36 samples of Smith's "just" talk that may aptly be understood as distributive justice.

FIGURE 1.2: THIRTY-SIX SAMPLES OF SMITH'S "JUST" TALK THAT MAY APTLY BE UNDERSTOOD AS DISTRIBUTIVE JUSTICE

TMS: equitable justice 62.2; so unjust are mankind 98.2; no just pretensions 115.4; justly merited the blame 116.5; act of justice 117.8; injustice of unmerited censure 121.15; justest eulogy 123.19; has so unjustly been bestowed 131.32; the deformity of injustice 137.4; unjust preference 142.13; what is just and unjust in human conduct 160.11; with exact justness 162.1; magnanimity, generosity, and justice 167.9; justly complain 172.4; justly refuse to lend 174.9; just magnanimity 176.11; from his humanity or his justice 184.10; perfectly just and proper 228.2; is justly condemned 244.16; is justly blamed 246.21; what he thinks, justice 255.35; unjust superiority 257.41; injustice which he does to himself 261.52; injustice of popular clamour 283.29; That other species of justice 297.11; exposed to unjust censure 311.10; the general rules of justice 330.8; just reason 336.26; justly condemned him 339.30; do them justice 339.31.

WN: justly complained of 726.9.

EPS: justly renowned 62.14; justly indeed 70.25; justly exposed 77.35; just occasion of suspicion 247.7; just panegyric 254.16.

The parallel between writing rules and moral rules

Smith helps us understand the difference between the rules of commutative justice and the rules of other virtues by drawing a parallel between moral rules and rules for writing:

> The rules of [commutative] justice may be compared to the rules of grammar; the rules of the other virtues, to the rules which critics lay down for the attainment of what is sublime and elegant in composition. The one, are precise, accurate, and indispensable. The other, are loose, vague, and indeterminate, and present us rather with a general idea of the perfection we ought to aim at, than afford us any certain and infallible directions for acquiring it. A man may learn to write grammatically by rule, with the most absolute infallibility; and so, perhaps, he may be taught to act justly. But there are no rules whose observance will infallibly lead us to the attainment of elegance or sublimity in writing; though there are some which may help us, in some measure, to correct and ascertain the vague ideas which we might otherwise have entertained of those perfections. And there are no rules by the knowledge of which we can infallibly be taught to act upon all occasions with prudence, with just magnanimity, or proper beneficence: though there are some which may enable us to correct and ascertain, in several respects, the imperfect ideas which we might otherwise have entertained of those virtues. (175-76.11)

Figure 1.3 depicts the parallel. The parallel is reiterated by Smith at the start of the final section of TMS (327.1-2).

FIGURE 1.3: THE PARALLEL BETWEEN THE RULES OF WRITING AND THOSE OF MORALS

	NATURE OF THE RULES	
	"precise and accurate"	"loose, vague, and indeterminate"
Rules of Writing	Grammar	"rules which critics lay down for the attainment of what is sublime and elegant in composition"
Rules of Conduct (Morals)	Commutative justice (CJ)	All other virtues: Distributive justice (DJ) and Estimative justice (EJ)
Feedback on how well your performance accords with the rules	Only negative (or neutral)	Negative and positive

Suppose you are a student with an assignment to turn in. If you turn in a blank piece of paper, though it commits no grammatical errors, you get an F. You must show regard not merely for the rules of grammar but also other rules of good writing.

Likewise, in sitting still and doing nothing, you might fulfill CJ. But the rules of prudence, magnanimity, beneficence, friendship, and so on are not grammar-like, but organized around propriety. Propriety is the "fair to middling" or "just OK" region within your reference group; performance above propriety is praiseworthy (positive) and below, blameworthy (negative) (TMS 26.9, 80.6). Sitting still and doing nothing, you must eventually flunk prudence and the other non-grammar-like virtues, even if you satisfy CJ.

Estimative justice, in E-E, for objects external to the estimator

In the Justices Paragraph, after treating CJ and DJ, Smith continues on to a third sense of the word *justice*, a sense that he does not name, which I call estimative justice (EJ):[9]

---

9. I had been using "esteem justice" until Austin Middleton suggested "estimative justice" to me, which I subsequently adopted. I feel that running a very close second to "estimative" is "evaluative," a term that would in some respects be better, and in some respects worse.

There is yet another sense in which the word justice is sometimes taken, still more extensive than either of the former, though
very much a–kin to the last; and which runs too, so far as I know,
through all languages. It is in this last sense that we are said to be
unjust, when we do not seem to value any particular object with
that degree of esteem, or to pursue it with that degree of ardour
which to the impartial spectator it may appear to deserve or to
be naturally fitted for exciting. Thus we are said to do injustice
to a poem or a picture, when we do not admire them enough,
and we are said to do them more than justice when we admire
them too much. (270.10)

Notice, first, that EJ is said to be "very much a-kin to the last," that is, to
DJ. The kinship, I believe, is, at least in part, that EJ is like DJ in having rules
that are loose, vague, and indeterminate; in often finding expression in figurative language; in very often entailing difficult and complex knowledge
problems; and in being susceptible to both positive and negative feedback.

Smith says that EJ is "still more extensive" than CJ or DJ. But its extreme
extensibility does not render it totally amorphous. Estimative jurisprudence
has the following logic:

1. Jim, the estimator, estimates an object;
2. Mary estimates the justness of Jim's estimation.

Like commutative jurisprudence and distributive jurisprudence, estimative jurisprudence is still about a person, Jim, taking an action, if only in
a loose, figurative sense of "taking" and a broad sense of "action." The action
is that of *estimating* the object. Smith uses the EJ logic quite pervasively. One
indication of such pervasiveness is that the noun *object(s)* occurs 228 times
in the final 1790 edition of TMS. In the preceding block quotation, Smith
gives two examples of an object for estimation: "a poem or a picture." Smith
says that Jim "does injustice" to them when he values or pursues them too
little, and "more than justice" when he admires them too much. In either
case we may say he estimates them unjustly.

Estimative justice, in E-E, for objects internal to the estimator

In the Justices Paragraph, after "a poem or a picture," Smith turns to objects internal to our own self. He writes: "In the same manner we are said to do injustice to ourselves when we appear not to give sufficient attention to any particular object of self-interest" (270.10). An object of self-interest might be one of Jim's own actions, interpretations, judgments, beliefs, habits, sentiments, purposes, or intentions. Anything of which consciousness is conscious is an object: an object of consciousness. In LRBL, Smith speaks of such "[i]nternal objects as passions and affections" (75).

Jim estimates the forest. But the estimation may be turned into an object of estimation: Jim estimates Jim's estimation of the forest. And then, at yet another moment, there is the Jim who estimates Jim's estimation of Jim's estimation of the forest. Earlier in TMS Smith writes: "The second is the agent, the person whom I properly call *myself*, and of whose conduct, under the character of a spectator, I was endeavouring to form some opinion" (113.6). Of these Jims, Smith says: "But that the judge should, in every respect, be the same with the person judged of, is as impossible, as that the cause should, in every respect, be the same with the effect" (113.6). Think of the Jims corresponding to the loops of a spiral, with a distinct subscript on each Jim. Such iteration can also be applied to Smith's analogy of cause and effect: We can inquire after the cause of the cause of the effect. Some say both spirals lead to God.

Treating an idea as the object of estimation, and applying EJ to such estimation, resembles the pragmatist idea that to say an idea is "true" is to say that it is worth holding, believing, considering, or giving weight to. For any action, such as buying toothpaste, it is natural for us to look for the knowing that inheres in the action. We understand that people buy toothpaste because they know of its utility to them in fortifying teeth and freshening breath. But EJ invites us to turn the matter around, to look for the action that inheres in knowing. Knowing entails interpretations, but, moreover, *judgment* regarding many things. We roll up the manifold responsibilities of judgment into an assessment as to how responsibly one estimates some idea X (e.g., "this toothpaste fortifies teeth"), how responsibly one forms and keeps associated beliefs. Jim's believing X entails not only an estimation on Jim's part of idea X; it also points to another object for estimation: Jim's responsibility or scruple in believing X.

Tri-layered justice: EJ blankets DJ, which blankets CJ

It might be contended that Jim's esteem is a sort of resource, a part of Jim's "own," and that EJ consists in Jim's distributing his esteem to various objects. It might be said, then, that EJ, too, is "the becoming use of what is our own." In this view, DJ swallows up EJ. But I incline against such a view.

In the three places in which Smith explicitly writes of "distributive justice," it is associated with: "proper beneficence," "charity or generosity," "the social virtues" (269.10), "the social and beneficent Virtues" (Fragment on justice, TMS 390), giving praise that is due, and again giving charity (in examples in LJ, 9). It seems that the objects of DJ attach to a set of persons; DJ would not apply to a poem, a picture, or an idea abstracted from any particular set of persons.

Moreover, to say that we have a supply of esteem points to distribute to the objects of the world usually works poorly, even as loose metaphor. Such a metaphor would need some notion of the budget constraint on esteem points, as well as some sense of the relevant objects over which such points are to be distributed. But, for EJ, we are talking about all manner of objects, including ideas. But ideas are not merely large in number, they are innumerable. As interpretative creatures, we create ideas as we go, such that one idea soon gives rise to others.

Ideas and sentiments form concatenations, and a single tweak or addition might render the larger concatenation deserving of a much different estimation. The tweak or addition makes for a new and distinct concatenation. Whereas DJ has a sense of confronting a robust set of objects—people, particularly those "connected" to us—over which one is to distribute one's social resources, with EJ we do not have much sense of a complete set of objects.

EJ is a more elementary operator than DJ; the minimal elements of EJ do not of themselves make for an act of distributing of one set of things (resources) to another set of things (objects). The minimal nature of EJ makes the requirements of its operation weaker and hence makes EJ "still more extensive" than DJ. In discussing the authority of the general rules of morality, Smith says that moral faculties, though a set of sensibilities, "bestow censure and applause upon all the other principles of our nature... It belongs to our moral faculties, in the same manner to determine when the ear ought to be soothed, when the eye ought to be indulged, when the taste ought to be gratified, when and how far every other principle of our nature ought either to be indulged or restrained" (165.5).

If one justice swallows another, it is EJ that swallows up both DJ and CJ. EJ is like a whale that swallows up all objects presented to its view. But DJ and CJ do not disappear inside the whale of EJ, because we too are inside the whale. There, within the whale, we perceive a rather clearly formed CJ and a vaguely formed DJ. The relationship might be diagrammed as in Figure 1.4:

FIGURE 1.4: TRI-LAYERED JUSTICE: CJ WITHIN DJ WITHIN EJ

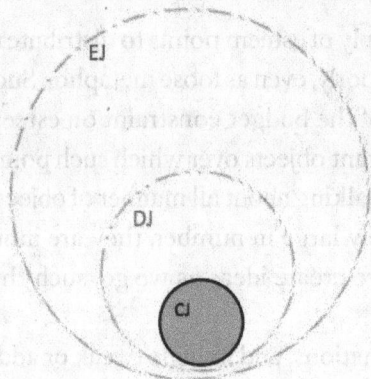

The EJ circle represents the outer boundaries of one's consciousness. Points within that space represent instances of human conduct. Any particular point is an instance of conduct, or a human action. The action can be assessed through three lenses: EJ, DJ, and CJ. But it is not always the case that all three are pertinent. Suppose Jim is deciding whether to donate $500 to a certain charity. We, as commutative jurisprude, would certainly be ready and able to comment on the CJ aspect of Jim's decision. But, really, it is hardly pertinent: Whether Jim does or does not make the donation, there is no real issue of CJ; the CJ aspect of donating to the charity is uncontested and uninteresting. Thus, that point is *outside of* the CJ circle, but *within* the DJ circle. The three circles are drawn to convey the nested nature of the *pertinence* of each lens of justice.

By the way, such lack of pertinence is on display when X tweets something obnoxious (but not violence inciting), and a journalist asks Y, an ally of X, what he thought of what X tweeted, and Y says: "I believe that everyone has the right to his opinion (or right to free speech)." That response is a dodge: The journalist asked Y to apply his DJ lens to X's conduct, but instead he applied his CJ lens.

Now consider a real matter of CJ, such as theft, trespass, or breach of contract. Any matter of CJ occasions a pertinent application of the DJ lenses. When Jim decides whether to mess with Albert's stuff, Jim is necessarily making a decision about the use of some of his own stuff (his hands, time, energy, attention, reputation, etc.); any matter that a commutative jurisprude takes up can also be taken up by a distributive jurisprude: Is Jim, in stealing bread from Albert, making a becoming use of his own? That question may be a live and debatable one. But, again, the converse is not true: Suppose Jim glimpses Albert flailing in a river, and leaps to his aid. That action can be treated as DJ, but CJ does not pertain in an important way. As far as CJ goes, Jim is simply and obviously satisfying the background default of not messing with anyone's stuff.

Every social act we take is making a use, a distribution, of our own, and, since we are under a perpetual duty to make a becoming use of our own, we may ask how we are doing, DJ-wise. But few of our social acts raise any issue as to whether we are violating CJ—messing with someone else's stuff. Yes, we are under perpetual duty to mind CJ, but that duty is of a very different nature, and usually is satisfied so simply, completely, and obviously that it isn't an issue at all. Your inner distributive jurisprude continually has eyes on what you are doing, and is constantly expressing to you approval or disapproval, if only of slight weightiness, as you negotiate the misty lines of propriety. In contrast, your inner commutative jurisprude is merely on call, and gets called in only when there arise hazards to the precise and accurate lines of CJ, hazards that trigger our violation-detector to emit alarm noises and flash red lights—as when Jim steals Albert's bread.

Likewise, any matter of DJ occasions a pertinent application of the

EJ lenses: Any decision about the use of one's own reflects estimations of objects. The diagram, then, depicts the moral embeddedness of all social engagement: Issues of CJ point to questions of DJ, which point to questions of EJ.

Meanwhile, actions lacking any social engagement, such as estimating a poem or a picture, may be regarded outside the DJ circle but within the EJ circle.[10] Suppose Robinson Crusoe is all alone on an island and with no prospect of returning to human society. And suppose we were we to apply the three lenses to his conduct. CJ would be entirely irrelevant, because there is no one else's stuff to mess with. DJ would be relevant only if we treated Crusoe as having a social relation with himself, which certainly has its place but is not what we usually have in mind when talking DJ or "social." I can certainly accept the statement, "Crusoe did a distributive injustice to himself"; I cannot accept the statement, "Crusoe did a commutative injustice to himself." Indeed, no one ever can do a commutative injustice to himself.

EJ, however, most certainly continues in pervasive application: Crusoe is still beheld by the universal beholder, and Crusoe would still be called to align his conduct with universal benevolence, even if the only virtue that remains for him is prudence. Prudence would still depend on estimating objects properly.

One might take a relatively expansive view of "social engagement" and expand the DJ circle toward EJ; such considerations would prompt a discussion of what it means for one person to have a "connexion" with another (269.10). Figure 1.5 indicates 57 samples of Smith's "just" talk that may aptly be understood as estimative justice in E-E.

---

10. Noteworthy in this connection is TMS (20–21.5), where Smith adds "a system of philosophy" to "a picture, or a poem."

FIGURE 1.5: FIFTY-SEVEN SAMPLES OF SMITH'S "JUST" TALK THAT MAY APTLY BE UNDERSTOOD AS ESTIMATIVE JUSTICE IN E-E.

TMS: just and proper, and suitable to their objects 16.1; the extent and superior justness 20.3; as just, as delicate and as precisely suited to its objects 20.4; nothing can be more just 90.11; Its self-evident justice 93.4; a more just sense 96.5; with some justice 97.2; the justest, the noblest, and most generous sentiments 106.3; most unjust resentment 107.4; just and equitable maxim 108.6; a just comparison 135.2; sense of propriety and justice 136.3; the just standard 139.8; applied with great justness 150.31; a just observation 150.32; not altogether just 157.3; those unjust passions 158.4;They Are Justly Regarded 161; may much more justly be denominated 165.6; justly places a double confidence 170.13; if just, and reasonable 187.11; so justly expose them 206–207.9; sometimes most unjustly 228.2; is justly called 233.16; this just indignation 240.9; seems justly to merit 240.9; justly feel themselves 249.27; the justness of his taste 252.30; sober and just esteem 254.32; justly observed 318.4; may very justly be considered 319.6; may justly be considered 320.9; uncommon and surprising justness 323.10; justness as well as delicacy 329.6; cannot indeed justly be considered 335.21; decisions to be just 339.33.

WN: may justly be considered 140.16; may very justly be regarded 282.16; just reason 621.73; justly observes 744.21; any just judgment 782.50; is perfectly just 873.9.

EPS: it is just 33.5; with justify them 48.1; justly conceived 65.18; justness of his corrections 88.55; unjust degradation 103.74; justly enough apprehended 120.1; justly passed 128.10; justly changed 128.10; justly observes 150.50; justified by examples 232.1; just arrangement 244.4; justness of their criticisms 248.7; just proportion 248.7; just arrangement 249.9; any just idea 251.12.

The topsy-turvy of justice paramountcy

In one sense CJ is paramount, because of its manifold specialness, its pillar-like importance, and its immanence in E-E; it is the justice that most often and most immediately calls loudly against violations. But in another sense it is lowliest because it is always dependent on DJ and EJ, and it is answerable to them; they are higher than CJ in that they provide the warrants for the presumption we give to CJ and they can override CJ (that is, it is they that authorize exceptions to CJ, as when stealing the bread is the right thing to do). The dependence of CJ on DJ and EJ throws an interesting light on Smith's remark that CJ is "what is peculiarly called justice" (TMS 82.9). Is it not peculiar that we call "justice" something which is in some instances is unjust in a larger sense?

A comprehensive perfection of EJ would be yet something else again

The operations of estimative jurisprudence can be applied to Jim's estimation of a poem, a picture, or any object whatever. I see Smith's discussion of EJ as consisting of, first, his expositing of the basic operation, and then, second, his saying that, according to Plato, as EJ may be applied to *any* of Jim's estimations, if Jim made an A+ in what seemed to be for practical purposes every application of EJ, Jim's conduct would be perfect. One might think of the A+ as a grade on Jim's eternal report-card, issued, as it were, in the life to come.

Smith speaks of an "object of self-interest," which, for Jim, means an object of more than passing interest; for example, the object might be a belief, habit, aspiration, or attachment of Jim's. Smith explains that in the EJ sense "we are said to do injustice to ourselves when we appear not to give sufficient attention to *any* particular object of self-interest" (270.10, italics added), and then proceeds to speak of "the perfection of every sort of virtue," which might be termed Platonic justice. I see EJ as an operation pervasively applicable and indeed pointing toward unfathomed depths.[11] But in itself the operation of EJ is minimal. It may be applied to some of Jim's estimations without treating the entirety of Jim's conduct. Even a quite imperfect person might estimate an object quite justly (cf. Griswold 1999, 232; C. Smith 2013, 785; Raphael 2001, 115, 123).

A jural equal who is of the governmental sector (cells A2, B2, C)

We proceed to the second row of the Justices Table. The row is labeled: Government actor as a sort of Equal, **not** *qua* Superior. This row accommodates governmental actors as owners or agents of owners of specific government resources, such as a street, a park, or a university. In such capacity, the government-sector actors act as an equal among equals. Thus this row basically follows the grooves of the previous row, for non-governmental equals.

Consider George Mason University, the state university in Virginia at which I am employed. I would be inclined to say that the university and its resources are owned (as opposed to being unowned), and I would be inclined to say that the owners are the residents ("the people") of Virgin-

---

11. As many scholars have noted, Smith's approach is nonfoundationalist (Griswold 1999, 165; Fleischacker 2004, 23-26; Rothschild 2004, 152; Haakonssen 2016, 61; and Klein 2016). The nature of EJ relates to such ethical nonfoundationalism.

ia. An alternative would be to say that the university is owned by the government of Virginia. But do the people own the government? Perhaps that makes sense.

It is obvious that government-sector ownership is usually quite different from normal private-sector ownership; that is one reason for breaking out a separate row. But it is the similar "equal-ness" that is important here: I suggest that such actors—such as the provost of the university—do not act as jural superiors. As owners or the agents of the owners of George Mason University, such actors make rules for the use of resources that they own. Yes, they may be huge players with tremendous economic and cultural influence; yes, they subsist greatly on tax-dollars, which are garnered by the initiation of coercion, but that, as it were, is outside their sphere of action as contained in the second row of the Justices Table. As an employee of George Mason University, I subsist in part on such tax-dollars, but I hardly think that that makes me either a jural superior or an initiator of coercion. In the narrow jural sense that concerns us here, *such government-sector actors do not mess with other people's stuff* (unless, of course, they do, like a burglar).[12]

The actions of a jural superior, in terms of CJ, DJ, and EJ (cells A3, B3, C)

The contrast to the equal-equal relationship (E-E) is the superior-inferior relationship (S-i). By definition, any actor that did not ever practice the open initiation of the violation of CJ would not be a jural superior. Thus, not only does a superior pursue rules that are beyond the grammar of CJ, he violates that grammar. A superior does things, often with authority, often with a legitimacy, and sometimes with the approval of the impartial spectator, that would be criminal by an equal or neighbor.

In S-i relations, the CJ-flipside—that is, others not messing with your stuff—Smith generally called "liberty" (sometimes, "natural liberty"). Smith expressed the flipside relationship between CJ and liberty quite clearly when he wrote of two government interventions: "Both laws were evident

---

12. At WN 866.7, Smith talks justice ("a just proportion") aptly interpreted as DJ in a government-sector-equal context.

violations of natural liberty, and *therefore* unjust…" (WN 530.16, italics added). Likewise, Smith acknowledges that government requirements to build a firewall and restrictions on the issuance of small-denomination bank notes are, in each case, "a violation of natural liberty," while he endorses them (WN 324.94). Edwin Cannan affirmed the flipside relationship when he introduced the following entry to the index of WN: "Natural liberty, violations of, unjust."[13]

One might ask: But if the boss at work has powers and prerogatives, and a superior authority, and yet does not violate CJ, why can we not say the same for the magistrate? The magistrate also enjoys a superior authority. His authority also resides within an organization of sorts, the polity, the rules of which, like those of the private organization, people are free to exit from and submit to voluntarily.

The suggestion, it seems to me, implies a configuration of ownership wherein the collectivity of the polity owns some kind of substratum upon which all privately owned property within the polity depends. Up from the collectively owned substratum stems a complex of contract, a complex that envelops those existing within the boundaries of the polity. If we accept such configuration of ownership, the reasoning has force; the polity would be organizational in that sense, and duly made laws that do things like, say, restrict the rate of interest that a lender can charge would not be violations of CJ. CJ "consists in abstaining from what is another's" (269.10), and, on the collectivist configuration, the owners of the vast club (e.g., the United States of America) would be satisfying that requirement. The club rules are their stuff, not some separate affairs of others.

I submit, however, that Smith tended to reject any such collectivist configuration. We may detect Smith's rejection of the collectivist configuration for example where he writes in WN of "the violence of law" and related expressions,[14] and in TMS of "fortunate violence" (253.30). Knud Haakonssen (1981, 96) notes that Smith recognized that taxation "involved forcible infringement of liberty, privacy, and property of individuals." Smith often

---

13. For that entry, Cannan cited pages that translate in the Glasgow/OUP/Liberty Fund edition to 157, 324, 530; see page 1057 of the latter. Incidentally, there on page 1057 of the latter, there should be an open-bracket before "Natural liberty."

14. See WN 525-526.4-5, 248.9, 285.31, 342.30, 372.32, 422.16, 586.52, 653.28.

declares duly enacted laws to be violations of the simple rules of CJ—as in many of the passages indicated in Figure 1.6—and violations of CJ's flipside in S-i, liberty. In this connection Smith even grows sarcastic, as when he writes about Englishmen's "boasted liberty" and how they "pretended to be free" (WN 660.47; 326.100).

FIGURE 1.6: TWELVE SAMPLES OF SMITH'S "JUST" TALK THAT MAY APTLY BE UNDER-STOOD AS COMMUTATIVE JUSTICE IN S-I.

TMS: laws of police, not of justice 341.37
WN: consistent with liberty and justice 145.27; natural liberty and justice 157.59; such violent injustice 326.100; and therefore unjust 530.16; ordinary laws of justice 539.39; Unjust, however, as such prohibitions 582.44; the natural system of perfect liberty and justice 606.44; of perfect justice 669.17; perfect liberty and perfect justice 674.28 [twice]; the ordinary principles of justice 826.6.

Following Hume, Smith rejected social contract (LJ 315–324, 402–404, 434–435), instead understanding political authority on Hume's conventionalist ideas. Perhaps relevant here is Smith's footnote in the Justices Paragraph regarding distributive justice: "The distributive justice of Aristotle is somewhat different. It consists in the proper distribution of rewards from the public stock of a community" (TMS 269.10n*). Peter Minowitz (1993, 50) comments: "Smith's decision here to employ a footnote, especially given the paucity of footnotes in *The Theory of Moral Sentiments*, suggests the distance he wishes to put between his own position and a more political approach to justice."[15] The configuration Smith subscribed to is non-collectivist. On the Smithian configuration, usury restrictions initiate coercion against people who have not themselves coerced anyone. Usury restrictions do not abstain from what is another's.

The affairs of the usurer and his trading partner are, *CJ-wise*, separate from the community, but they are not separate in other terms. The atomism of CJ does not imply atomism in the other justices; it does not imply an ethical atomism. Figure 1.4 showed CJ nested within DJ nested within EJ: We are ethically embedded. As numerous scholars have noted (see Chapter 2), Smith taught a presumption against violation of CJ by superiors, a

---

15. Incidentally, that is the last substantive footnote of TMS, and the last note of Rousseau's *Discourse on Inequality* (1997, 221–222) also concerned distributive justice and affirmed a collectivist approach.

presumption of liberty, but the presumption admits of exceptions. In fact, Smith endorsed the usury restrictions of his society.

In pondering an exception to the principle, Smith is sometimes found talking of the polity in organizational terms:

> The expence of government to the individuals of a great nation, is like the expence of management to the joint tenants of a great estate, who are all obliged to contribute in proportion to their respective interests in the estate. In the observation or neglect of this maxim consists, what is called the equality or inequality of taxation. (WN 825.3)[16]

But such talk is figurative. Smith uses such figures, not to trace out the lines of CJ, but to explore the vague rules of estimative justice, which may indeed trump CJ. Indeed, on the page preceding the "great estate" passage, Smith speaks of "the people contributing *a part of their own private revenue* in order to make up a public revenue to the sovereign or commonwealth" (WN 824.21, italics added). Smith's talk of the polity as a great estate is metaphorical in a manner rather like when he suggests, in espousing "the liberal system," that the different states of Europe "so far resemble the different provinces of a great empire" (WN 538.39). Figure 1.7 indicates 11 samples of Smith's "just" talk that may aptly be understood as estimative justice in S-i.

FIGURE 1.7: ELEVEN SAMPLES OF SMITH'S "JUST" TALK THAT MAY APTLY BE UNDERSTOOD AS ESTIMATIVE JUSTICE IN S-I.

WN: the just liberty 138.12; a just proportion 620.71; as just as it is generous and liberal 678.38; It is unjust that 815.3; without any injustice 815.4; without injustice 815.5; The evident justice and utility 827.7; equally just and equitable 834.20; most unjust and unequal 893.55; not contrary to justice 944.88; ought justly to be charged 946.92.

Earlier I quoted Smith referring to two laws that "were evident violations of natural liberty, and therefore unjust." Smith then adds directly:

---

16. Cf. Fleischacker 2004, 194, who also quotes the "great estate" passage and tends rather to ascribe the collectivist configuration to Smith.

"and they were both too as impolitick as they were unjust. It is the interest of every society, that things of this kind should never either be forced or obstructed" (WN 530.16; see likewise Corr. 241). I propose that we read this as Smith saying: Both laws violated CJ, and, moreover, were estimatively unjust. Again, Smith allows that EJ can trump CJ. He is pointing out that in the matter of the two laws referred to, that is not the case.

Likewise, when Smith allows that taxes may be used to defray the expenses of roads or schools "without any injustice" (WN 815.4; and "without injustice" in 815.5), that is not a CJ commentary on either taxation or such spending, but an EJ commentary on such spending (or perhaps on the DJ of a government-sector equal). Just prior, Smith writes of related matters in terms of *propriety* ("There is no impropriety" 814–815.2): Propriety is a feature of the aesthetic sort of rules that are beyond CJ; it is not an important feature of CJ's grammar-like rules. And directly following the second "without injustice," in his final words on schooling, he says that the expense might perhaps be left "with equal propriety" entirely to voluntary action (WN 815.5; on this matter see Drylie 2016). Smith's bracketing of the two without-injustice remarks with two propriety remarks signals that he was talking justice beyond CJ.

In the Justices Table, in the superior row, for the DJ column I write "Not applicable." I propose that we see Jim as not owning anything in his capacity as a jural superior, and therefore DJ not applying to the jural superior. I think that such a suggestion can be made to work with some creative expounding of the multiple facets of Jim and his world, using the other rows, notably the government-sector equal row.

The following passage illustrates policy as an object of EJ: "[T]he praises which have been bestowed upon the law which establishes the bounty upon the exportation of corn, and upon that system of regulations which is connected with it, are altogether unmerited" (WN 524.1). Smith says "unmerited," but he might just as well have said unjust: People unjustly praise, or estimate, the bounty. There are two ways to talk about a jural superior's policy in terms of justice: (1) CJ, that is, does the policy initiate messing with other people's stuff? and (2) EJ, that is, would a belief in it or a habit of affirming and espousing it be estimatively just?

Concluding remarks

Many scholars have read Smith as though he confined his justice talk to CJ, while many have read otherwise. Such disparities in readings evince a contrariety residing in *justice* in Smith's work. Although parts of Smith's texts, examined in isolation, give the impression of his favoring that justice talk be confined to CJ, Smith embraced and pervasively practiced talking all three senses of justice. This chapter has offered explication of the three senses and advanced the idea of such embrace by Smith.

If there is merit here, it leaves us with the question: Why didn't Smith make his justice polysemy clearer, and clarify pervasively in the instant, by prominently using modifiers (as in, CJ, DJ, EJ)? If I were to approach the question, I would begin with Arthur Melzer's four purposes or motives to esotericism: defensive, protective, pedagogical, and political (Melzer 2014).

CHAPTER 2

The Presumption of Liberty in Adam Smith

In Smith's time, it was understood that exceptions do not destroy the liberty principle's principlehood. But later, some would "Ah ha!" exceptions, challenging liberals to articulate the basis, or foundation, upon which they made any such exception:

- "So you *admit* that your principle is not self-justifying!"
- "Where do you draw the line?"
- "Your statements are normative, not positive."
- "How can you claim to be doing science?"

Many scholars have drawn up lists of Smith's exceptions to the liberty principle. Scholars debate what is to be placed on the list, and what to make of the items on the list.

In this short and simple chapter, I emphasize the principle *to which* they are exceptions. What I wish to emphasize is that the exceptions are exceptions; they are to be regarded as exceptional. If we can establish that Smith maintained and propounded a presumption of liberty, we can proceed more assuredly on the supposition that he was a classical liberal in his moral and political outlook—and hence disposed against the governmentalization of social affairs.

The liberty principle says: In a choice between two reforms (one of which may be no-reform), with one reform higher in liberty than the other, the higher-liberty reform is the one that is more desirable from the point of view of a universal benevolent beholder. The liberty principle qualified by "by and large" makes the liberty maxim. Belief in the maxim makes a presumption. The presumption places the burden of proof on the contravener of principle. It is like the presumption of innocence: We maintain the presumption of innocence, even while recognizing that not everyone is innocent.

In an article noted for documenting Smith's departures from, or exceptions to, the liberty principle, Jacob Viner wrote:

> There is no possible room for doubt, however, that Smith in general believed that there was, to say the least, **a strong presumption** against government activity beyond its fundamental duties of protection against its foreign foes and maintenance of justice. (Viner 1927, 219, bold added)

It is true that Smith sometimes endorsed exceptions to the liberty principle; he sometimes equivocates and argues in ways that point to inconsistent positions, for example, on education and on usury, and he sustained polysemy in key words, notably *justice* and *nature/natural*. But the prime meanings of liberty and (commutative) justice are quite sufficiently clear to understand and confirm the statement above from Jacob Viner.

Likewise, here are some other "presumption"/"burden of proof" quotations from Smith scholars:

- J. Shield Nicholson (1885, 557–8): "Adam Smith has said that in *almost all cases* to direct private people how to employ their capital is hurtful or useless..."
- Samuel Hollander (1973, 256): "Throughout the *Wealth of Nations* Smith makes use of a **presumptive** case in favour of laissez-faire based upon the 'natural right' of individuals not to be interfered with."
- Jeffrey Young and Barry Gordon (1996, 22): "The **burden of proof**, however, still lies with those who would suspend commutative justice" (bold added).
- Charles Griswold (1999, 295): "A **burden-of-proof** argument suffuses Smith's writing in political economy; the state may intervene in all sorts of ways, but those who would have it do so are required to show why it should in this par-

ticular instance, for how long, in precisely what fashion, and how its intervention will escape the usual dangers of creating entrenched interest groups and self-perpetuating monopolies" (bold added).

- Craig Smith (2013, 796): Smith "points us toward a **presumption** against the state and a **presumption** in favour of private action by voluntary association of individuals" (bold added).

- James Otteson (2016, 508): "He [Adam Smith] is willing to allow that there might be cases in which the state should take on duties beyond those of the night watchman, but the default is against such interventions, and **the burden of proof** falls on those recommending them to show why an exception should be made."

Here are some passages that support Viner's claim that Smith believed in a "strong presumption" against the role of government extending beyond its "fundamental duties":

To give the monopoly of the home-market to the produce of domestic industry, in any particular art or manufacture, is in some measure to direct private people in what manner they ought to employ their capitals, and must, in almost all cases, be either a useless or a hurtful regulation. (WN 456.11)

In general, if any branch of trade, or any division of labour, be advantageous to the public, the freer and more general the competition, it will always be the more so. (WN 329.106).

To hinder, besides, the farmer from sending his goods at all times to the best market is evidently to sacrifice the ordinary laws of justice to an idea of public utility, to a sort of reasons of state; an act of legislative authority which ought to be exercised only, which can be pardoned only in cases of the most urgent necessity. (WN 539.39)

Both laws were evident violations of natural liberty, and therefore unjust; and they were both, too, as impolitic as they were unjust. It is the interest of every society that things of this kind should never either be forced or obstructed. (WN 530.16)

What is the species of domestic industry which his capital can employ, and of which the produce is likely to be of the greatest value, every individual, it is evident, can, in his local situation, judge much better than any statesman or lawgiver can do for him. The statesman who should attempt to direct private people in what manner they ought to employ their capitals would not only load himself with a most unnecessary attention, but assume an authority which could safely be trusted, not only to no single person, but to no council or senate whatever, and which would nowhere be so dangerous as in the hands of a man who had folly and presumption enough to fancy himself fit to exercise it. (WN 456.10)

There are many passages—too numerous to cite—where Smith clearly favors liberty, even "perfect liberty." One example is what he says of the school of French Oeconomists (Physiocrats): "in representing perfect liberty as the only effectual expedient for rendering this annual reproduction the greatest possible, its doctrine seems to be in every respect as just as it is generous and liberal" (WN 678.38; see also 116.1).

And there are quite a few passages in which Smith pounds the fist for liberty, such as at 138.12 ("plain violation of this most sacred property") and 582.44 ("the most sacred rights of mankind") and 188.27 ("In both regulations the sacred rights of private property are sacrificed to the supposed interests of publick revenue"). At 687.50-51 he expounds "the obvious and simple system of natural liberty," wherein "Every man, as long as he does not violate the laws of justice, is left perfectly free to pursue his own interest his own way, and to bring both his industry and capital into competition with those of any other man, or order of men." Smith then describes the three functions of government.

Smith imputed a kind of legal positivism to Thomas Hobbes and explained the errors of "so odious a doctrine" (TMS 318.3). He also condemned Colbert's management of the French economy "upon the same model as the departments of a public office," and contrasted it with "allowing every man to pursue his own interest in his own way, upon the liberal plan of equality, liberty, and justice" (WN 664.3).

Wesley Clair Mitchell ([1949], 1) said, in lectures from the 1930s, that Smith "set forth with masterly lucidity the proposition that the wealth of the nation would grow most rapidly if the government practiced a minimum of interference with the operations of private people". There are many, many passages in Smith's writing suggesting what might be called Smithian growth theory, that liberty and security of property conduce to economic growth.

Smith himself chides others for pretending to have a presumption of liberty but not upholding it. After describing and condemning the mass of interventions for bounties, subsidies, and restrictions, he writes: "It is unnecessary, I imagine, to observe, how contrary such regulations are to the boasted liberty of the subject, of which we affect to be so very jealous; but which, in this case, is so plainly sacrificed to the futile interests of our merchants and manufacturers" (WN 660.47).

Free-market economics in Smith's classroom

Besides saying that Smith advanced "the general view which we now usually characterize by the French phrase *laissez faire*," Mitchell ([1949], 70) adds, "apparently from the beginning of his teaching." Smith's lecture notes from the early 1760s provide a special window on Smith's sensibilities. They are a record of what he said about domestic policy to his students at the University of Glasgow, who were mostly teenagers (Scott 1937, 28). The eminent professor seeks to edify them in a basic outlook for domestic policy, a way of formulating and estimating the objects of public policy. What does Smith put across?

In such context, Smith would not be much concerned about how his words would have sounded to those beyond the immediately congregated. His words might travel somewhat, as a student might scrawl a transcription, which might pass hand to hand or be duplicated by hand. Still, the transcribed lecture notes are somewhat like a surreptitious recording of a private lecture. It provides a candor and casualness that we do not have in the works composed and released by Smith for publication.

In the "police"—or policy—part of the 1763–1764 jurisprudence course, we find, tax-supported night-watchman functions aside, virtually no exceptions to the liberty principle. The liberty principle is advanced less eloquently but more steadily than in WN. Smith does not serenade his students; the tone, rather, tends towards one not unknown to free-marketeer instructors of economic principles: benignant and mirthful confidences about the world's systematic illiberal follies and hypocrisies. He tells the students time after time that, as far as policy goes, the best available option is liberalization and freer enterprise. For example, he roundly endorses free banking, mentioning none of the exceptions found in WN. At virtually every turn, the answer to, *And what is the best course for policy?*, is freer enterprise, even for crime prevention! (See LJ 486–87.) The closest thing to an exception in the entire domestic-policy part of the 1763–64 course comes in discussing disadvantages of a commercial spirit, where Smith merely remarks: "To remedy these defects would be an object worthy of serious attention" (541). His recommendations for policy reform are devoid of restrictions on voluntary affairs and of government as a more active player in social affairs. The outlook that Smith imparted to his teenage students was one presumptively opposed to the governmentalization of social affairs.

I do not mean to suggest that all of WN's equivocations, exceptions, and inconsistencies are to be regarded as rhetorical ploys and hence discounted. But I do suggest that Smith believed that the liberty principle and "the liberal plan" are challenging. They challenge not only entrenched interests and popular prejudices, but primordial human instincts. He recognized and anticipated reactionary distaste for liberal ideas. Yet he wanted the engagement of his works to be broad, long-lived, and irenic. He assures us that he was no man of system, that he was not proposing a rationalistic application of the liberty principle. His published works not only taught Solonic political moderation, they practiced it (Clark 2021).

In fact, in *other* parts of the 1763–1764 jurisprudence course (and in the 1762–1763 course), Smith mounts arguments for positions that he himself seems to consider contraventions of (commutative) justice and therefore of the liberty principle. For example, Smith indicates that he does not consider it a breach of (commutative) justice to decide not to raise, or even to abandon, one's child (LJ 449, 172), and likewise to divorce or take multiple wives (ibid., 442, 150f.), and yet he argues against both, invoking overall-liberty arguments particularly for prohibiting polygamy. Nonetheless, when he turns to domestic policy or "police," the pro-liberalization aspect is remarkably steady.

Michael Clark (2021) explains that Smith "held liberty as a central principle, but also that he adopted an approach of strategic yielding and caution. Smith associated this accommodating approach with the Athenian official Solon, who put forth laws that attempted to be 'the best that the people can bear.'" Clark's article is titled "Adam Smith as Solon: Accommodating on the Edges of Liberty, Not Abandoning It." Clark says that we need to see Smith as Solon, "accommodating where necessary" (Clark 2021, 739).

CHAPTER 3

Mere-Liberty in David Hume

By Daniel Klein and Erik W. Matson

Hume's work presents interpretive difficulty. "The difficulty is not so much in regard to [Hume's] arguments taken singly," wrote Norman Kemp Smith ([1941]), "but in regard to their bearing upon one another, and upon the central positions which they are intended to support" (79).[1] Donald Livingston (1984) argues that such a mode is a central part of "the way [Hume] does philosophy" (1984, 35). Livingston writes, "philosophical insight is gained by working through the contrarieties of thought which structure a drama of inquiry." The idea is expressed in the title of Annette Baier's book, *A Progress of Sentiment: Reflections on Hume's Treatise* (1991).

To study Hume is to study the contrarieties. The most dramatic contrariety of the *Treatise* concerns the word *reason*: What Hume often refers to as reason—probable (or moral) reasoning from ideas of cause and effect —is explicitly deemed *unreasonable* according to another meaning he at times employs.[2]

Another contrariety resides in *natural*. Hume says that (commutative) justice is an artificial—not natural—virtue, yet, "in another sense of the word [*natural*]," "as no principle of the human mind is more natural than a sense of virtue; so no virtue is more natural than justice" (T 3.2.1.19). Whether it be on *reason* or on *natural*, a just interpretation must synthesize the relevant passages.

---

1. For other remarks on the difficulty of interpreting Hume, see, e.g., Passmore (1951, 1); Forbes (1975, ix); Selby-Bigge (1975, vii).

2. Cf. T 1.3.6. For an elaboration of this contrariety, see, e.g., Winters 1979; Millican 1998; Matson 2017a.

Livingston's "contrariety" adage also pertains to *liberty*. Like *reason* and natural, the word *liberty* in Hume is polysemous and paradoxical. Liberty's various formulations, usages, and accompanying modifiers support varying interpretations of its signification, as evidenced by different readings in the secondary literature.[3]

We argue that a central meaning, here dubbed *mere-liberty*, is the individual's dominion over her person, property, and freedom of association (giving rise to associated promises due to her). Governmental trenchings on such dominion (taxes, restrictions, etc.) are violations of mere-liberty. But for Hume sometimes it is right and good to violate mere-liberty; mere-liberty is defeasible. Some mere-liberty violations (whether they be features of the status quo or hypothetical reform thereto) are conducive to the long-run or overall state of mere-liberty. Mere-liberty depends on protection and support. Hume says that "A great sacrifice of liberty must necessarily be made in every government" (EMPL 40), and he does not consider society-without-government a relevant option.

Hume was born in 1711. By the time of his maturity, Britain was a stable polity (Plumb 1967). Hume developed his political outlook upon a supposition of stable polity: "liberty is the perfection of civil society." But "authority must be acknowledged essential to its very existence" (EMPL 40). When looking back on British history, or elsewhere, Hume might favor the establishing of authority over and against axiomatic scrupling about mere-liberty—thus his favor for the Tudors' suppression of the barons, the Henrician Reformation, and other steps toward jural integration, stable polity, and capacious government. "[I]n all governments there is a perpetual intestine struggle...between Authority and Liberty; and neither of them can ever absolutely prevail in the contest" (EMPL 41; see also H VI, 533).

We do not assert that Hume makes a singular, supreme objective of overall mere-liberty. Mere-liberty was not a maximand. We contend only that overall mere-liberty figures prominently in Hume's political sensibilities. Accordingly, political objects, including norms embodying cer-

---

3. Speaking to the liberty contrariety, Miller (1981) writes that "the absence of arbitrary coercion... is one of Hume's main use of the term... But Hume also, without warning, uses 'liberty' in two other ways: to mean simply the absence of constraint (particularly in matters such as freedom of speech and religious belief), and to describe one particular form of government, which he labels 'free'" (149).

tain political tenets and principles, may be understood in light of their historically situated tendency to serve overall mere-liberty: Objects well serving mere-liberty—for example, norms of clear and predictable rules, constraints on royal prerogative, increased republicanism, specific rules for court or parliamentary procedure, the power of the purse ("withdrawing supplies;" H I, 475; see Sabl 2012, 191), abolition of the Court of Star Chamber ("There are needed but this one court in any government, to put an end to all regular, legal, and exact plans of liberty"; H IV, 263)—*et cetera, et cetera*—are then associated with liberty and freedom.

We might speak of our car as "transportation," but strictly speaking our car is an input to transportation. A car has aspects, uses, and significance apart from transportation, and the word *transportation* has a meaning independent of cars. *Moving things from one place to another* may be posited as the *essential* meaning of *transportation*. Now, upon that, conceive a category of *contributory* meanings: Things thought to contribute to (or be conducive to) the moving of things from one place to another; thus, cars are designated "transportation." Finally, conceive a category of *parallel* meanings;[4] a parallel meaning of *transportation* is exile to Australia. We interpret Hume's polysemous "liberty" talk with an eye to see mere-liberty as essential, some as talk of political objects contributory to that, and some parallel.

Others, too, see mere-liberty in Hume. Frederick Whelan (1985) acknowledges multiple concepts of liberty in Hume, emphasizing the primacy of the "'liberty of spontaneity,' or the freedom to act in accordance with one's will without external coercion or constraint" (88).[5] Nicholas Capaldi (1990) says, "Hume was concerned about…the liberty that arises

---

4. In relation to a posited essential meaning X of word W, we might see three categories of parallel meanings: (1) Meanings that, accepting X as essential, signify things perceived as contributory to X but that *our speaker* (of word W) does *not* perceive as particularly contributory to X. (2) Meanings that posit as essential a meaning other than X, say some other meaning Z. (3) Meanings that, accepting Z as essential, signify things perceived as contributory to Z.

5. Although Whelan (1985) clearly sees the mere-liberty formulation in Hume, referring to it at one point as "negative" liberty that is opposed to violence (88n), he underscores Hume's focus in politics on "rules, and the corresponding obligation to obey rules, that are necessary for social order" (358). Thus Whelan's general position: "Hume's political philosophy upholds liberty only under law, or within the confines of the various artifices that are the focus of his analysis; and within this framework his emphasis is not so much on liberty as it is on the order that is the more fundamental and universal product of artifice" (359).

from justice" (197). Russell Hardin (2007) speaks of Hume's liberty "in the sense of political freedom to do as one pleases with one's life and to engage in whatever economic activity one wishes" (185). Thomas Merrill (2015) writes that "the object or purpose of political institutions, Hume suggests, is individual liberty" (137, see also 118).

But the literature on Hume's politics by no means reliably sees mere-liberty as central in Hume. Other scholars treat certain meanings of "liberty" as central that, in our construal, are contributory, and they give little expression to mere-liberty. Thus, mere-liberty has often been too faint—absent, obscure, perhaps disguised—in the secondary literature on Hume's politics. Figure 3.1 shows works that speak to the meaning of liberty in Hume but are shy on mere-liberty, and snippet quotations of what the author highlights as what Hume meant by "liberty." The present paper is offered as friendly criticism of such works for their going too light on mere-liberty in Hume. The present paper is also offered as a general exposition of mere-liberty in Hume.

FIGURE 3.1: WORKS THAT SPEAK TO THE MEANING OF LIBERTY IN HUME BUT ARE SHY ON MERE-LIBERTY

	what is highlighted as central in Hume's meaning of liberty
John Valdimir Price (1966)	"individual activities and expressions of ideas that are not inimical to the stability of the government" (141)
Friedrich Hayek (1967)	"general and inflexible laws" (117f)
Duncan Forbes (1975)	"the security of the individual under the rule of law" (87, also 88, 153); "general and equal laws" (154f); "the absolute rule of law" (170, 181)
David Miller (1981)	"the absence of arbitrary coercion" (148)
John B. Stewart (1992)	"civil liberty entails a rule of law; it requires established rights with respect to economic activity, speech, religion, and so forth" (232)
Donald Livingston (1998)	"uncoerced by the arbitrary will of another," "a government of Laws, not of Men," "Law must be known, regular, and predictable," "the rule of law" (182f)
Andrew Sabl (2012)	"strategies and institutions for limiting the power that accrues to those who hold power under conventions of authority" (16); "general and inflexible laws" (206)

We do not mean to impute any sort of philosophical essentialism to Hume. We contend simply that mere-liberty was central and vital in Hume's "liberty" talk. The three categories of meanings—essential, contributory, and parallel—help to organize our argument.

The essential and contributory meanings not only correlate empirically but interrelate conceptually: Government laws are predicated on background configurations of ownership and operative principles of voluntary association, and "rule of law" often speaks of the predictability or generality *of a restriction thereto*. Because of the correlations and interrelations between essential and contributory meanings, it is little wonder that they get jumbled up together.

We start with mere-liberty as essential in Hume's thinking about liberty, anchored in the exposition of (commutative) justice in the *Treatise*. As we proceed to the wide range of "liberty" talk in Hume, we argue that mere-liberty can be seen in much of it, and that much may be understood as contributory. Figure 3.2 represents the idea that mere-liberty is central to Hume, and that it depends on a constitutional setting of established institutions.

FIGURE 3.2: MERE-LIBERTY AT THE HEART OF HUME'S THINKING ABOUT LIBERTY

HUME'S CONSTITUTION OF LIBERTY

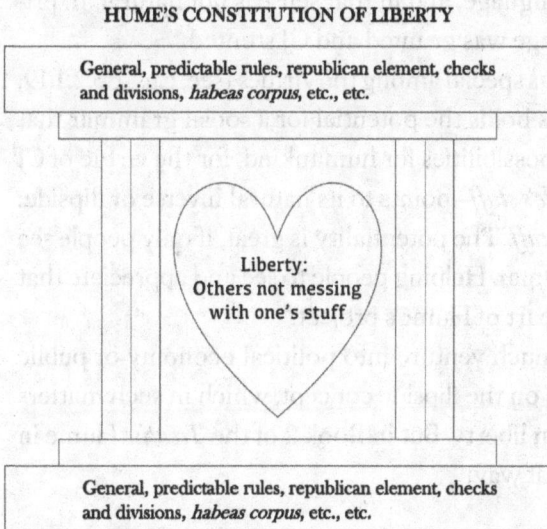

General, predictable rules, republican element, checks and divisions, *habeas corpus*, etc., etc.

Liberty:
Others not messing with one's stuff

General, predictable rules, republican element, checks and divisions, *habeas corpus*, etc., etc.

Liberty Fund hosted an exchange among five scholars (Hart 2018). Capaldi and Daniel Klein concur on the centrality of mere-liberty in Hume, while Chandran Kukathas[6] and Andrew Sabl dispute that contention, with Mark Yellin perhaps leaning to their side. The present chapter draws on Klein's entries in that exchange but adds much new material.

---

6. Kukathas writes: "My deeper concern, however, is with Klein's conception of liberty as 'others not messing with one's stuff.' I see nothing in Hume that comes remotely close to conceiving of liberty in this way."

Mere-liberty: The flipside of commutative justice

The virtue of *not messing with other people's stuff* is called by Hume simply "justice," and never "commutative justice." We proceed to speak of it as commutative justice. We abbreviate commutative justice as CJ.

It is Book 3 of the *Treatise* that contains Hume's profound and path-breaking exposition of CJ. The exposition is pathbreaking not for identifying CJ and understanding it as precept against messing with other people's stuff—that has a rich provenance, notably Grotius,[7] whom Hume salutes (EPM App. 1 fn. 63). It is pathbreaking for other reasons. Hume explains that social evolution selects property/contract rules for their ability to deliver precision and accuracy in ordinary life; such precision and accuracy is an emergent, selected-for feature (see, e.g., EPM 3.2.34–3.2.45). The evolutionary process is one of "insensible gradations," but any property/contract rule or principle that emerges "admits not of degrees" (T 3.2.6.8). Later, Adam Smith would liken that feature to grammar (TMS 175.11, 327.1). In its being extended beyond one's person and immediate possessions, the social grammar of CJ is evolved, like language, and in that sense is not natural. In primeval communities, language was grunted and CJ stunted.

Hume taught that CJ was special among the virtues (see, e.g., T 3.2.1.19; EPM 3.2.48). Its specialness holds the potential for a social grammar that opens up remarkable new possibilities for humankind, for the virtue of CJ —*not messing with other people's stuff*—points to its natural inverse or flipside: *others not messing with one's stuff.* The potentiality is great, if only people see and respect the social grammar. Helping people to see and appreciate that social grammar is a major part of Hume's project.[8]

The *Treatise* does not much venture into political economy or public policy; it does not expound on the flipside concept, which in such matters would mean expounding on liberty. But in Book 2 of the *Treatise* Hume in fact uses "liberty" in just that way:

---

7. On Grotius, search http://oll.libertyfund.org/people/hugo-grotius on "abstain."

8. Incidentally, yet other things in the Treatise, about CJ, that are pathbreaking include: (1) the teaching that the adoption of such rules is necessary for a society to advance (and in that sense such rules constitute a set of natural conventions) (T 3.2.6; T 3.2.8.3); (2) the very phraseology of *convention* in the sense distinct from compact, contract, or consent; and (3) that the conventionalist understanding of CJ has a parallel in a conventionalist understanding of political authority (T 3.2.7; EMPL 481, 489).

'Tis sufficient to observe on this occasion, that property may be defin'd, *such a relation betwixt a person and an object that permits him, but forbids any other, the free use and possession of it, without violating the laws of justice and moral equity.* If justice, therefore, be a virtue, which has a natural and original influence on the human mind, property may be look'd upon as a particular species of *causation*; whether we consider the **liberty** it gives the proprietor to operate as he pleases upon the object, or the advantages, which he reaps from it. (T 2.1.10.1; italics original, boldface added)

A few other pertinent "liberty" instances arise in the *Treatise*, as when the first pages praise England as an exceptional "land of toleration and of liberty" (T Intro.7). But what is paramount is to see that Book 3 of the *Treatise* is indeed pregnant with the idea of mere-liberty as flipside of CJ, and even quietly expresses the liberal sentiment that Hume would later expound.

Although it is somewhat obscure, Hume assumes self-ownership as a sort of natural property (exactly like Friedman 1994), and goes from there. He writes:

There are three different species of goods, which we are pos-sess'd of; the internal satisfaction of our minds, the external advantages of our body, and the enjoyment of such possessions as we have acquir'd by our industry and good fortune. (T 3.2.2.7)

The third species of goods, possessions, pose great problems to early man "from their looseness and easy transition from one person to anoth-er." Thus, men "must seek for a remedy, by putting these goods, as far as possible, *on the same footing with the fix'd and constant advantages of the mind and body.* This can be done after no other manner, than by a convention" (T 3.2.2.9; italics added).[9] Thus Hume assimilates ownership of possessions to ownership of one's own person. "Hume's conception of liberty(ies) is derivative from his conception of the individual" (Capaldi, in Hart 2018).

---

9. Alas, Forbes (1975, 86) overlooks the self-ownership implied by T 3.2.2.7–9.

The *extending* of CJ principles *beyond* one's own person and most immediate possessions was said to be "artificial": We suggest that Hume took
self-ownership to be natural. In the *Treatise*, self-ownership finds other
glancing expression, as when he says that war puts at stake "the most considerable of all goods, life and limbs" (T 3.2.8.1). His autobiographical essay
"My Own Life" suggests self-ownership in its title and recounts "the great
decline of my person" caused by illness at the end of his life (EMPL xl). In
the essay on suicide, Hume would seem to presuppose self-ownership when
speaking of "our natural liberty" and "native liberty" (EMPL 588 n6, 580),
and in another essay he speaks of the English government's obligation "to
secure every one's life" (EMPL 12).

Adam Smith capsulized CJ as "abstaining from what is another's" (TMS
269.10), a formulation that predates Hume. For a brief formulation, we prefer *not messing with other people's stuff* (for reason stated in footnote 4 of the
first chapter of this book). But to analyze the text of the *Treatise*, we recur
to the phraseology of *abstain*.

In discussing justice, Hume uses *abstain* and its cognates nine times,
making clear that "abstaining from what is another's" fits Hume's conception of CJ (boldface added in the following):

> *Wherein consists this honesty and justice, which you find in restoring
> a loan, and **abstaining** from the property of others?* (T 3.2.1.9; ital-
> ics original)

> [M]en, in the ordinary conduct of life, look not so far as the pub-
> lic interest, when they pay their creditors, perform their prom-
> ises, and **abstain** from theft, and robbery, and injustice of every
> kind. (T 3.2.1.10)

> Instead of departing from our own interest, or from that of our
> nearest friends, by **abstaining** from the possessions of others, we
> cannot better consult both these interests, than by such a con-
> vention [abstaining from the possessions of others]; because it
> is by that means we maintain society, which is so necessary to
> their well-being and subsistence, as well as to our own. (T 3.2.2.9)

[T]he sense of interest has become common to all our fellows, and gives us a confidence of the future regularity of their conduct: And 'tis only on the expectation of this, that our moderation and **abstinence** are founded. (3.2.2.10)

After this convention, concerning **abstinence** from the possessions of others, is enter'd into, and every one has acquir'd a stability in his possessions, there immediately arise the ideas of justice and injustice; as also those of property, right, and obligation. (T 3.2.2.11)

'Tis certain, that no affection of the human mind has both a sufficient force, and a proper direction to counter-balance the love of gain, and render men fit members of society, by making them **abstain** from the possessions of others. (T 3.2.2.13)

Afterwards a sentiment of morals concurs with interest, and becomes a new obligation upon mankind. This sentiment of morality, in the performance of promises, arises from the same principles as that in the **abstinence** from the property of others. (T 3.2.5.12)

[T]his external relation [first occupation] causes nothing in external objects, and has only an influence on the mind, by giving us a sense of duty in **abstaining** from that object, and in restoring it to the first possessor. (T 3.2.6.3)

...the obligation to **abstain** from the possessions of others... (T 3.2.8.6)

The duty of CJ tells a person to abstain from a neighbor's stuff. Reciprocally, the neighbor has *a right to exclude* other's from messing with her stuff. The logic is plain in Hume as when he writes: "...particular goods are to be assign'd to each particular person, while *the rest of mankind are excluded* from their possession and enjoyment" (T 3.2.3.1, italics added).[10] There is no denying that logic in Hume, and he is schematic in talking "abstaining."

The concept of abstaining necessarily implies certain boundaries. There is every reason to think that those same boundaries would operate in Hume's understanding of government vis-a-vis the governed. One's stuff is one's own; it is *not* enveloped within a social contract (T 3.2.8.3-3.2.8.5; EMPL 465–487, 489). The government is treading on one's stuff whenever it does anything we would call treading if done by a neighbor. "A man's property is suppos'd to be fenc'd against every mortal, in every possible case"T 3.2.1.16).

That is not to deny that we make an important distinction between government treading and robbery; we do. The idea is not that government should never tread; again, "A great sacrifice of liberty must necessarily be made in every government" (EMPL 40). But a sacrifice of liberty is a sacrifice of liberty—even if it serves liberty overall. Liberty depends on authority, and authority depends on violations of liberty, so *liberty depends on violations of liberty*—a paradox to be appreciated, refined, naturalized.

Hume favors violations of liberty as necessary for authority—stable polity, etc.—but seems otherwise to maintain a strong favor for liberty, a presumption of liberty. As Capaldi puts it: "Those who would seek to limit liberty have the *onus* of showing that (a) a particular [voluntary] action is harmful and (b) curtailing that action will not have even more harmful consequences" (in Hart 2018). Indeed, the *Treatise* quietly indicates such presumption:

> No one can doubt, that the convention for the distinction of property, and for the stability of possession, is of all circumstances the most necessary to the establishment of human society, and that after the agreement for the fixing and observing of this rule, **there remains little or nothing to be done** towards settling a perfect harmony and concord. (T 3.2.2.12; italics added)

---

10. Gregg (2009) and Robinson (2016) elaborate the exclusion conception of property in Hume's Scottish predecessors Gershom Carmichael and Francis Hutcheson, and Robinson (2017) touches on Hume in treating the same in Adam Smith.

As Hardin (2007) and Sabl (2012) richly appreciate, Hume had uncanny insight into focal points, mutual coordination, and convention, prefiguring Thomas Schelling (1960) and David K. Lewis (1969). Hume made a crucial part of the arc from natural jurisprudence to what Smith would express as "the liberal plan of equality, liberty, and justice" (WN 664). That commutative justice and liberty are flipsides is signaled by Smith, for example, when he says of two restrictions: "Both laws were evident violations of natural liberty, and *therefore* unjust"(WN 530, italics added). Here it is entirely appropriate to assimilate Hume to Smith—we *dis*agree with Sabl when he writes "the common tendency to assimilate Hume to Smith on these matters rests on low and eroding ground" (in Hart 2018). Smith, in the LJ, writes frequently of ownership being extended to objects as propertization advances (LJ 10, 16, 19–23, 27, 34, 38, 39, 207, 308, 309, 432. 434, 460, 466, 467, 468). Contrary to what Sabl writes, assimilating Hume to Smith sheds light on the liberalism of Hume's *Essays* and the *History*.

Indeed, Hume says that if every man had sufficient sagacity to see the interest he has in observing justice and equity, and sufficient strength of mind, "there had never, in that case, been any such thing as government or political society, but each man, following his **natural liberty**, had lived in entire peace and harmony with others" (EPM 4.1; boldface added). Hume is imagining a fictional world in which people have natural conventions about not messing with other people's stuff, *observe those conventions*, and, therefore, each man enjoys "natural liberty": Others not messing with one' stuff.

Other modern scholars also assimilate Hume to the natural jurisprudence tradition

Because our claim—that mere-liberty is central in Hume—has met with resistance (see Hart 2018), we invoke leading scholars on the connection we are drawing from natural jurisprudence to mere-liberty. Stephen Buckle (1991) writes that the natural jurisprudence tradition developed formulations of duties intended to specify "not only a morally inviolable realm which it is the purpose of political society to protect, but also the place of the individual within the social order" (vii). A number of scholars have held that Hume's political thought may be seen as continuing the tradition, albeit with different metaphysical underpinnings (Forbes 1975, 16–17, 26–27). Knud Haakonssen (1981) writes: "Hume was undoubtedly very much influenced by modern natural law theories in Grotius, Pufendorf, and others. But his real genius was to combine the strands of his inheritance into a completely new sort of natural law theory—for, indeed, he is quite willing to use that label, provided we let him fill in the contents himself" (12; see also Haakonssen 1996, 118). Buckle (1991) says, "Hume can be recognized to be an important contributor to the natural law tradition" (ix), "Hume observes that his theory of property is much the same as Grotius's.... [T]here is no bar, and substantial support, for accepting his claim, and therefore for recognizing his theory as a contribution to the modern theory of natural law" (295).

In Grotius, with whom Hume associates his own theory of property and justice,[11] natural rights are understood as stemming first from people's "natural drives or instincts for self-preservation, and, second, [from] right reason or sound judgment of what is *honestum*, that is, what makes life with others possible" (Haakonssen 1996, 27; italics original). From the notion of self-preservation, Grotius derives the perfect right of self-ownership; from the criterion of right reason comes the necessity of property and contract, without which society would not be possible. Together, self-ownership, property, and contract in Grotius form the complex of *one's own*, corresponding to the Latin *suum*. "[Natural right] in the strictest sense is, then, every action which does not injure any other person's *suum*, which in effect means that it is every *suum* which does not conflict with the *sua* of others" (Haakonssen 1996, 27). The most basic duties of justice consist merely in abstaining from every other person's *suum*.

Unlike Grotius and his natural law followers, Hume does not define property or justice in terms of natural rights or theological foundations. Rather, he frames property as a mental relationship of persons and objects, and justice as the ensuing moral sentiment to abstain from the property of others. It is in the negation of invasion—*not* messing, abstaining—that

---

11. "This theory concerning the origin of property, and consequently of justice, is, in the main, the same with that hinted at and adopted by GROTIUS" (EPM App. 1, f. 63).

liberty must be understood. Mere-liberty is implied by the moral precept or injunction to abstain from what is another's. Haakonssen (1996) says that for Hume "The object of just laws is thus **individual *liberty***, and, since the most obvious and most endangered expression of **such *liberty*** is the acquisition and use of property, justice is centrally concerned with property and, it follows, with contracts" (117, italics added).

The flow from the commutative justice of natural jurisprudence to the mere-liberty of liberalism is acknowledged. J. G. A. Pocock (1983) writes that "the child of jurisprudence is liberalism" (249), and Dugald Stewart (1854) noted that "the systems of *natural jurisprudence* compiled by Grotius and his successors" were "the first rudiments of pure ethics and of liberal politics taught in modern times" (26).

Pinning down the content of mere-liberty

The mere-liberty formulation is *others not messing with one's stuff. That formulation has inside of it* the evolved historicity of the grammar-like content of:

1. what counts as "stuff,"
2. what makes it "one's,"
3. what counts as "messing with" it.

Hume's *Treatise* is especially rich in discussing the second facet of CJ, that is, what it is that makes a thing Jim's: Hume says that Jim's ownership derives from a lineage based on the principles of possession/occupation, prescription, accession, succession, and transference by consent (T 3.2.3). Other works in jurisprudence treat also what counts as stuff and what counts as messing with it. For example, Smith's *Lectures on Jurisprudence* explains that land became susceptible to ownership only in the age of agriculture (LJ 20-22, 409, 460), and he explains various types of wrongs that might be done to one's stuff.

Just as every language community may have its own language with its own grammar, every community can have its own way of settling the three matters listed above. To a great extent, the community's particular rules of CJ bubble up from its history of equal-equal relationships; but also, as Hume notes, governmental institutions ("municipal laws") may "fix what the principles of human nature have left undetermin'd" (T 3.2.3.10 n75.13)—just as government policy sometimes resolves or alters particulars of the grammar of a national language. Although it is crucial to recognize the distinction between equal-equal jural relationships and superior-inferior jural relationships, it is wrongheaded to think of those two living completely separate lives: Natural conventions of equal-equal relationships certainly play the primary role, but some particular rules or boundaries are affected by government lawmaking. Both realms of jural relationships play a role in pinning down and filling out the details of that society's social grammar of CJ.

Social life establishes within that community a social grammar of *not messing with other people's stuff.* The injunction or precept against messing is a necessary convention among jural equals; if CJ is grossly unsettled or unheeded, the society will degenerate. Hence, among viable communities, amidst a diversity of historicity, a diversity of social grammars, there obtains a uniformity in the general formulation: All viable communities uphold the general precept against messing with other people's stuff.

Now consider the set of societies in which, furthermore, a superior-inferior—or, governor-governed—relationship can be said to function as a coherent, integrated system. For all such societies, we have a uniformity, also, in applying the following crucial principle: a type of action in the superior-inferior jural relationship is an initiation of coercion if (and only if) such action in equal-equal jural relationships is an initiation of coercion. If your neighbor "taxed" you (i.e., extorted wealth from you) or "regulated" your freedom of association (i.e., stalked and assaulted you in private life), we darned-well would regard that as an initiation of coercion, and so we do call it an initiation of coercion when done by government (though we do not call it "extortion" or "assault").[12]

Historicity pins down "stuff," "one's," and "messing with," yielding operative concepts of both commutative justice and liberty. The Hume-Smith formulations maintain that taxation and government interventions are initiations of coercion, are violations of liberty; such semantics check their

---

12. Note that not seeing taxation and government restrictions as voluntary depends on properly theorizing the configuration of ownership; see Klein 2011.

advocates by placing upon them a burden of proof. The government may not much respect liberty, but *the concept* is operative there nonetheless: it requires only coherence in the social grammar of that society's equal-equal relationships, as well as the aptness of saying that a superior-inferior jural relationship prevails there.

Uniformity amidst diversity: It is precisely in the uniformity, in all such societies, that the ideas of CJ and mere-liberty can be said to *transcend historicity*. They are natural conventions to all such societies. As Charles Griswold put it, CJ "is neither free from historicity nor reducible to it" (2006, 185; see likewise Haakonssen 1981, 43-44). CJ and liberty need historicity to pin down the specifics of the social grammar, but as general formulations they achieve a uniformity pervading all such societies.

Jural dualism (E-E and S-i), as opposed to either jural monism or jural pluralism

Today, speaking of "*the* government" feels natural to us. Within the modern nation-state there is an integration of the, e.g., municipal, county, provincial, national authorities. It is natural enough for us to understand that each of us has jural relationships with our neighbors and other jural equals, and that each of us has jural relationships with the government, which clearly does things that our jural equals cannot. The modern nation-state is a polity of *jural dualism*, which is to say, the existence of only two kinds of jural relationships, equal-equal (abbreviated E-E) and superior-inferior (S-i).

But human experience has, arguably, found itself in conditions of jural monism, that is, *only* equal-equal, in the simple society of the ancestral band of the Paleolithic, giving us instincts to jural monism that die hard (Hayek's two-worlds hypothesis and atavism thesis about modern collectivist politics; see Hayek 1976, 1978, 1979, 1988). Jural monism is in our genes. It is an instinct that has to be *overcome* (see ch. 8).

In recent millennia, human experience has found itself in conditions of jural pluralism beyond dualism: That is, our ancestors, Moses to Machiavelli, knew life of multiple and *non-integrated* jural authorities: Families, clans, master-slave relationships, tribes, barons and lords, ecclesiastical institutions, multiple and often unstable kings and chieftains, all grating against one another, a jural mishmash that defies the simple "jural superior" of the modern nation-state. In the *History*, Hume speaks of the old times of jural pluralism when he says:

> In the ancient feudal constitution, of which the English partook with other European nations, there was a mixture, not of authority and **liberty**, which we have since enjoyed in this island, and which now subsist uniformly together; but of authority and anarchy, which perpetually shocked with each other, and which took place alternately, according as circumstances were more or less favourable to either of them... During an unpopular and weak reign, the current commonly ran so strong against the monarch, that none durst inlist themselves in the court-party; or if the prince was able to engage any considerable barons on his side, the question was decided with arms in the field, not by debates or arguments in a senate or assembly. (H V, 556, Note [J]; see also 533)

Sabl puts it vividly in his excellent *Hume's Politics: Coordination and Crisis in the History of England*:

> In the feudal era, they [England's barons] did not support the rule of law because in its absence they themselves were law. Civilization was a matter of bringing the barons, through a mix of force and bribery, to believe that great wealth and status among fellow subjects, under equal laws, was more desirable than a lawless and miserable domination over slaves. This was eventually a change in identity: barons became gentlemen. (Sabl 2012, 65)

As Robert Bucholz (2003) puts it, Britain saw the formation of *imperium*. In this case, *imperium* is the nation-state's supervening and integrating of jural affairs. The formation of such jural imperium is a chief theme of Hume's *History of England*. Britain was early to jural imperium (which does not preclude competing court systems) and consequent jural dualism. In the *History*, Hume is quite consistently favorable toward developments in the direction of imperium and consequent jural dualism (other passages related to the imperium theme are found at I, 254; II, 525; III, 49, 51, 73-77, 80; IV, 384, 406, 414).

The realization of jural dualism—the modern, integrated, stable nation-state—is key to mere-liberty: It is only by taking the social grammar of CJ as operative in the society's E-E relationships and applying that to *its system of S-i relationships* that mere-liberty is pinned down and becomes meaningful within that historical context. But that move is not so possible when society does not have an S-i system. In the fog of jural pluralism, there is bound to be less clarity in translating E-E principles to form a concept of "liberty" that is operative within the constellation of plural jural powers. Indeed, under jural pluralism, it may not even make sense to speak of a system of E-E relationships.

Moreover, the very fact that, under jural pluralism, such powers are apt to be battling each other is likely to leave liberty on the back-burner. Under jural pluralism, then, there is not only the primary problem, the *conceptual* fog, but a secondary practical problem: The fog of war. Hume's astounding understanding of focal points, mutual coordination, and convention enabled him to cut through the fogs, to see how the new (Plumb 1967) emergent condition of a stable and jurally integrated nation-state enabled a new focal vision for the polity. Hume, Smith, Franklin, Burke, Madison are among the convention-savvy civilizational leaders who cultivate the vision. They built upon the anticipations of men like Grotius and Locke, who were not yet in a situation in which stable integrated polity could be presupposed.

The accretion of jural integration occurred at the same time that political philosophy was shifting from social cohesion in the higher things to the emergent, post-Westphalia focus on the lower things that were worked out in natural jurisprudence, a refocusing that comported with (1) growing toleration in high-things differences, (2) concomitant abstract ideas like earnings (honest, CJ-abiding income), increasingly sanctified in evolving Christianity and justified in the liberal theory of virtue (e.g., in Britain, Perkins, Baxter, Defoe, Locke, Addison, Steele, Butler, Hutcheson, Hume, Smith), (3), liberal economic theory and Smith's "liberal plan," and (4) the approval of innovation, and (5) the great enrichment (McCloskey 2016). The vision cultivated by Hume et al. was not just the nation-state, but inspiration and formulations for a *liberal* nation-state—a plan practical and lucrative to most, not least the Exchequer, but also virtuous: "A commercial humanism had been not unsuccessfully constructed" (Pocock 1985, 5). Perhaps deliberately downplaying concomitants which tended toward social discohesion (DelliSanti 2021), Hume and Smith made such appeal to all honest gentlemen (Merrill 2015).

Thus, jural integration, jural dualism, brings liberty into focus: Others, including the government, not messing with one's stuff. That essential meaning is used to formulate reforms and to compare them (including the no-reform option), thus keeping thought and discussion anchored in what we know and practice, the status quo. The liberty principle (if Reform 1 rates higher in liberty than Reform 2, then prefer it to Reform 2) is defeasible; Hume wrote with approval of government's providing of bridges, harbors, canals, fleets, and armies (T 3.2.7.8) and of forced sharing in special cases of extremity (EPM 3.18). But Hume and Smith make a maxim of the liberty principle.

Hume and Smith considered the constitutive elements that contribute or conduce to relative liberty—rules certainty and generality, representative government, divided powers, checks and balances, and so on. The adjective "regular," as in "regular liberty," it seems, implied something like jural integration (see Carmichael 1724, 159–161, channeling Pufendorf). The word *liberty* is often used by Hume as descriptive of such contributory political-science and constitutional elements. Both essential and contributory meanings must be seen in Hume's "liberty" discourse.

If mere-liberty depends on jural integration and stable, established authority, then it is no wonder that Hume sees a regular system of mere-liberty as something of only late distillation in the history of England. Forbes puts it pithily: "if liberty and the constitution are modern, the Stuarts, or the first two at least, could hardly be blamed for trying to destroy something which did not then exist" (1975, 263). Hume basically endorses the integrative work of divine right monarchy, but is then glad of how it was reconstituted, in fitful succession, by "opinion" associated with such things as print culture, commerce, and not least Puritan enthusiasm (Merrill 2018).

Liberty in the History, Vols. 1–6

The contrarieties that resides in *liberty* are most in evidence in the six-volume *History*. Our consideration of that massive work can here be only smattering and slapdash—and we confess to being inexpert in the *History*.

Kukathas reports that Hume uses "liberty" about 700 times in the *History* (Hart 2018). Often it comes with modifiers, thus "personal liberty," "civil liberty," "political liberty," "English liberty," "established liberty," "general liberty," "public liberty," etc. Hume frequently writes of the system/plan of liberty, often with "regular." Here we do not attempt to nail down the meanings of the various expressions. As argued in the foregoing, Hume's moral and political philosophy authorizes our seeing mere-liberty as central, even primary.

Mere-liberty is connoted in the following expressions:

- *liberty of thought/conscience/religion*: I, 393; III, 136, 189, 212, 266, 289, 322, 342, 384, 433; IV, 19, 150, 168, 211; V, 115, 125; VI, 71, 88, 139, 184, 250, 254, 364, 377, 389, 398, 482.

- *liberty of press/speech*: III, 345; IV, 140, 180, 285; V, 91, 92, 130, 190, 240; VI, 540, 542.

- *captives/prisoners/slaves recovering their liberty/being restored to liberty/etc.*: I, 142, 143, 149, 172, 224, 231, 260, 265, 291, 384, 396, 398, 401, 402, 403, 409, 469; II, 48, 58, 58, 61, 62, 79, 89, 93, 113, 124, 187, 190, 191, 244, 253, 259, 260, 330, 334, 387, 417, 424, 472, 488; III, 22, 35, 36, 67, 70, 75, 159, 162, 163, 164, 166, 167, 174, 175, 229, 240, 270, 294, 296, 297, 305, 379, 382, 405, 406, 407, 428; IV, 7, 8, 50, 80, 98, 124, 128, 130, 132, 156, 157, 171, 180, 190, 198, 201, 202, 232, 296, 327, 335; V, 62, 63, 74, 216; VI, 9, 13, 33, 88, 124, 133, 228, 327, 371, 529.

In the following cavalcade of comments on vols. 1–6, we chiefly highlight passages *where an idea of mere-liberty is salient*, putting such ideas in **boldface**. In treating each volume, we highlight passages in the order in which they come in the volume.

Volume I

One of the important meanings of liberty is a political community's not being dominated by a foreign power or hegemon. That meaning is metaphorically analogous to our essential meaning: If we regard that community metaphorically as a human being, then the foreign power is messing with that being's stuff. In such fashion, the being's being free from a foreign hegemon might be regarded as a meaning that is merely parallel to our essential meaning. But hegemony may well obstruct the achieving of jural dualism, or in other ways militate against mere-liberty, and so being free from a foreign hegemon might be seen as a *contributory* meaning. (Of course hegemony could go the other way, too, or lead to an absorption that undoes "foreign.")

Early in Volume I, one of the last composed, Hume writes: "And the Britons had now, during almost a century, enjoyed their *liberty* unmolested, when the Romans, in the reign of Claudius, began to think seriously of reducing them under their dominion." Upon Roman invasion, "the [Britons], disarmed, dispirited, and submissive, had left all desire and even idea of their former *liberty* and independence" (H I, 7,11; italics added). We are inclined to read liberty here as chiefly a condition of political independence, but a mere-liberty meaning is perhaps reasonable as well.

In the same volume, Hume speaks of Alfred the Great's division of England into counties and smaller localities for the purpose of regulating the administration of justice. Alfred's scheme, in the chaotic wake of the Danish invasion, hindered legal mobility, a move which Hume says would "be regarded as destructive of **liberty** and commerce in a polished state" (H I, 77). But, Hume continues, Alfred's scheme was "well calculated to reduce that fierce and licentious people under the salutary restraint of law and government...and nothing could be more popular and liberal than his plan for the administration of justice" (H I, 77). Thus, Hume suggests here that counter to what one in a developed, stable political order might think, Alfred's plan for the administration of justice, which again hindered free movement, was at the time conducive to mere-liberty. Direct reductions in mere-liberty spelled augmentations in overall mere-liberty. Hume writes:

On the whole, notwithstanding the *seeming liberty* or licentiousness of the Anglo-Saxons, the great body, even of the free citizens, in those ages, *really enjoyed much less true* **liberty**, than when the execution of the laws is most severe, and where subjects are reduced to the strictest subordination and dependence on the civil magistrate. The reason is derived from the excess itself of *that* **liberty**. Men must guard themselves at any price against insult and injuries; and where they speak, and where they receive not protection from the laws and magistrate, they will seek by submission to superiors, and by herding into some private confederacy, which acts under the direction of a powerful leader. And thus all anarchy is the immediate cause of tyranny, if not over the state, at least over many individuals. (H I, 169; italics added).

Here we see elements of jural pluralism and unstable polity in Hume's explanation of why early Britons "really enjoyed much less true liberty."

It was somewhat likewise later under the Normans, who were "incapable of any true or regular liberty; which requires such improvement in knowledge and morals, as can only be the result of reflection and experience, and must grow to perfection during several ages of settled and established government" (I.254). Yet the people "had indeed arms in their hands, which prevented the establishment of a total despotism, and left their posterity sufficient power, whenever they should attain a sufficient degree of reason, to assume true **liberty**" (I.254).

Hume clearly means mere-liberty when he says that King Henry I "sometimes deprived his subjects of the **liberty** of hunting on their own lands, or even cutting their own woods" (I.277). He says that some of the articles of the Great Charter "provide for the equal distribution of justice, and **free** enjoyment of property; the great objects for which political society was at first founded by men, which the people have **a perpetual and unalienable right to recal**, and which no time, nor precedent, nor statute, nor positive institution, ought to deter them from keeping ever uppermost in their thoughts and attention" (445).

Volume II:

Writing of the late 13th century, Hume says:

> Though the inhabitants of the country were still left at the disposal of their imperious lords; many attempts were made to give more security and **liberty** to citizens, and make them enjoy unmolested the fruits of their industry. Boroughs were erected by royal patent within the demesne lands: **Liberty** of trade was conferred upon them... (H II, 105)

King Edward laid his "oppressive hand on all orders of men":

> He **limited** the merchants in the quantity of wool allowed to be exported; and at the same time **forced** them to pay him a duty of forty shillings a sack, which was computed to be above the third of the value. He **seized** all the rest of the wool, as well as all the leather of the kingdom, into his hands, and disposed of these commodities for his own benefit: He **required** the sheriffs of each county to supply him with 2000 quarters of wheat, and as many of oats, which he permitted them to **seize** wherever they could find them. The cattle and other commodities, necessary for supplying his army, were **laid hold of without the consent of the owners**...(H II, 117)

In discussing the maneuvering by barons and other around the king and political charters to ensure "against all impositions and taxes without consent of parliament," Hume writes of "the attachment, which the English in that age bore to **liberty**, and their well-grounded jealousy of the arbitrary disposition of Edward" (H II, 119-121).

Later, Hume speaks of foolish price restrictions following a bad season: "The parliament, in 1315, endeavoured to fix more moderate rates to commodities...and laws, instead of preventing [scarcity], only aggravate the evil, by **cramping** and **restraining** commerce. The parliament accordingly, in the ensuing year, repealed their ordinance, which they had found useless and burdensome" (H II. 177).

In the valediction (518-25) at the end of Vol. II (the last to be written):

> Violence generally prevailed, instead of general and equitable maxims: The pretended **liberty** of the times, was only an incapacity of submitting to the government: And men, not protected by law in their lives and properties, sought shelter, by their personal servitude and attachments under some powerful chieftain, or by voluntary combinations.
>
> The gradual progress of improvement raised the Europeans somewhat above this uncultivated state; and affairs, in this island particularly, took early a turn, which was more favourable to **justice** and to **liberty**. Civil employments and occupations soon became honourable among the English…. (522)

> [T]he distinction of villain and freeman was totally, though insensibly abolished, and that no person remained in the state, to whom the former laws could be applied.
>
> Thus *personal* **freedom** became almost general in Europe; an advantage which paved the way for the encrease of *political or civil* **liberty**, and which, even where it was not attended with this salutary effect, served to give the members of the community some of the most considerable advantages of it. (H II, 524)

In the previous passage, perhaps "political or civil liberty" signifies a institutionalized system of recognizing and protecting mere-liberty, while "personal freedom" signifies either the mere reality that one's stuff is not being messed with by others (irrespective of whether such freedom is institutionalized) or associated features such as personal capability, independence, or autonomy. We share two more notable quotations:

> It [the pre-Tudor period] required the authority absolute of the sovereigns, which took place in the subsequent period, to pull down those disorderly and licentious tyrants [the barons], who were equally averse from peace and from freedom, and to establish that regular execution of the laws, which, in a following age, enabled the people to erect a regular and equitable plan of **liberty**. (H II.525)

Above all, a civilized nation, like the English, who have established the most perfect and most accurate system of **liberty** that was ever found compatible with government, ought to be cautious in appealing to the practice of their ancient ancestors, or regarding the maxims of uncultivated ages as certain rules for their present conduct. (H II:525)

Volume III:

In reviewing the reign of Henry VII, Hume provides a several-page catalogue of policy developments affecting commerce. Hume's drift is clearly and consistently against governmentalization. Hume reports approvingly that "the nobility and gentry acquired a power of breaking the ancient entails," and disapprovingly ("how unreasonable and iniquitous" that "Severe laws were made against taking interest for money"; "Even the profits of exchange were **prohibited**"; "Laws were made against the exportation of money, plate, or bullion" (H III, 77); "It was **prohibited** to export horses"; "no bows were to be sold at a higher price than six shillings and four-pence"; "Prices were affixed to woollen cloth, to caps and hats"; and "the wages of labourers were regulated by law" (78). Hume clearly speaks mere-liberty: "*these matters ought always to be left* **free**, *and be entrusted to the common course of business and commerce*" (78, italics added).[13] And our free-marketeer is not finished: "One great cause of the low state of industry during this period, was the **restraints** put upon it"; "These absurd **limitations** proceeded from a desire of promoting husbandry"; "All methods of supporting populousness, except by the interest of the proprietors, are **violent** and ineffectual" and "One check to industry in England was the erecting of corporations; an abuse which is not yet entirely corrected" (79).

About 55 pages later, Hume once again issues a general maxim endorsing liberty in commerce and the arts:

[T]he constant rule of the magistrate, except, perhaps, on the first introduction of any art, is, **to leave the profession to itself,**

---

13. Sabl (in Hart 2018) suggests, rather, that this is an "offhand line" and that it does not significantly attest to mere-liberty in Hume.

and trust its encouragement to those who reap the benefit of it. The artizans, finding their profits to rise by the favour of their customers, encrease, as much as possible, their skill and industry; and as matters are **not disturbed by any injudicious tampering**, the commodity is always sure to be at all times nearly proportioned to the demand. (H III, 135; boldface added.)

Hume presents the general maxim so as to address a policy measure that he highlights as an exception to it. There follows a passage well known because Adam Smith reproduced it in *The Wealth of Nations* (790-791). The passage suggests that in the 16th century (if not more generally) there was good reason for the "wise legislator" to prevent "the interested diligence of the clergy," by bribing "their indolence," through a "fixed establishment for the priests" (136; and he seems to endorse a state church in the Perfect Commonwealth essay, 525). Still, the general principle is "to leave the profession to itself"— to not mess with its people's stuff. The drift of Hume's essays about commerce and the jealousy of trade is clearly and consistently opposed to the governmentalization of social affairs. As Russell Hardin (2007) put it: "he thinks that government should be kept small and not intrusive, as he argues in his varied essays on economics" (200; see also Stewart 1992, 178ff).

Hume writes that Henry VIII "published an edict for a general tax upon his subjects, which he still called a loan…This pretended loan, as being **more regular, was really more dangerous to the liberties of the people**, and was a precedent for the king's imposing taxes without consent of parliament" (H 3:148). Notice, "more regular" may not mean more liberty, and can even mean less liberty.

But Hume seems to be glad of the Henrician Reformation, on the whole. He says about "the catholic religion": "Papal usurpations, the tyranny of the inquisition, the multiplicity of holidays; all these **fetters on liberty** and industry were ultimately derived from the authority and insinuation of monks" (H III, 227).

At 330–31 there are more free-market comments (like those at 77–79), and such words as "fixing," "permitting," "confining," "excluding," and "prohibited" all imply a mere-liberty notion.

Volume IV:

Hume speaks of Elizabeth "allowing a **free** exportation of corn" (48).

Hume treats Peter Wentworth's "premeditated harangue" and says in his own voice: "it seems to contain a rude sketch of those principles of liberty, which happily gained afterwards the ascendant in England" (178). Hume's summary of the harangue shows both mere-liberty and established-rule/parliamentary ideas. Hume also says that "Wentworth better understood the principles of liberty" (180). We return to Wentworth below.

Speaking of Elizabeth's use of purveyance (that is, forced hospitality), Hume notes that payment "was often distant and uncertain" and continues: "so that purveyance, **besides the slavery of it**, was always regarded as a great burthen, and being arbitrary and casual, was liable to great abuses" (272). Most significant here is the word *besides: Besides* the uncertainty and arbitrariness, there is the sheer slavery of it.

At 344-46 Hume again decries market interventions under Elizabeth, particularly monopolies. The words "restraints," "extorted," "free themselves," and "restrained" all imply mere-liberty. Hume then says such restrictions embarrass certain prepossessions about the degree of "**liberty** possessed under the administration of Elizabeth" (346). Hume then notes:

> It was asserted, that the queen inherited both an enlarging and a restraining power; by her prerogative she might **set at liberty** what was restrained by statute or otherwise, and by her prerogative she might restrain **what was otherwise at liberty**.... (346)

Hume here clearly draws a contrast between liberty and established statute. (See also Note [HH], 411f.)

At 367 Hume speaks of "branches of prerogative, which are now abolished, and which were, every one of them, **totally incompatible with the liberty of the subject**." Sounds to us like mere-liberty.

By the way, at 380, it is quite interesting that Hume baldly reports in a paragraph consisting solely of one very short sentence: "In the fifth of this reign was enacted the first law for the relief of the poor." No comment—just as Smith never weighed in on the poor law (apart from the related settlement restrictions) in his otherwise quite comprehensive review of public policy.

Volume V

Hume says about the times at the start of James I: "In England, the love of freedom, which, unless checked, flourishes extremely in all liberal natures, acquired new force, and was regulated by more enlarged views, suitably to that cultivated understanding, which became, every day, more common, among men of birth and education" (H V:18). At 20–21 we find free-market remarks, including the endeavor "to **free** trade from those **shackles**," "patents for monopolies…extremely **fettered** every species of domestic industry," the Commons attempted "to give **liberty** to the trading part of the nation," and an attempt "to **free** the nation from the burthen of purveyance." Recovering from their lethargy in the face of the assertion of absolutism, they "were resolved to secure **liberty** by firmer barriers, than their ancestors had hitherto provided for it" (40).

Hume writes of a bill in Parliament under James I:

> Advantage was also taken of the present good agreement between the king and parliament, in order to pass the bill against monopolies, which had formerly been encouraged by the king, but which had failed by the rupture between him and the last house of commons. This bill was conceived in such terms as to render it merely declaratory; and all monopolies were condemned, as contrary to law and to the known **liberties** of the people. It was there supposed, that every subject of England had **entire power to dispose of his own actions, provided he did no injury to any of his fellow-subjects**; and that no prerogative of the king, no power of any magistrate, nothing but the authority alone of laws, **could restrain that unlimited freedom.** The full prosecution of this noble principle into all its natural consequences, has at last, through many contests, produced that singular and happy government, which we enjoy at present. (H V, 114)

The parts in boldface ring mere-liberty. That the "full prosecution" of the "noble principle" that "the authority alone of laws [as opposed, that is, to merely royal prerogative], could restrain that unlimited freedom" does not imply that the government that fully prosecutes such principle will necessarily liberalize as thoroughly as Hume thinks desirable, yet it remains perfectly sensible that Hume would applaud the full prosecution of the principle, and believe such full prosecution essential to producing "that singular and happy government, which we enjoy at present."Also, in Hume's note to the passage (Note N, 560), Hume speaks of the law recalling patents of monopolies as "establishing principles very favourable to liberty." Hume is using *liberty* in the mere-liberty sense.[14]

In reflecting on James I, Hume remarks on developments *since 1625*: "By the changes, which have since been introduced, the **liberty** and independence **of individuals** has been rendered much more full, intire, and secure; that of the public more uncertain and precarious"(128). Notice that the liberty *of individuals* is said to have become not only more "secure," but more "full" and "intire." Thus, even for a law that leaves civil rights perfectly certain and predictable, there remains the further issue of how *fully* or *entirely* liberty is adhered to by the laws that are instituted.

At page 160 Hume says of a key group of parliamentarians, including Thomas Wentworth, Robert Philips, Edward Coke, and John Selden: "Animated with a warm regard to liberty, these generous patriots...." At page 177 Hume emphasizes that forced loans "however authorized by precedent, and even by statute, were a violation of **liberty**." People were riled up by "violations of **liberty**" (187, 202); "Their **liberties**, they believed, were ravished from them"" (186). At 189-91 Hume quotes Philips and Wentworth at length, and mere-liberty is conspicuous in their words. At 194-95 Hume channels the "partizans of the court": "it were surely much better for human society to be deprived of **liberty** than to be destitute of government." Sketching three types of puritan, Hume says that one were "the political puritans, who maintained the highest principles of **civil liberty**-"(212).

Volume VI

Speaking again of commerce, the free-market Hume says "the monopoly was gradually invaded, and commerce encreased by the encrease of **liberty**"(148).

---

14. Sabl (in Hart 2018) offers a reading of the passage (H V: 114) quite contrary to ours.

Remarks on Scotland suggest that there is more to liberty than being free from arbitrary power of the prince: "The Scottish nation, though they had never been subject to the arbitrary power of their prince, had but very imperfect notions of law and **liberty**; and scarcely in any age had they ever enjoyed an administration, which had confined itself within the proper boundaries" (223). In remarks on the Dutch, Hume indicates that authority comes before liberty: "De Wit, too pertinacious in defence of his own system of liberty, while the very being of the Commonwealth was threatened..." (268).

Hume writes of "the rigours exercised against conventicles," of the "enormous outrage" of quartering mercenaries to enforce it, and of how, furthermore, "chicanery was joined to tyranny" (328-29). "If...a protestant church [that] approaches towards unlimited authority were so tyrannical, how dismal its final establishment; when all dread of opposition shall at last be removed by mercenary armies, and all sense of shame by long and inveterate habit?" (331).

Hume explains that the Jesuits believed that they would be able to convert the English population if they were to obtain "toleration"and then "entire liberty" (340). Discussing habeas corpus, Hume says that it "seems necessary for the protection of **liberty**." He also comments: "It must, however, be confessed, that there is some difficulty to reconcile with such extreme **liberty** the full security and the regular police of a state, especially the police of great cities" (367). "The **liberty** of the subject, which had been so carefully guarded by the great charter, and by the late law of habeas corpus, was every day violated by their arbitrary and capricious commitments" (385).

In general remarks on the 1688–89 revolution, Hume clearly indicates that liberty means more than simply established, predictable government:

> The revolution forms a new epoch in the constitution; and was probably attended with consequences more advantageous to the people, than barely freeing them from an exceptionable administration. By deciding many important questions in favour of **liberty**, and still more, by that great precedent of deposing one king, and establishing a new family, it gave such an ascendant to popular principles, as has put the nature of the English constitution

beyond all controversy. And it may justly be affirmed, without
any danger of exaggeration, that we, in this island, have ever since
enjoyed, if not the best system of government, at least the most
entire system of **liberty**, that ever was known amongst mankind.
(H VI, 531)

Hume concisely expresses the authority-liberty theme, as reflected in
the spirited Whigs and their opponents:

> Compositions the most despicable, both for style and matter have
> been extolled, and propogated, and read; as if they had equalled
> the most celebrated remains of antiquity [Hume's note: Such as
> Rapin Thoyra, Locke, Sidney, Hoadley, &c.]. And forgetting that
> a regard to **liberty**, though a laudable passion, ought commonly
> to be subordinate to a reverence for established government, the
> prevailing faction has celebrated only the partizans of the for-
> mer, who pursued as their object the perfection of civil society,
> and has extolled them at the expence of their antagonists, who
> maintained those maxims, that are essential to its very existence.
> (H VI, 533)

Hume makes the remarkable suggestion that moderation and accom-
modation might have avoided much of the great turmoil of seventeenth-cen-
tury England:

> Indeed, could the parliaments in the reign of Charles I. have
> been induced to relinquish so far their old habits, as to grant that
> prince the same revenue which was voted to his successor, or had
> those in the reign of Charles II. conferred on him as large a reve-
> nue as was enjoyed by his brother, all the disorders in both reigns
> might easily have been prevented, and probably all reasonable
> concessions to **liberty** might peaceably have been obtained from
> both monarchs. But these assemblies, unacquainted with pub-
> lic business, and often actuated by faction and fanaticism, could
> never be made sensible, but too late and by fatal experience, of

the incessant change of times and situations. (535)

Page 540 provides a valuable paragraph on the liberty of the press, which reminds us that liberty emerged fitfully and was still being "perfected" well after the close of Hume's narrative:

> The **liberty** of the press did not even commence with the revolution. It was not till 1694, that the restraints were taken off; to the great displeasure of the king, and his ministers, who, seeing no where, in any government, during present or past ages, any example of such **unlimited freedom**, doubted much of its salutary effects, and probably thought, that no books or writings would ever so much improve the general understanding of men, as to render it safe to entrust them with an indulgence so easily abused. (H VI, 540)

Remark on Vols. 1-6: We see here copious textual evidence that mere-liberty was not merely a denizen of Hume's abstract speculative thought, but a core concept of his historical analysis. Alongside that essential meaning, many contributory meanings are seen. *The History of England* is a narrative of the evolution of liberty, in its plexus of meanings.

Operose Machines 'R' Us

In our view, in the hands of some authors, the idea of mere-liberty has been oversimplified, ill-formulated, dogmatized, and wrongheadedly justified—problems evinced in the writings of Murray Rothbard, for example. When handled without proper delicacy, the idea of *other's not messing with one's stuff* is sure to put people off. Mere-liberty is surrounded by great taboos, leaving it neglected and overlooked (Cf. EMPL 41).[15]

Maintaining and advancing our liberal inheritance depends on getting liberalism right, and that depends on coming to terms with complications,

---

15. On Hume's possible motives to esotericism on liberty, see Klein's final entry in Hart (2018). DelliSanti (2021) explores such motives in treating economic innovation in the thought of Adam Smith. Diesel (2021) offers an esoteric reading of Smith on usury.

qualifications, holes, paradoxes, areas of vagueness, and other embarrassments in the central idea of liberty (that is, mere-liberty) and in the claims
made for it. Maintaining our liberal inheritance depends on knowing and
showing that mere-liberty survives the embarrassments.

To return to the diagram that appears at the start of this chapter (Figure 3.2): There, liberty is presented in *a heart*. But that is the heart of *the
liberal's* operose intellectual "machine."[16] In terms of the social ways of life
espoused by the liberal, mere-liberty is better understood as a *backbone*, as
something which lends structure or grammar to social experience. And
grammar capacitates beauty, heart-warming beauty. Firming up that backbone is the heart of the liberal's intellectual operoseness.

Yes, authority, stability came first, and in that sense Hume was, as a
voice for his own day, an establishment political philosopher (Forbes 1975,
91; Matson 2017b). But *as a policy analyst or political economist*, Hume upheld
a presumption of liberty, a definite directional bent, even while also according a presumption to the status quo. Indeed, those two presumptions are in
tension when it comes to a reform that would liberalize the status quo, but
such are the embarrassments of liberal politics.

Hume knew that philosophy was a problem in managing embarrassments. Philosophical decisions "are nothing but the reflections of common
life, methodized and corrected" (EHU 12.3.25), and common life, both
under government and among equals, certainly understands the grammar-like idea of other's not messing with one's stuff. Our responsibility is
to find less-embarrassing philosophical formulations, work with them, and
strive to improve them—as Hume himself says, "the heart of man is made
to reconcile contradictions" (EMPL, 71).

---

16. The "operose machine" metaphor comes from Smith (TMS 182), in a passage that relates inti-
mately to Hume's Conclusion to Book I of the *Treatise* (see Matson and Doran 2017).

CHAPTER 4

Convention without Convening

By Erik W. Matson and Daniel Klein

C hoice is affected consciously by deliberation and subconsciously by a complex of norms, social expectations, and habits of thought. These norms, expectations, and habits are often called "conventions." Conventions structure economic issues—traditions concerning the use and possession of resources, the perceived legitimacy and hence feasibility of public policy, cultural dimensions of consumption like fashion. But what exactly are conventions?

A large-scale textual search shows that up to the time of David Hume's *Treatise of Human Nature* (1740) nearly all usage of the word "convention" meant the convening of persons to discuss or deliberate on a matter, or an agreement or resolution so arrived at—that is, a compact, contract, covenant, promise, or matter of consent.[1] In his *Enquiry Concerning the Principles of Morals*, Hume himself acknowledged such meaning to be "the most usual sense of the word" (EPM Appendix 3.7). The *Treatise* advances another meaning, however, one that does not necessarily entail a convening nor a contract, compact, promise, or agreement. Hume emphasizes that feature. He says that a person may adopt a rule or "convention" to abstain from another's possessions from "a general sense of common interest." Hume says: "This convention is not of the nature of a *promise*: For even

---

1. With the help of Jonathan Matt, to whom we are grateful, we have conducted a systematic search of texts in English (including translations of Hugo Grotius, Samuel Pufendorf, etc.) at Liberty Fund's Online Library of Liberty. The coverage includes all thinkers in the following groups at the Liberty Fund site: "17th Century Natural Rights Theorists," "18th Century Commonwealthmen," "The Levellers," "Pre-Smithian Economists," "The Philosophical Radicals," "The Protestant Reformation," "Puritans," and "The Scottish Enlightenment." The resultant 800-row Excel file shows the text containing "convention."

promises themselves…arise from human conventions… In like manner are languages gradually establish'd by human conventions without any promise" (T 3.2.2.10). Language did not originate in the resolutions of convening syndics, since such syndics would presumably have to have had some language to conduct such deliberations.

The point about convening syndics is made by W.V. Quine in his Foreword to David K. Lewis (1969), *Convention; A Philosophical Study*. Building on Hume and Thomas Schelling, Lewis beautifully develops a definition (78) of convention "along the lines of Hume" (3). Figure 4.1 shows Lewisian convention and consent to not be coextensive. Language is largely the child of convention, not consent or compact. In the yellow area are located also our duties to justice, [2] political authority, and those which correspond to the entire class of what Hume calls the "artificial" virtues. Of course, it is not only "convention" that was and is polysemous. "Consent" and "agreement" are also somewhat polysemous. But from the haze of meanings and connotations, Lewis highlights a set of meanings that accords with Figure 4.1. Figure 4.1 is along the lines of Hume, as it is along the lines of Lewis. Although there remain instances of the older meaning of "convention" in Hume's works (instances of what he calls the "usual sense" of the term), his use of "convention" to mean Lewisian convention is central and widespread in his thought.

FIGURE 4.1: HUME'S AND LEWIS'S CONVENTION WITHOUT CONSENT/COMPACT.

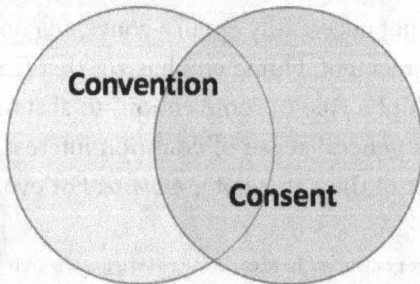

---

2. We mean "commutative justice" in Adam Smith's (TMS 269) sense of the expression, which is the primary sense in which Hume uses the term "justice." For an exposition of the three senses of justice maintained by Smith, see Chapter 1.

Hume scholars have long recognized the importance of convention and the so-called "artificial virtues" in his thought. Hume helps us see how and why certain character traits and behavioral tendencies, such as honesty and allegiance to political authority, which are conventional rather than instinctive, emerge and subsequently are moralized in advanced societies (Mackie 1980, 2–3; 87–91). The insight is among his significant achievements: "Hume's most important contribution is his theory of 'convention'" (Livingston 1991, 161), a contribution that makes him "a glorious inventor in moral and social theory" (Baier 1988, 757). Reading Hume along with Lewis gives us a vocabulary with which we can better appreciate and articulate the innovativeness of Hume's theory of convention.[3]

A main purpose of this chapter is to contribute to that appreciation, and to rearticulate and extend Hume's innovative analytical framework for thinking about the unformalized duties and obligations—sometimes glossed as *institutions* or *culture*—underlying social interaction. After summarizing Lewis, we will treat Hume's account of the emergence of the conventions of language, justice, and political authority in broadly Lewisian terms.

A second purpose is to develop, from Hume's thought, a notion we call "natural convention": a natural convention is a social practice whose concrete form in time and place is conventional in a Lewisian sense, but whose generalized form is necessary, and hence natural, for more advanced social organization. The concept of natural convention clarifies the meaning of Hume's claim that, although justice is "artificial," it is nonetheless part of the "laws of nature"; it is "obvious and absolutely necessary" and "inseparable from the species" (T 3.2.1.19). In the language of game theory, the concept of natural convention shows how conventions of property in Hume have elements of both cooperation and mutual coordination (cf. Barry 2010; Binmore 2005, 48; see also Hart [1961], 199). Our discussion of natural convention casts light on the similitude between Hume and the modern natural law tradition. Hume does not frame his discussion of the "laws of nature" (T 3.2.1.19) in theological terms. But his argument from

---

3. Other works in Hume scholarship up to 2012 that highlight similitude between Hume and Lewis on convention include: Ardal (1977); Charron (1980); Sugden (2005 [1986]; 2011); Vanderschraaf (1998); Hardin (1999; 2007), and Sabl (2012). For an attempt to develop an economic theory of institutions from Lewis's ideas, although without reference to Hume, see Schotter (1981).

the facts of human nature to the necessity of certain forms of social rules and moral values for the survival and advancement of society beyond a primeval social state leads him to put forth a social and political theory that parallels the natural law tradition in important ways.

The chapter concludes by offering evidence on Hume's semantic innovation. We report the results of a largescale text search of Liberty Fund's Online Library of Liberty on uses of "convention" before Hume. Although we find prefigurings of Hume's Lewisian ideas of convention prior to Hume, especially in Gershom Carmichael and Francis Hutcheson, they are few and faint. A sense of convention without convening indeed appears to have been quite original to Hume, a product of his intellectual creativity and boldness.

Lewisian convention

David K. Lewis (1969) develops a definition of convention.[4] He drew inspiration and ideas from Thomas Schelling, and emulated his discursive game-theoretic style. Lewisian convention begins with formal games, but as it develops it takes on looser formulations.

Considering a strategy profile in a game, Lewis defines "coordination equilibrium," and it is useful to contrast that with Nash equilibrium. Nash equilibrium can be described as a strategy profile that is a set of best responses. In the prisoner's dilemma, the strategy profile (defect, defect) is a Nash equilibrium. Coordination equilibrium goes further: Not only does some individual Jim like what he is doing given what everyone else is doing, but, further, he likes what each person is doing given what everyone else (including himself) is doing. This second aspect helps to ensure a certain "coincidence of interests" (14). Thus, Jim not only finds his own choice to be a best response, he also finds the choice of each of the others "agreeable," in the sense that he is glad of that choice, against the background of the remainder of the strategy profile. Lewis captures the two aspects of the definition as follows: "Let me define a *coordination equilibrium* as a [profile]

---

4. Lewis (1969) arrives at his final definition of convention on page 78. Thereafter in the book he contrasts convention with several other concepts and then employs his analysis to address issues of the conventionality of language and to clarify issues of analyticity.

in which no one would have been better off had any one agent alone acted otherwise, either himself or someone else" (14). Every coordination equilibrium is a Nash equilibrium, but the converse is not true: (defect, defect) in the prisoner's dilemma is not a coordination equilibrium because each player would prefer that the other choose "cooperate."

All players find a coordination equilibrium to be "agreeable" in the sense just stated, but that does not mean everyone finds it particularly good or satisfactory. In fact, it may not even be Pareto efficient. Everyone driving on the left side of the road might be a coordination equilibrium. But if cars have the steering column on the left, then everyone driving on the right would make everyone better off. Thus, in the first case, when everyone drives on the left, each behaves agreeably, but the whole strategy profile, relative to one that has everyone driving on the right, is agreeable to no one, nor to an impartial spectator outside the game.[5] But the requirements of coordination equilibrium do not consider such multi-party changes to the strategy profile being tested.

Lewis adds the qualifier "proper," to avoid oddities arising from ties in payoffs. He then defines "coordination problems" (22): "situations of interdependent decisions by two or more agents in which coincidence of interest predominates and in which there are two or more proper coordination equilibria" (24). Some people have taken multiplicity of Nash equilibria to be the defining feature of a coordination problem.[6] But in "Chicken," for example, there are two Nash equilibria {(hawk, dove), (dove, hawk)}; neither is a coordination equilibrium because in each the person playing dove would prefer that the other also play dove, so "Chicken" is not a coordination problem. A coordination problem is represented by "Battle of the Sexes" or "The Road Game."

In defining convention, Lewis chaperones the reader through a progress of philosophizing. He works through a series of preliminary definitions (42, 58, 76). He notes problems of each, finds the need to define common

---

5. The Schelling-Lewis coordination discussed here is mutual coordination, as opposed to concatenate coordination, which is about what a spectator of the whole concatenation finds pleasing (Klein 1997; 2012, 37–77).

6. For example, Murphy (2010, 119, 122) suggests that multiple Nash equilibria is the defining characteristic of a coordination problem.

knowledge, revises, sometimes by loosening requirements, arriving at a fourth and final definition given in two versions (78–79).[7]

In developing his definitions, Lewis speaks of a regularity in a recurrent situation. At first, he explicitly makes the recurrent situation a coordination problem (42). But subsequently the form of the recurrent situation is loosened (68–69) and quantifications are relaxed—for a few odd birds or malefactors, "children and the feeble-minded," etc. (75). In defining some regularity R to be a convention Lewis adds the presence of an alternative possible regularity R', to capture the idea that "there is no such thing as the only possible convention" (70). Built into the definition of convention, then, is a sense of a possible alternative agreeable way of behaving in the recurrent situation.

Regularity in a recurrent situation is one reason why a one-off matter of consent, the keeping of a *particular* promise or contract, would not, in that limited aspect, be convention: Fulfilling that particular contract is not a regularity in a recurrent situation. That is one reason why the pink area in Figure 4.1 is not subsumed within the yellow area.

Lewis offers another reason why even a promise pertaining to a recurrent situation might not qualify as a convention (84). Promising itself might alter preferences so as to make conforming to what was promised sufficiently *un*conditional, precluding the existence of (or even just common knowledge of the existence of) the sort of alternative regularity required for his definition of convention.

The relaxation of quantification and the loosening of form to a broad idea of a recurrent social situation have the result that the word "coordination" does not appear in Lewis's final definition of convention. But the spirit of Lewis's coordination formulations (e.g., "coordination equilibrium," "coordination problem") is very much preserved. Digesting those formal definitions is the way to ascend to Lewis's (78) final definition of convention.

The matter of a possible alternative convention R' helps to clarify the statement that commutative justice is conventional: Within a context, the observed system (regularity) R of commutative justice is a convention, for,

---

7. The second version of the final definition simply specifies indices ($d_0, d_1, d_2, d_3, d_4, d_5$) to express degree, in lieu of "almost any instance," "almost everyone conforms," etc. in the first version.

within that same context, many an alternative (R') would also be a possible convention. That among neighbors commutative justice is a necessary or natural convention may be taken to mean that conformance to *some* such conventional system (R, R', or some other) must exist. It is not commutative justice's existence, as opposed to nonexistence, that is conventional, but rather the observed system of commutative justice, as opposed to some other system of commutative justice, notably a more primitive system now superseded, particularly by extensions of propertization. We can say that commutative justice is a "natural convention" in the sense that necessarily, for any surviving community, a commutative-justice convention must exist among neighbors and other jural equals.

Here is Lewis's final definition of convention:

> A regularity R in the behavior of members of a population P when they are agents in a recurrent situation S is a *convention* if and only if it is true that, and it is common knowledge in P that, in almost any instance of S among members of P,
>
> 1. almost everyone conforms to R;
> 2. almost everyone expects almost everyone else to conform to R;
> 3. almost everyone has approximately the same preferences regarding all possible combinations of actions;
> 4. almost everyone prefers that any one more conform to R, on condition that almost everyone conform to R;
> 5. almost everyone would prefer that any one more conform to R', on condition that almost everyone conform to R',
> 6. where R' is some possible regularity in the behavior of members of P in S, such that almost no one in almost any instance of S among members of P could conform both to R' and to R. (78)

Regarding "the population P": Note that P might be a religious sect, an ideological group, an ethnic group, etc. subsisting as a subset of wider society. The common knowledge assumption implies that the members of *P* have a sense of their mutual belonging to *P* (Lewis 1969, 43, 44, 61–68). Part of the art of deploying the convention concept is seeing the population *P* of those party to the convention (77).[8]

The definition in no way requires that the convention *R* emerged from any sort of convening; it need not be a conforming to a compact or agreement. It is possible that the behavior (think, strategy profile) specified by *R* had been agreed to in a compact, but there is no necessity of it having done so. When it hasn't, we have an agreeable regularity without agreement. We can call such a convention an *emergent* convention.

In fact, if *R* originated in an agreement (an "oath"), it might be the case that conforming to *R* is *not* a convention, for a reason already alluded to and which Lewis states as follows: "we might all prefer *un*conditionally to conform to *R*, each determined that even were the others to break their oaths and conform to some alternative regularity *R'*, still he would rather keep his oath" (84). Hence, adherence to regularity *R* may not qualify as convention. Note, however, that *behind* the fulfilling of that compact is a deeper regularity in *another* sort of recurrent situation, about keeping such oaths under such circumstances, and that that regularity is convention. For the regularity that starts with a compact, Lewis says: "We have a convention only after the force of our promises has faded to the point where it is both true and common knowledge that each would conform to some alternative regularity *R'* instead of *R* if the others did" (84). He notes, however, that if, at the original convening, "we agreed by exchanging *conditional* promises binding us to conform to *R* only if others did, or by exchanging noncommittal declarations of intent, the resulting regularity would be a perfectly good convention *at once*" (84, italics added).

What is of chief interest is the yellow region outside the pink in Figure 4.1: Lewis elucidates convention without convening. Next we draw on Lewis to cast light on Hume's groundbreaking analyses of language, justice, and political authority. Then we consider Hume's semantic originality speaking

---

8. Seeing the relevant population is critical to Lewis's conclusions about analyticity. At the end he writes: "I have given an account of the proper kind of analyticity—analyticity relative to a population of language users" (207).

of convention in a Lewisian mode, a mode not requiring or entailing a literal convening or resolution.

Hume's Lewisian convention

Hume's thought has been increasingly appreciated in light of game theory. Ken Binmore (1998, 506) claims Hume to be "the first person to recognize that the equilibrium ideas now studied in game theory are vital to an understanding of how human societies work... He even anticipated modern game theorists in seeing constitutional reform as a problem in mechanism design." Peter Vanderschraaf (1998, 217 n2) points out that Hume anticipates the concept of Nash equilibrium, the knowledge conditions required to reach equilibrium, and the social and psychological mechanisms for selecting an equilibrium among a multiplicity. Many of these game theoretic insights orbit around Hume's discussion of convention, a concept he uses to explain social phenomena ranging from the synchrony of oarsmen, justice, language, money, political authority, gallantry, norms of chastity, and rules of traffic.[9]

There is debate over the precise meaning of "convention" in Hume. Indeed, as with so many other key concepts in Hume ("reason," "nature," "liberty," "sympathy," etc.), there appears to be a multiplicity of meanings and scholarly interpretations. Robert Sugden ([1986], 149) claims to follow Hume in differentiating between (1) conventions of coordination, which evolve out of repeated games of pure coordination, (2) conventions of property, which evolve out of repeated play of games resembling Chicken, and (3) conventions of reciprocity, which emerge from playing tit-for-tat strategies in a repeated prisoner's dilemma.[10] John Latsis (2009) finds in Hume "a concept of convention (convention1) that relies on linguistic interaction and the adoption of conditionally binding principles" (229) and a "convention (convention2) [that is] independent of linguistic practice" (231). Brian Barry

9. For a list of conventions in Hume, see Hardin (2007, 85).

10. J. L. Mackie (1980, 88–91) seems to view conventions of reciprocity as the main sort of convention in Hume. He emphasizes the "experimental spirit" by which conventions are spread throughout a population (89). Recognizing themselves in a recurring situation, individuals attempt what they take to be mutually beneficial actions, continuing in those actions if others cooperate.

(2010, 375–76) reads into Hume distinct "coordination conventions" and "cooperation conventions." Most recently, Sabl (2012, 31–34) distinguishes in Hume between "ordinary conventions" (e.g., property, allegiance), "fundamental conventions" (political authority), and "pseudo-conventions" (e.g., religious and political beliefs).

We recognize that there is polysemy in Hume's convention talk. But we argue that the Lewisian sense of convention is pronounced and central to Hume's analysis, an interpretation shared by Lewis (1969, 3, 48) himself. We point to the historical originality of that sense of convention to Hume's thought. With perhaps some small qualifications, we agree with Hardin (2007, 83): "it is clear that the meaning [of convention that Hume] has in mind is that of Lewis's analysis."

Hume first articulates his understanding of convention in Book 3 of the *Treatise* over the course of his nested accounts of justice, promise-keeping, and political authority. His key move, which he makes at the outset, is to distinguish his new understanding of convention from convention-as-compact or consent. Convention "is not the nature of a *promise*: For even promises themselves...arise from human conventions" (T 3.2.2.10). Promises—the practice of holding to one's word—themselves are conventions in the sense which he is to explicate. We have no congenital inclination to keep our word but learn from childhood that the reciprocal practice of promise-keeping is useful, expected, and widely maintained in certain circumstances. Like justice, promise-keeping or fidelity is for Hume beyond the primeval society, or "artificial."

After separating his sense of convention from promise-keeping, Hume continues:

> I observe, that it will be for my interest to leave another in the possession of his goods, *provided* he will act in the same manner with regard to me. He is sensible of a like interest in the regulation of his conduct. When this common sense of interest is mutually express'd, and is known to both, it produces a suitable resolution and behaviour. And this may properly enough be call'd a convention or agreement betwixt us, tho' without the interposition of a promise; since the actions of each of us have a reference to

those of the other, and are perform'd upon the supposition, that
something is to be perform'd on the other part. (T 3.2.2.10; italics in original)

The problem of justice in the text surrounding this passage bears some
likeness to a Prisoner's Dilemma (Vanderschraaf 1998, 218; Barry 2010,
376). The facts of scarcity and limited benevolence mean that each individual faces certain incentives to take the possessions of others, and have
others not take hers. On such incentives alone, knavery is a strictly domi-
nant strategy; if mutually pursued, it leads to wretchedness—a Hobbesian
jungle. A more desirable outcome can be achieved by "convention," which
Hume describes as a social practice predicated upon mutual interest and
reciprocal expectations of abstaining from one another's possessions. When
enough individuals form such expectations and believe others expect likewise, the convention of abstaining becomes a self-sustaining norm. Over
time our experience "assures us still more, that the sense of interest has
become common to all our fellows, and gives us confidence of the future
regularity of their conduct: And 'tis only on the expectation of this, that
our moderation and abstinence are founded" (T 3.2.2.10).

Hume's requirement that conventions be of mutually recognized common interest corresponds to Lewis's (1969, 78) first three stipulations that
regularity R is a convention if and only if (1) "almost everyone conforms to
R," (2) "almost everyone expects almost everyone else to conform to R," and
(3) "almost everyone has approximately the same preferences regarding all
possible combinations of action." In another Lewisian passage Hume writes:

Every one expresses this sense [of interest in mutual abstention]
to his fellows, along with the resolution he has taken of squaring
his actions by it, on condition that others will do the same. No
more is requisite to induce any one of them to perform an act of
justice, who has the first opportunity. This becomes an example
to others. And thus justice establishes itself by a kind of *convention
or agreement*; that is, by a sense of interests suppos'd to be common to all, and where every single act is perform'd in expectation
that others are to perform the like. (T 3.2.2.22; italics added)

Note that Hume here says "convention or agreement" (he says the same at T 3.2.2.10). We have noted that a coordination equilibrium is mutually "agreeable," in the sense that no player dislikes what any player is, taken individually, doing. We suggest that Hume's "agreement" here be understood as mutually agreeable. In Hume's *Enquiry Concerning the Principles of Morals*, agreeableness is a cornerstone of his account of virtue. It means immediately pleasing; it does not there imply an action of agreeing between persons. As "convention is not the nature of a *promise*" (T 3.2.2.10), neither is "agreement" in the sense that it is here used. "Agreement" for Hume is polysemous, as is "convention."

The distinction that some scholars draw in Hume between coordination and cooperation conventions (e.g. Sugden [1986]; Barry 2010), with justice (and property) being an example of the latter, touches on an important point: commutative justice, as we note above, in its generalized form ("abstaining from what is another's") is not, in a sense, a proper Lewisian convention. To justice we can add that language and government *in their generalized forms* are also not proper Lewisian conventions.

By the fifth element of Lewis's definition, to be a convention in a recurring situation S, regularity R must stand in relation to an alternative regularity R' such that

> almost everyone would prefer that any one more conform to R', on condition that almost everyone conform to R', where R' is some possible regularity in the behavior of members of P in [recurrent situation] S, such that almost no one in almost any instance of S among members of P could conform both to R' and to R. (Lewis 1969, 78)

But in the case of commutative justice there is no alternative regularity R' to abstaining from another's goods, such as "not abstaining from another's goods," that would satisfy the agreeableness conditions of Lewis's definition of convention. It is because there is no agreeable alternative regularity to *some* general form of commutative justice that justice in Hume is sometimes treated as a convention that resolves something like the Prisoner's Dilemma.

Sabl (2012, 32) considers all "ordinary conventions"—which include justice and government (but not constitutional conventions, which falls under what he calls "fundamental conventions")—as "natural," in the sense that they "respond to partiality and short-sightedness that are everywhere and always present in human nature."[11] With respect to justice and government, *some* degree of cooperation is presupposed in even speaking about society beyond the primeval stage of history. It is, again, difficult to maintain that such cooperation is "conventional," at least in a colloquial sense, in that without it, advanced social life could simply not exist. Without rules of mutual forbearance, "what point could there be for beings such as ourselves in having rules of *any* other kind?" (Hart 2012, 194).

It is along such lines that Hume asserts that the "artificial" virtues—i.e., virtues that do not spring from primeval instinct—are "natural." He even speaks of justice as part of the "*laws of nature*" because he sees that an established practice of generally abstaining from others' goods and persons is "obvious and absolutely necessary" and "inseparable from the species" (T 3.2.1.19; italics in original). For any society that gets beyond the primeval, it is natural for us to expect to find within it both some form of commutative justice and governance extending beyond whatever primitive form of commutative justice (e.g., ownership in our persons) and governance (e.g., family hierarchy) we might use in construing the primeval society.

As with justice, there is likewise no alternative regularity R' to shared meaning in communication. Thus language, to which Hume explicitly compares the convention of justice (T 3.2.2.10), likewise, is also in one sense not "natural." We are not born speaking language. In primeval existence even the grown-ups would have practiced a grammar extremely primitive. As Hume put it, in his *Letter from a Gentleman to his Friend in Edinburgh*, "Sucking is an Action natural to Man, and Speech is artificial" (published in Hume 2007a, 430). But in another sense, language is clearly "natural," and therefore not conventional. Like justice, Hume would likely maintain that language is also "obvious," "absolutely necessary," and "inseparable" from advancement of the species (T 3.2.1.19). One cannot imagine beyond-pri-

---

11. A similar point is made by H. L. A. Hart (2012 [1961], 193–200) in his discussion of "the minimum content of natural law."

meval society without it—there is no *R* to replace shared meaning and communication beyond whatever grunting, chanting, and gesturing marks the primeval society.

But emphasizing property and government and language as cooperative might obscure their important coordinative aspect. There *is* Lewisian convention in the practice of one concrete form of commutative justice as opposed to another, just as there is proper Lewisian convention in submitting to one political regime as opposed to another, and in speaking one language rather than another.[12] With respect to justice, Hume says, "Sometimes the interests of society may require a rule of justice in a particular case; but may not determine any particular rule, among several, which are all equally beneficial" (EPM 3.2.31). What can be seen as the properly conventional element of justice comes down to rules of ownership and contract or consent: who owns what (conventions of possession), how ownership can change hands (conventions of transfer), what counts as messing with another person's stuff, how promises or contracts are communicated, what counts as breach, and so on. In the case of government, the conventional element comes down to the form of government and the particular persons who are perceived to possess legitimate political authority. Hume says the rules of justice and authority are determined in time and place (T 3.2.3, T 2.3.8), anticipating the idea pioneered by Schelling and developed by Lewis of salience as a factor in determining convention.

"Natural" and "artificial"

Hume's thinking involves an idea of a primeval condition—"primeval" being an ascription applied to the rudimentary social state of humankind, not the nature of the organisms of that social state, which, at least according to Hume, is broadly constant through time (EPM 8.1.7; Forbes 1975, 102-121; Berry 1982). In one sense the word "artificial" simply denotes developments after the primeval state. An "artifice" is any social practice that was not present in the primeval human state, and hence is not "natural." But if we allow "natural" to mean a normal sort of development attending a con-

---

12. Lewis (1969, 48) himself seems to pick up on Hume's theory of property along such lines.

dition beyond the primeval state, it makes sense to speak of certain artifices as "natural" in beyond-primeval human societies. Hume's remarks in the *Treatise* about meanings of "natural" seem to be along just such lines as these we are suggesting (T 3.1.2.8, 3.2.2.19).

How might we delineate between normal and non-normal developments from the primeval state? What artifices are to be considered "natural"? The main facet of the delineation must have reference to universality. An artifice can justly be considered "natural" if it appears everywhere "inseparable from the species" (T 3.2.2.19), derived or developed in response to universal aspects of human nature. A subtler facet of the delineation, however, involves a conscious semantic decision based on our assessment, as theorists, about what social practices and virtues are worth naturalizing. When we theorize about society from the idea of the primeval social condition, we the theorists invest the primeval condition with various potentialities. We affirm some potentialities as proper and conducive to human advancement (e.g., property, free speech) over others (e.g., slavery, violations of the rule of law), and theorize accordingly.

The word "natural" then is polysemous, bearing simultaneously at least three meanings or connotations: (1) *of the primeval condition*; (2) *a normal or regular feature in the career of humankind*; (3) *worth normalizing or "naturalizing."*

Natural convention: Extending natural property

We think Hume would have done well to have referred to language, government, and commutative justice, beyond their primitive instantiations in the primeval state, as instances of natural artifice or "natural convention." We define a natural convention as a social practice whose concrete form in time and place is conventional in the Lewisian sense, but whose generalized form is necessary, and hence natural, to social development beyond the primeval state.

Hume provides a homey example. It is natural for animals, such as birds and humans, to build shelters. Shelters are natural. But humans develop conventions as to particulars of their shelters. Hume writes in the *Enquiry Concerning the Principles of Morals*:

All birds of the same species in every age and country, built their nests alike: In this we see the force of instinct. Men, in different times and places, frame their houses differently: Here we perceive the influence of reason and custom…. [A]ll houses have a roof and walls, windows and chimneys; though diversified in their shape, figure, and materials.

After writing of the variety of conventions in home construction, Hume writes: "A like inference may be drawn from comparing the instinct of generation and the institution of property."

In view of the naturalness of property and justice, it may be misleading to frame certain conventions as things which we "collectively invent" (Baier 1988, 757; see also Mackie 1980, 5). The inventive or "artificial" aspect of the natural convention of justice pertains only to the precise way in which the rules of property manifest, not to the broad underlying form of justice—abstaining from what is another's. Hume indicates the general point when, speaking of political authority, he says: "'Tis interest which gives the general instinct; but 'tis custom which gives the particular direction" (T 3.2.10.4). Interest and instinct are "natural" and "general"; but *any actualization of those interests and instincts*—any actualization of what we interpret as natural rights —will depend on "particular direction"—or the conventions of actual social existence. Put differently, the idea of natural right has *built within* it a clause about recurring to and applying what, in actual social existence, happen to be the pertinent conventions of commutative justice. The concept of "natural convention" then helps reconcile nature and convention, and corrects the error of violently separating, or demarcating, between them.[13] Indeed,

---

13. Our notion of "natural conventions" relates to Binmore's idea of "natural justice," although like Hume we eschew discussion of "social contracts." Binmore (2005, 48) observes that "it is natural that a human society should have a social contract [i.e., rules of justice enforced by an established political authority], but its actual social contract is an artifact of its cultural history." H. L. A. Hart advances similar ideas in his discussion of the minimum content of natural law. Some "minimum forms of protection for persons, property, and promises […] are indispensable features of municipal law," although the exact features of municipal law differ in time and place (Hart 2012 [1961], 199). Natural conventions have both universal and particular aspects. The universal aspects derive from the principles of human nature; the particular aspects derive from varying ways in time and place that these universal aspects find concrete expression in different societies (e.g., different forms of political arrangement, rules of possession, language, etc.).

in the wilds of human society, once we understand the "natural" part of natural conventions, we may feel aesthetic pleasure in encountering, as Francis Hutcheson ([1725], 30) put it, "the uniformity amidst an almost infinite Variety." The variety lies in the variety of conventions actualizing the "natural" principle.

Many scholars now take Hume to be an extension of the natural law tradition of Hugo Grotius, Samuel Pufendorf, John Locke, and Francis Hutcheson, albeit an extension with different philosophical underpinnings (Forbes 1975, 16–17, 26–27; Buckle 1991, 295; Haakonssen 1996, 118; see also Hart [1961], 191). Hume in fact explicitly links his theory of justice to Grotius in the *Second Enquiry*.[14] He sometimes lends himself to misinterpretation in relation to natural law, however, especially with respect to self-ownership. Miller (1980, 268), for instance, says, "whereas Locke wishes to show that property is a natural right, Hume's view is that the rules of property, like the institution itself are conventional artefacts which cannot be grounded on the *supposed* right of self-ownership" (italics added). It is true that Hume doesn't articulate a concept of "self-ownership" as such. Neither does he embrace the Lockean formulation of mixing one's labor with a resource (T 2.3.2). But it is nonetheless clear that Hume takes there to be a special kind of natural property in oneself from which conventional aspects of justice and property extend.

Hume's position on natural property in one's person may be helpfully compared with ideas in David Friedman (1994; see also Sugden [1986], 95–101). Friedman claims that "the laws and customs of civil society are an elaborate network of Schelling points" (9). In elaborating his position, he suggests that our bodies may be considered a kind of "natural property" in that we have—and are recognized by others to have—superior knowledge and control of them:

> I can control the motions of my body by a simple act of will.
> You can control its motions by imposing overwhelming force,
>   by making believable threats to which I will yield, or in various

---

14. "This theory concerning the origin of property, and consequently of justice, is, in the main, the same with that hinted at and adopted by GROTIUS" (EPM Appendix 1 n63).

other ways. Controlling it may be possible for both of us, but it is cheaper and much easier for me. In this sense, we may describe my body as my natural property. (Friedman 1994, 14)

The same applies to external objects. Natural property on the basis of knowledge and control extends from mind and body to, for example, "my gun—because I know where I hid it and you do not. Even land may be natural property to some extent if my detailed knowledge of the terrain makes it easier for me to use or defend" (14).

Hume articulates a similar logic. He distinguishes between "three different species of goods, which we are possess'd of; the internal satisfaction of our minds, the external advantages of our body, and the enjoyment of such possessions as we have acquir'd by our industry and good fortune" (T 3.2.2.7). He says that the third species (external possessions) is naturally less secure than the other two: it is subject to "looseness and easy transition from one person to another." We must therefore "seek for a remedy, by putting these [external] goods, as far as possible, on one and the same footing with the *fix'd and constant advantages of the mind and body*" (T 3.2.2.7; italics added). From this passage it is clear that Hume sees the internal satisfaction of our minds and the advantages of our body to naturally be our own (a "species of goods, which we are possess'd of"). They are our own in that their advantages are "fix'd and constant." They are fixed and constant because the relation that mind and body bear to our sense of self is constant and the knowledge and power we have in relation to our mind and body are unique. Such uniqueness derives from the fact that the demarcation between mine and yours is plain, or salient, prior to social conventions. As Baier (1991, 136) put it: "Since we can see the separateness of human bodies (once the umbilical cord is cut), we know what makes one person different from another." Once we know what makes one person distinct from another, we immediately have a sense of self and dominion over a sphere of "mine" as opposed to "yours," a sphere which in the first instance, consists of mind and body. Sympathy connects you and me, even in the primeval state, but nourishment will get to my stomach only by putting the food into my mouth.[15]

Hume's thinking on our natural property in mind and body comes across clearly in his discussions on the passion of pride in Book 2 of the *Treatise*: "[N]ature has given to the organs of the human mind, a certain disposition fitted to produce a peculiar impression or emotion which we call *pride*: To this emotion she assign'd a certain idea, *viz.* that of *self*, which it never fails to produce" (T 2.1.5.6). Pride is produced through a "double relation of ideas and impressions" (T 2.1.5.5). The two ideas in this relation are of the self and of a related object. The two impressions are the pleasant feeling evoked by perceiving the object and the pleasurable impression that arises from associating the object uniquely with one's self; that second impression is the pleasurable passion of pride. We feel pride if we associate a pleasing object uniquely with ourselves. I feel pride in a shirt in perceiving it to be pleasing and to be mine.

Although the causes of pride (the specific ideas of objects that cause pride) are "prodigious [in] number" (T 2.1.3.5), they are limited in time and place by certain principles of mind. An important limiting principle is that the pleasant object must "be very discernable and obvious, and that not only to ourselves, but to others" (T 2.1.6.6). To be proud, we must not only feel that an object that we connect with ourselves is pleasing; we must also believe that others feel that it is pleasing and connected with ourselves.[16]

Virtues for Hume are durable qualities of the mind that lead to useful and agreeable outcomes. He says they are "the most obvious" causes of pride (T 2.1.7.7), because we clearly recognize them as our own. We—"the soul"—feel, instinctively, that our virtues are the product of *our* agency, *our* responsibility.[17] We take pride in them because we believe that we are the

---

15. Hume's language throughout his writing affirms the idea of self-ownership as natural. In the *Treatise*, he says that war puts at stake "the most considerable of all goods, life and limbs" (T 3.2.8.1). His autobiographical essay "My Own Life" suggests self-ownership in its title; he recounts "the great decline of my person" caused by illness at the end of his life (EMPL, xl). In his essay on suicide, Hume would seem to presuppose self-ownership when speaking of "our natural liberty" and "native liberty" (EMPL, 588 n6, 580). In another essay he speaks of the English government's obligation "to secure every one's life" (EMPL 12).

16. On pride in Hume see Matson (2021, 853–56); Taylor (2015, 37–50).

17. In Book 1 of the *Treatise* Hume compares the soul to a republic (T 1.4.6.19). For other remarks on the soul, see T 2.1.3.3, 2.1.3.5, 2.1.5.4; DP 3.6, 6.12.

only credible claimants of their being. We believe that others perceive our virtues similarly because we connect virtues that are not our own with the agency and responsibility of others. Baier (1991, 136) says, "we must see other persons in relation to what is theirs, and ourselves in relation to what is ours, in precisely the same way."

The case is the same with our bodies. "Whether we consider the body as a part of ourselves, or assent to those philosophers, who regard it as something external, it must still be allow'd to be near enough connected with us to [cause pride]" (T 2.1.8.1). Our bodies naturally cause us pride because we connect them with our idea of self. We believe that others connect them with ourselves because we connect other bodies with other selves.

Together with his comments about mind and body being "species of possessions" that are "fix'd and constant" (T 3.2.2.7), Hume's treatment of pride, and the psychology of the passion more generally, supports the view that we have a kind of natural property in ourselves. The notion of natural property in oneself is a central facet of our consciousness, and an indispensable element in our social interaction. Understanding the particular logic of self-ownership in Hume sheds light on Knud Haakonssen's (1981, 12) claim that Hume's "real genius was to combine the strands of his [natural law] inheritance into a completely new sort of natural law theory—for, indeed, he is quite willing to use that label, provided we let him fill in the contents himself." Hume would seem to dissent from theological ideas found in some natural law discourse about the ends of humankind and the nature of human flourishing. Yet Hume still manages to give "good sense to the terminology of Natural Law" (Hart [1961], 191) by emphasizing how its essential elements (protection of person, property, and promises due) are, given the facts of human nature, necessary for the survival and advancement of the species beyond the primeval state (cf. Forbes 1975, 59–90).

Moving forward from the primeval stage of history, the conventional rules that make up a community's specific conventions of ownership extend outward from a person's body and mind. The historical dimension of property in the first stage of human society and its subsequent *extension* comes across nicely in transcribed notes of Adam Smith's lectures on jurisprudence, (Smith 1982a, 20, 460). Recall that the extension idea is implicit in Hume's claim that we seek to place external "goods, as far as possible, on one and the same footing with the fix'd and constant advantages of the mind and body" (T 3.2.2.7). One might rephrase Hume's statement as "we seek to extend the constant advantages of the mind and body to external goods." The idea of the extension of property from the self in Hume and Smith is parallel to Bart Wilson's elaboration of property as an imaginary extension of our sense of self into external objects. Rather than seeing a "thick dividing line between our physical body and the environment surrounding it," Wilson (2020, 15) suggests that we in fact project ourselves, to an extent, *into* tools, food, possessions, estates, and so forth. We naturally "emphysicalize the concept of mine" (123). Wilson's valuable neologism "emphysicalize" is like the words *embody, embed, embolden.*

In his analysis of the extension of property from the soul or self, and the emergence of particular conventions of property, Hume shows the Lewisian dimension of his analysis. Following Thomas Schelling, Lewis emphasizes the role of salience as a means for selecting between potential conventions.[18] Salience refers to a thing's focal or conspicuous aspect. A salient element is one which "stands out from the rest by its uniqueness in some conspicuous respect. It does not have to be uniquely *good*; indeed, it could be uniquely *bad*" (Lewis 1969, 35; italics in original). In situations where communication is not possible, coordination between individuals with overlapping interests can be achieved if they share perceptions of salience. Schelling (1960, 55–56) famously wrote of two individuals meeting at Grand Central Station at 12:00 PM, because each person would have reason to believe that the other might have a similar perception.

In the context of the rules of property, Hume uses salience first to explain the emergent convention of present possession. "'Tis evident, therefore, that men wou'd easily acquiesce in this expedient, *that every one continue to enjoy what he is at present possess'd of*" (T 3.2.3.4; italics in original). Although Hume says that the right of present possession might be a matter of "public utility," he "suspect[s], that these rules are principally fix'd by the imagination, or the more frivolous properties of our thought and conception" (T 3.2.3.4 n71). Possession is a "frivolous" matter in that although

---

18. The similarity of Hume's concept of salience to Schelling's and Lewis's has been treated by Sugden (2005 [1986], 96; 2011). On the importance of salience in Hume's account of political authority, see Sabl (2012).

we share perceptions of what constitutes possession, we often find it very difficult to define what possession is in precise terms (T 3.2.3.7). Hume, however, falls back on a commonsense idea of possession as the division of goods according to which we each have the right to what we presently control and historically have had control over: "what has long lain under our eye, and has often been employ'd to our advantage, *that* we are always the most unwilling to part with" (T 3.2.3.4). So long as there exist largely coextensive perceptions of "long" and "often been employ'd to our advantage" in a community, conventions of possession emerge and self-sustain. Hume's criterion of advantage and long possession relate to superiorities in knowledge. Recall Friedman's (1994, 14) comment: "We may describe my body as my natural property. The same description applies to my gun —because I know where I hid it and you do not".

Hume's treatment of the conventions of occupation, prescription, accession, and succession proceeds in similar fashion. Those conventions serve as a lineage for present ownership. Occupation refers to the rule of first possession, which, in the early stages of society, keeps resources from being in "suspense" and thus prevents "violence and disorder" (T 3.2.3.6). When first possession cannot be used, prescription ascribes ownership on the basis of long possession: the memory and effectiveness of first possession fade into the background over time. Accession holds that a person owns the produce of her property, e.g., the fruits of her garden (T 3.2.3.10). Succession acknowledges that "the [deceased] person's children naturally present themselves to the mind" (T 3.2.3.10). There is no necessary logic that dictates these principles as conventions behind the determination of ownership. But they are salient.

As for issues of contract and consent, again Hume sees salience in a certain "*form of words*" and "signs" used in agreements (T 3.2.5.10; italics in original). The same exact point is, again, made in Friedman (1994, 8): "[T]he agreement itself…is thereafter itself a Schelling point… The signing of a contract establishes a new Schelling point."

Political authority: The conventionalist view

Political authority is another natural convention. The granting of authority to *some* party is necessary for the advancement of society.[19] "Liberty," Hume says, "is the perfection of civil society; but still [political] authority must be acknowledged essential to its very existence" (EMPL, 40). The convention-al aspect of political authority speaks to the form of government and the particular persons in power. As with conventions of ownership, there are multiple forms of political organization and innumerable potential politi-cal leaders that meet the agreeableness criterion of Lewisian convention. Also, like Lewisian conventions, established forms of political authority might not be very good; it could well be the case that society on the whole would benefit from a regime change or new political leadership. The special challenge with political authority, however, is effectively changing conven-tions, a challenge that Hume thinks is generally difficult to meet: "It is not with forms of government, as with other artificial contrivances; where an old engine may be rejected, if we can discover another more accurate and commodious" (EMPL, 512). For this reason, Forbes (1975, 91) has said that Hume had an "establishment political philosophy." Hume appreciates the coordinating tendencies of the status quo, especially in a relatively stable polity. Although he recognized myriad problems with Hanoverian Britain, he sought to support the Hanoverian Settlement upon the recognition that opting for an imperfect but stable political order is most often better than striving for constitutional perfection.[20] Although a liberal with respect to ordinary policy reform, Hume, like Smith and Edmund Burke, was con-servative with respect to *polity* reformation.

In elaborating the principles by which political authority is established, Hume rejects social contract theory. He explicitly criticizes the notion that political authority is founded on consent, tacit or otherwise (see T 3.2.8.9, EMPL, 465–92). To the contrary, he maintains that most contemporary political authorities have a violent, non-contractual history: "there scarce is any race of kings, or form of a commonwealth, that is not primarily founded on usurpation and rebellion" (T 3.2.10.4). His telling of political authority relies on convention. The particular manifestations of political authority—

---

19. It should be noted that Hume takes the natural conventions of justice and the rules of property to precede the institutions of government (T 3.2.10.2).

20. On the relationship between what Forbes calls Hume's "establishment political philosophy" with his presumption of liberty in political economy, see Matson (2019, 44–47).

i.e., its Lewisian aspect—are selected on the basis of salient features of certain regimes and individuals, features that lead members of the polity to perceive them as authoritative. In the *Treatise* he outlines five such features: long possession, present possession, right of conquest, right of succession, and positive law (T 3.2.10). None of these principles dominates the others; together they lead to the emergence and endurance of particular political regimes. Along such lines, Sabl (2012) richly interprets Hume's *History of England* as an account of the emergence of political authority and stability.

In the area of political authority, some seem to take the agreeableness criterion of convention (see T 3.2.2.22) as grounds for labeling Hume a "contractarian." David Gauthier (1979, 13), for example, interprets Hume in terms of "hypothetical contractarianism," whereby "systems of property and government are legitimated in terms of the consent they would receive from *rational* persons in a suitably characterized position of free choice" (italics in original). Bimore (2005, 29) makes a similar semantic decision, speaking of "Hume's insight that a social contract can be seen as a largely unrecognized consensus to coordinate on a particular equilibrium of the game of life." Robert Sugden argues that his own approach "to normative economics" is "both Humean and contractarian," and that the answer to the question "can a Humean be a contractarian?" is "yes" (Sugden 2013, 61; see also Sugden 2009).

In our view, labeling Hume as a "contractarian" of any sort is problematic.[21] Hume of course criticized the Whig social contract theorists of his day, arguing that they misunderstood the nature and historical origins of political authority in general, and British political authority in particular. He viewed eighteenth-century social contract theory, as Livingston (1998, 129) puts it, as "intrinsically absurd," a species of "false philosophy." Those who interpret Hume as a contractarian accept his dismissal of eighteenth-century Whig contractarianism. But they argue that the label is still apt, so long as we understand the term "contract" somewhat loosely, taking it as widely synonymous, as Sugden (2013, 64–68; 2018, 33–37) does, with the concept of "mutual advantage."

---

21. For further discussions on Hume and contractarianism, see Whelan (1994); Hardin (2007); Salter (2012).

We of course take no issue with interpreting some of Hume's ideas in terms of mutual advantage (although agreeableness might be more apt since conventions by no means assure maximal mutual advantage or even Pareto efficiency). But we deny that such an interpretation provides grounds for labeling him a contractarian or assimilating him into the contractarian tradition. The point of speaking in the language of contractarianism tends to be "to assert the *voluntarism*," rather than the usefulness, "of our participation in society under an actual government" (Hardin 1990, 36; italics added). Hume has no such illusions. Political authority might be beneficial, and our mutual submission to existing political authority is to our mutual advantage. And it is from a sense of mutual benefit that conventions of political legitimacy arise, conventions that are subsequently moralized into broader opinions about the rightness of allegiance. But to treat our mutual submission of political authority as a matter of "contract" of any type is to downplay the fact that actual political authority in the course of human affairs is essentially a matter of coercion and acquiescence.[22]

The semantics of contractarianism, from a Humean point of view, obscure the nature of actual political authority and practice (cf. Livingston 1998, 128–29). Hume felt that the myth of the "social contract" was unworthy partly because the terms and conditions of the supposed contract are themselves unclear and paradoxical (Klein and Clark 2010), even on a Lockean view of those terms and conditions. The terms and conditions are, in the wilds of human society, readily reinterpreted or simply dispensed with. "When we assert, that all lawful government arises from the consent of the people, we certainly do them a great deal more honour than they deserve" (EMPL 478). Hartmut Kliemt (2021) writes: "Referring

---

22. Anthony de Jasay (2010) criticized Sugden (2009), saying that one cannot be a contractarian without embracing some form of social contract theory, a theory that "goes right against the Humean grain" (de Jasay 2010, 401). Hume's position entails the idea of acquiescing to institutionalized coercive political power, not contracting or agreeing with others to constitute that power. In framing Hume's conventionalist account of acquiescing to political authority as "contractarian," or something that "might reasonably be called" a matter of "implicit agreements" (Sugden 2013, 65), one goes against Hume and, we think, undermines understandings and semantics that are vital to liberal civilization. That said, we join Sugden (2013, 62–63) in saying that de Jasay errs in aligning Hume with "ordered anarchy" (de Jasay 2010, 402). Nowhere in Hume do we see sentiments that would deny legitimacy to governmental authority, per se, or savor the abolition of the state—Hume would see such sentiments as a species of political enthusiasm and "false philosophy."

to state action as the result of 'coercion' rather than a 'conceptual contract' may not only be theoretically but also practically preferable."

Hume's originality in convention without convening

In this last section we provide evidence on Hume's semantic originality in his convention talk. *The Oxford English Dictionary* makes clear that the verb "convene," meaning to come or bring together, emerged in the 15th century, and with it the noun "convention," meaning the act of convening or a resultant agreement. Again, Hume noted that such was "the most usual sense of the word" (EPM Appendix 3.7). We have captured all text showing "convention" in abundant texts inventoried from the Liberty Fund Online Library. Our coverage includes all thinkers included under the following groups at the Liberty Fund website: "17th Century Natural Rights Theorists," "18th Century Commonwealthmen," "The Levellers," "Pre-Smithian Economists," "The Philosophical Radicals," "The Protestant Reformation," "Puritans," and "The Scottish Enlightenment." The text search is not a definitive demonstration of Hume's originality. But given the wide range of relevant literature archived by Liberty Fund, it presents compelling evidence. (The resultant spreadsheet from the text search may be obtained from either Matson or Klein.)

Baier (1988, 762) points to the conceptual originality of Hume's theory of convention, which we have attempted to articulate in conversation with Lewis. She sees some hints of Hume's theory of the artificial virtues (which are conventions) and their corresponding duties in Thomas Hobbes, Samuel Pufendorf, and John Locke. "The very term 'artificial'," she notes, "would to Hume's first readers evoke Hobbes's version of Leviathan…as an automaton, or artificial animal" (762). Hobbes, and perhaps especially Pufendorf and Locke, see contract as "more basic or 'primary' than other moral modes" (768). But the morally authoritative features of contract are largely taken for granted in their thinking, not explicated as they are in Hume. Contracts, Hume points out, presuppose authority; they cannot in themselves be invoked to explain it (Livingston 1998, 129). As for semantic practice, Locke and Pufendorf appear to use "convention" only in the usual sense. Hobbes scarcely uses the term. Other relevant authors using convention in the "usual sense" of a convening, include John Milton, James Harrington, John Lilburne, Andrew Fletcher, John Trenchard, Thomas Gordon, and Johann Gottlieb Heineccius (translated into English).

A significant step toward the Humean usage of convention comes in texts that refer to conventions that are "tacit." Writers had used "tacit" when distinguishing between explicit and implicit/tacit contract or compact. The phrase "tacit convention" emerged because people had started to use the word *convention* for the agreement, contract, covenant, or compact produced by a convening.

The Glasgow professor Gershom Carmichael (1672–1729) seems to have been one of the first to use "tacit" with the word "convention." Carmichael ([1724], 87–90, 372) notably speaks of tacit convention as the basis for semantics, the meaning of words. He also steps toward a Humean understanding of promises. He recognizes that promises are "conventional" but that calling them conventional does not imply an actual convening. If the virtue of promise-keeping derives from convention, "when and how do men enter into that convention? … I fully agree that convention is not to be denied in this question. The only difficulty about it is, when and by what means the convention was entered into" (88). There appears in his thought also glimmers of common knowledge, although they are not developed: "Each man, in addressing another person…makes a tacit agreement with him to use words in the sense which he thinks will be understood by him" (88; cf. T 3.2.2.22). As for political authority, Carmichael affirmed a Lockean consent theory (147, 152, 164), "given expressly or tacitly" (152). But he does not seem to use the idea of "tacit convention" in this connection.

In treating jurisprudence among equals, Carmichael ([1724], 112–17) gives considerable attention to a notion of "quasi-contract" *(quasi ex contractu)*. Quasi-contract is a concept from Roman law used to assess non-contractual obligations—i.e., cases in which a person can be said to owe another without having entered into a contract. The concept of quasi-contract in Roman law was used, for example, to establish compensatory obligation in cases when a person incurred an expense in protecting another's property, without his or her knowledge, during an emergency (see editor's note at Carmichael 2002, 112). Carmichael draws a line between quasi and tacit contracts, noting that quasi contracts are contractual only in a purely ficti-

tious sense: "Quasi contracts must not be confused with *tacit* contracts. In
tacit contracts consent is argued to have occurred in actual fact on the basis
of some action or nonaction; but in quasi contracts consent is pretended for
the sake of equity" (113; italics in original). Obligations by quasi-contract
are no more derived from a contract than those by delict or damage (113).

Some of these conceptual elements were used by Carmichael's student
Francis Hutcheson. Like Carmichael, Hutcheson ([1747], 170–72; 1755, 2:8,
21, 31,33) spoke of "tacit convention" in relation to the meaning of words.
Hutcheson ([1747], 241) also used the idea of quasi-contract to understand
political authority: "They are bound therefor [*sic*], whether they consent or
not;" here the 1747 English translator (whose identity is unknown) adds in
a note: "This is an obligation *quasi ex contractu*" (italics added; see also 275;
see also 1755, 2: 231, 233). In treating political authority, Hutcheson, again
broadly Lockean, suggests quasi- contract as the metaphorical "consent"
involved in political authority. Some of Hutcheson's (1755, 2:31, 33, 234,
300, 352, 368) talk of "tacit convention" and of "importing" a convention
sounds very Humean. To the extent that Hutcheson is saying that so-called
political consent is quasi-contract, and quasi-contract is not contract at all,
we may see Hutcheson as either watering down political-consent theory
or even quietly distancing himself from it. He is taking steps away from a
Lockean contractarianism, toward Hume and his rejection of social contract theory. Note, however, that although Hutcheson was Hume's senior
by 17 years, the two works containing these discussions of political authority were published *after* Hume's *Treatise*. [23]

Hutcheson died in 1746. His *System* was published in 1755, but draft
material for it had circulated privately among his friends as early as 1737
(Turco 2007, x). It is not unreasonable to think that in the matters treated
here he may have been influenced by Hume, and we do not know what
changes may have been made to the draft materials. In 1742 Hutcheson sent Hume a copy of his *Instituto Compendiaria* (which was translated

---

23. Hume sent Hutcheson Book III of the *Treatise* in manuscript in 1739 and it was published in 1740. It
is likely that Hume paid a visit to Hutcheson in the winter of 1739–40 (Turco 2007, xviii). Hutcheson
(2007) was first published in Latin in 1742 and a second revised edition in 1745, and the English translation in 1747. Hutcheson died in 1746. Hutcheson (1755) was brought forward by his son, also named
Francis.

and published in English in 1747 as *A Short Introduction to Moral Philosophy*). In response, Hume wrote to Hutcheson, complimenting his Latin, but reproaching Hutcheson for his fear of basing "any thing of Virtue from artifice and human Conventions" (Greig 1932, 33–34; referenced in Turco 2007, xix), a reproach that may well have led Hutcheson to meditate on Hume's own ideas. Furthermore, we cannot rule out that handlers of the 1755 *System* themselves tweaked the material in Humean ways.

As for convention after Hume, we have not made a study. It would seem that Hume did advance a new meaning of "convention." In our Excel file it is remarkable how abundantly Rousseau used these terms in the Humean sense in *Emile, or On Education* (1762) and, to a lesser extent, in *The Social Contract* (1762). The Humean sense also seems to appear in Edmund Burke and Dugald Stewart (1854, 1:134, 176, 178). The adjective "conventional" rises steadily after 1810, to the much more widespread usage of today. "Conventional" seems to naturally carry a spirit of convention in the Humean sense; things that are "conventional," in a colloquial sense, are understood to be customary, normal, usual, etc., not agreed upon by resolution or literal convention.

Examining the Liberty Fund texts reinforces Hume's innovativeness in his analysis of convention with the Lewisian meaning. Neither Carmichael nor Hutcheson seems to provide any significant "convention" discourse with hints at the Lewisian meaning. In establishing the Lewisian meaning, Hume transcended the expression "tacit convention;" he never used it in his published works.[24] By definition, Lewisian conventions are regularities in behavior *that are common knowledge*, so what would "tacit convention" mean? The "tacit" is in one sense redundant: the regularity is conventional, so people don't need to enunciate it. And in another sense inapt: people could enunciate the regularity, at least in vague terms, if called to.[25]

---

24. For the sake of completeness and future reference, note that Hume uses the words "tacit" and "implicit" to modify "promise," "consent," or "agreement" in the following instances in his *Treatise*: T 3.2.3.6, 3.2.8.3, 3.2.8.9. In his *Essays*, he uses "tacit" in connection with "promise," "consent," or "agreement," only critically in "Of the Original Contract" (EMPL, 465–487). "Implicit" is not used in such a way in the *Essays*. Neither "tacit" nor "implicit" are used to modify these terms in his *Enquiries*.

25. The reader is encouraged to check "tacit convention" in Google's Ngram Viewer.

CHAPTER 5

Conservative Liberalism: Smith, Hume, and Burke as Policy Liberals and Polity Conservatives

Adam Smith suggested that *Wealth of Nations* (WN)'s practical teachings make "the science of a legislator" (468.39). A legislator presupposes a legislature. WN does not instruct us in designing legislatures.

If one were to draw from Smith a distinction between the science of a legislator and the art or science of designing legislatures, it might correspond to a distinction between *subconstitutional* and *constitutional*. But I speak instead of *policy reform* and *polity reformation*. I avoid "constitution" because it may connote an articulated frame of government, but, more importantly, I understand polity as something broader and more organic than the constitutive parts of the government, the formal laws, definitions, structures, and jurisdictions of a society. I also mean (at least in some degree) its manners, ways, character, and culture. Laws have to be interpreted; interpretations flow in part from customs, attitudes, and ways of life. Actions that significantly affect the polity raise issues of polity reformation. I propose to call Hume, Smith, and Burke "conservative" on polity reformation—though by no means otherwise purely neutrally so.

While the three are conservative on polity reformation, I call them "liberal" in policy reform. "Policy reform," as used here, presupposes that there is an approximation to a stable, integrated, and reasonably functional polity and refers to narrower change for the better. Americans, Britons, and others today are accustomed to stable integrated polity, but such had not been assured in Britain until sometime in the 1720s, after which the system of government became "adamantine" (Plumb 1967, xvii).

In this chapter I further narrow our special sense of "policy reform." The concept presupposes a stable integrated polity, but is also qualified further as follows:

1. *We narrow* to issues best thought of as issues of *domestic* policy.

2. *We narrow* by abstracting from how reforms might affect the norms, cultures, practices, and institutions that constitute the polity and its manner of proceeding: Such abstracting-from is most suitable when the reforms under discussion simply *do not much* affect those things. In this respect, especially, "policy reform" in our narrowed sense sometimes does *not* coincide with "policymaking," because sometimes workaday policymaking too much affects the polity to warrant the confining of our estimating of it to the "science" of policy reform in our narrowed sense.

As indicated, policy reform in our narrowed sense is to be understood in contradistinction to *polity reformation.* A large reform in immigration policy, for example, may significantly alter (or may be widely thought to significantly alter) the electorate and norms surrounding the functioning of the polity, so the issue of mass immigration has a significant polity-reformation aspect to it. We may say likewise about schooling, since there are significant soulcraft and politycraft aspects to schooling. But most economic regulation and many other policy issues have only a faint aspect of polity reformation, and can principally be thought of as policy-reform issues. For any given policymaking issue, we pragmatically draw a wavy line beyond which the polity-reformation aspect is too considerable to treat the issue as one of mere policy reform.

I cannot help but sometimes use the word *policy* in the plain-language sense of policy issuing from government, irrespective of polity reformation. The reader must cope here with *policy* polysemy.

There is a sense in which a human entity—a human being, a family, an organization, a network, a polity, a society, humankind—is partly defined by its doings. For example, Smith spoke of proper beneficence as a *becom-*

ing (TMS 270.10).

But we pervasively distinguish what an entity *does* and what it *is*. Policy reform, in our narrowed sense, is within the realm of what the polity *does*, and polity reformation is about changes in what the polity *is*. Within the ontology of a polity there is a historistic element—but only an element. We do not allow historicity to drive us into ontological infinitesimals. Nor do we absorb all history into Parmenides' one unchanging being. Human ontology is always elusive.[1] I do not attempt to delineate clearly the ontology of polity, nor of reformations thereto.

The polity conservatism of Hume, Smith, and Burke was not purely neutral: Their liberalism was, in their context of domestic politics, primary, and that liberalism would be cautiously favored, and the contrary disfavored, in matters of polity reformation. Still, the salient feature of their posture on polity reformation was conservatism.

In the following quotation from Burke, I have, where indicated, snipped away and altered terminology, but it comports with his meaning: "[T]here is a manifest marked distinction...between [polity reformation] and [policy reform]. The former alters the substance of the objects themselves.... Reform is, not a change in the substance [of the polity]..., but a direct application of a remedy to the grievance complained of" (1992, 290). Broadly speaking, polity reformation considers changes *to what the polity is*, and policy reform considers only changes *in what the polity does*.

The proposition that Hume, Smith, and Burke were liberal in policy reform and conservative in polity reformation is not novel. It accords, for example, with the "three-sided comparison" of David Miller (1981, 196), which finds among the three men "substantial similarities in outlook...: a belief in economic freedom, a belief in social hierarchy, and a commitment to the political establishment of eighteenth-century Britain." Duncan Forbes (1975) explained that Hume was "a post-revolutionary, establishment political philosoph[er]" (91), but that does not imply an establishment policy analyst (Matson 2019, 44–47). Like his two friends, Hume was a liberal reformer. Donald Livingston (1995, 158) speaks of "the humanistic, histori-

---

1. An as-yet-unactualized potential human entity is not actual, but what about the potentiality? Is it not actual? Does not the potentiality inhere in the human entity today? Indeed it does, but we analysts will have difficulty in coming to agreement on what the currently inhering potentialities are.

cal, rhetorical, and virtue-centered liberalism of Hume, Smith, and Burke." Hume, Smith, and Burke are repeatedly listed together by Friedrich Hayek as representative of the liberalism he stands for (Hayek 1948, 4–7; 1960, 55; 1967, 160). A book title uses the same expression I do for the affinity between Hayek and our troika: *Hayek's Conservative Liberalism* (Gissurarson 1987).

I worry about my own twisting of Hume, Smith, and Burke. Yet I press on. As for my classical-liberal motivation, I hope that Smith was right when he said that "[f]rankness and openness conciliate confidence" (TMS 337.28). The six ascriptions—both liberal and conservative to all three, Hume, Smith, and Burke—are little more than asserted. I exposit an interpretation.

To understand renovations being made to a building, it is good to understand the kind of order that the renovator hopes to establish, secure, and foster. Burke (1992) writes to a French correspondent in 1789: "Permit me then…to tell you what the freedom is that I love." That freedom is liberal policy; and that is *why* Burke is so opposed to the goings-on in France: They will not conduce to "practical liberty" (7, 11). Burke "opposed the French Revolution on liberal and pluralist grounds" (Himmelfarb 2004, 72; likewise O'Brien 1992, 608). By understanding Hume, Smith, and Burke's sensibilities in policy reform, we have a better sense of what their judgments would aim for, long-term.

The foregoing talk of conservative liberalism is underpinned by big ideas in jural theory and political theory. In the next four sections of this chapter, I briefly exposit those big ideas. W. R. Scott (1923) wrote: "Adam Smith was truly great because he stood, more than anyone else, more than most people understand even now, for *liberty* for a man to make the best of his enterprise, of his labour or of his capital *within the fabric of a stable and well organised State*" (143, italics added). In that sentence, the two key concepts are italicized by me. The next four sections offer big ideas about those two concepts and how they interrelate.

The source of liberalism

"The child of jurisprudence is liberalism," wrote J. G. A. Pocock (1983, 249), and Dugald Stewart made similar remarks (1854, 26; cf. 183, 171). In particular, as stated above, commutative justice enables liberty.

Smith maintained three senses of justice, one being commutative. (The others, distributive and estimative justice, are discussed in Ch. 1.) Smith summarizes the basic precept of commutative justice as "abstaining from what is another's" (TMS 269.10). I prefer to say *not messing with other people's stuff.* Smith gives his most definite description of commutative justice's "most sacred laws" (TMS 84.2) as not messing with other people's person, property, and promises due (thus my "stuff" includes promises due, or obligations by consent or contract).[2]

Smith exposits the specialness of commutative justice. The rules of the precept are grammar-like, "precise and accurate," at least as compared to the rules of other virtues. On these matters, Smith is like Hume, who copiously talks "abstain" (as in "abstaining from what is another's") in the *Treatise* and explains that the rules of commutative justice evolve to be precise and accurate (T 3.2.6.7–8; EPM 3.2.34–3.2.45). In Hume's presentation, the most essential constituent of "stuff," one's person, is understated, but self-ownership is affirmed, even presupposed, and folded into "property" (T 3.2.2.7-9). Hume's description of commutative justice ("three fundamental laws of nature," T 3.2.6.1) aligns with Smith's threefold "most sacred laws." In line with Knud Haakonssen (1981, 12; 1996, 27, 117–8) and Stephen Buckle (1991, vii, ix), we see that Hume and Smith are in these regards developing their own expressions of the natural jurisprudence tradition: The "stuff" held sacred by commutative justice corresponds to one's own, *suum*, in Grotius, Pufendorf, and others.

Just as the grammars of languages vary, so too do commutative-justice "grammars." The parsing of "messing with other people's stuff" varies to some extent by time and place. But any society that gets beyond primeval must have a beyond-primeval system of not messing with other people's

---

2. At several points Smith also indicates "reputation" as something covered by commutative justice, that is, as something constituent of what I'm calling one's "stuff." Bonica and Klein (in Ch. 6) make the case that in as much as Smith does affirm reputation as constituent of stuff, he means only a very basic "simple" reputation that amounts to a right against detractions that put the estimated party in jeopardy of invasion of person, property, and promises due.

stuff, just as it must have a beyond-primeval language.[3]

The jural logic of one's own

Jural dualism means there are two kinds of jural relationships: equal-equal, like you and your neighbor, and superior-inferior, or governor-governed (Diesel 2020). In both dimensions in commercial society, Smith sees the flipside of the duty of commutative justice (not messing with other people's stuff) in the correlated claim of right: others not messing with one's stuff. This is *liberty*. Liberty is others, particularly the government, not messing with one's stuff.

Smith writes in WN of "the violence of law" and related expressions,[4] and in TMS of "fortunate violence" and "irresistible force": we "submit," "are taught to acquiesce"—not consent!—to "those superiors" (253.30). Smith often declares duly enacted laws to be violations of the simple rules of commutative justice and its flipside, liberty.[5] Smith recognized that taxation "involved forcible infringement of liberty, privacy, and property of individuals" (Haakonssen 1981, 96). As for Hume, the critic of social contract, it is the same, and likewise for Burke. Burke's "convention" talk (e.g., Burke 1999a, 151) is principally the sort that does not imply a convening (Lewis 1969; ch. 4 of the present book). Burke's prescription talk for political authority is the borrowing from Hume's conventionist reasoning (in the *Treatise*) on ownership of property. Burke (1999a, 20–21) wrote: "Prescription is the most solid of all titles, not only to property, but, which is to secure that property, to Government."

---

3. Matson and Klein (ch. 4 of the present book) pushes against the idea that, even in the *Treatise*, Hume really meant to say that in the primeval state there was no effectual sense of property at all. The point becomes clear in Smith's jurisprudence, where he says that following the primeval hunter stage, property is further *extended*.

4. For "violence of law" and like remarks see WN 525-526.4-5, 248.9, 285.31, 342.30, 372.32, 422.16, 586.52, 653.28, 647-648.17.

5. Most notably at WN 530.16 but for other instances of Smith identifying laws violating commutative justice/liberty see Figure 1.6 of the present book. Smith grows sarcastic, as when he writes about Englishmen's "boasted liberty" and how they "pretended to be free" (WN 660.47; 326.100). Smith's maintenance of the jural logic of one's own is marked by "of its own accord" and "of their own accord," which occur 28 times in WN. I read Smith's discussion of the ethics of keeping a promise made to a highwayman (TMS 330-333) as esoteric homiletics about our obligations to government.

As for Burke's talk of "contract" and "compact," that belongs to a rejection of contractarianism. What he means is custom likened to a "virtual" contract (1992, 160), "by the spirit of philosophic analogy" (1999a, 122), and it is an assenting to God, "the source and original archetype," "the great primaeval contract of eternal society…connecting the visible and invisible world," expecting "oblation of the state itself," that is, the oblation of the state to God (1999a, 193, 195; cf 1999b, 305), "the sovereign of the world" (1999a, 264). This contract is "social," *not* in the sense that society's members all enter into a contract (either with one another or with the government), but rather in the sense that the contract's principal terms, so to speak, correspond with our striving to act to the betterment of society. By faith in God and his work, our contract with God involves a social orientation. Doing our best to advance the social good will corresponds with our being becoming in God's eyes. It inheres in the "deal" we make with God for his approval. As for relations among humans, Hume, Smith, and Burke saw the institutionalizing of the initiation of coercion as the hallmark of jural superiority within the polity, nowadays called "the government." In conforming to conventions of political authority, people acquiesce to the initiation of coercion.

Liberty is likewise somewhat historistic. But that does not subvert the grammar-like reasoning of commutative justice and liberty—*the jural logic of one's own*. The "logic" is pinned down within any modern jural-dualistic society by the following principle: A type of action in the superior-inferior jural relationship is an initiation of coercion if (and only if) such action in equal-equal jural relationships is an initiation of coercion. Yes, what counts as initiation of coercion among equals varies with historical context, but whatever any particular jural-dualistic context recognizes as initiation of coercion among equals will, on the jural logic of one's own, pin down what counts as such when done by the jural superior. If your neighbor "taxed" you (i.e., extorted wealth from you) or "regulated" your freedom of association (i.e., stalked and assaulted you in private life), we darned-well would regard that as an initiation of coercion, and so we do call it an initiation of coercion when done by government (though we do not call it "extortion" or "assault").[6] This logic takes the historistic element onboard, and domesticates it.

Hume likewise works with flipside notions. Erik Matson and I use the phrase "mere-liberty," because Hume speaks of "liberty" with many a modifier. We argue that mere-liberty is for Hume the *essential* notion of liberty, whereas other notions are *contributory*, in the sense that they contribute to a regular system of liberty, as a car contributes to transportation and is often spoken of as transportation. Along the lines offered by Nicholas Capaldi (1990),[7] mere-liberty is at the heart of the aspiration of a liberal constitution, ascribed to Hume, Smith, and Burke. In Figure 5.1, all rectangular shapes represent institutions that are contributory to the to mere-liberty, which is the heart, the essence, of liberty.

FIGURE 5.1: THE CONSTITUTION OF LIBERTY

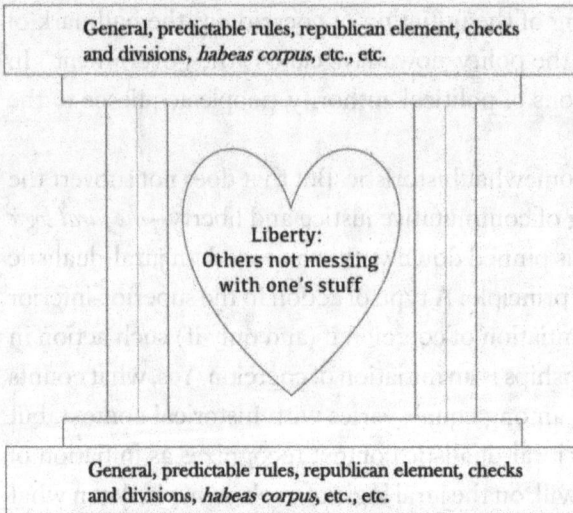

General, predictable rules, republican element, checks and divisions, *habeas corpus*, etc., etc.

Liberty:
Others not messing
with one's stuff

General, predictable rules, republican element, checks and divisions, *habeas corpus*, etc., etc.

In any particular society, the set of conventions that constitute political authority may interpenetrate those that constitute commutative justice/liberty, but neither of those two sets of conventions is subsumed within the other. Government entitlements such as Medicare do not count as commu-

6. Note that not seeing taxation and government restrictions as voluntary depends on properly theorizing the configuration of ownership; see Klein 2011.

7. There is no real disagreement between Capaldi and us (Matson and me), but I'm not thrilled with the leaning that Capaldi does on the words "arbitrary" and "autonomy," preferring rather to get down to the staples of commutative justice. Capaldi and I were allied on these matters in a multipart exchange (Hart 2018).

tative-justice "stuff": were the government to decide to roll back certain entitlement programs, that rolling back would not be a messing with anyone's stuff in the commutative-justice/liberty sense. Likewise, the franchise, access to government-sector employment or participation (e.g., for Catholics or Dissenters), and many other rights involved in the government rules that govern government resources are not—here we abstract away from any taxation upon which such rights may depend—constitutive of commutative-justice "stuff" (though, as always, they do belong to the two other senses of justice).

The liberty principle and the liberty maxim

The liberty principle says: In a choice between two reforms (one of which may be no reform at all), the one that rates higher in liberty better serves universal benevolence. If it seems weird to think that two reforms can readily be ranked in terms of liberty, realize that a key aspect of Smithian policy-reform liberalism is the tendency *to formulate policy issues so as to be able to do just that*.

But Smith did not maintain the liberty principle as an axiom. Rather, it is defeasible. As Burke put it: "Nothing, certainly, can be laid down on the subject that will not admit of exceptions" (1999c, 90; cf 1992, 91). The troika held that the principle holds only *by and large*—making *a maxim*. Thus, they give liberty a presumption, which like any presumption can be overcome when the prosecution overcomes the burden of proof.

Smith hedges and refines his discourse due to his sensitivity to many paradoxes and subtleties, including:

- Some of the exceptions come because the greater direct-liberty option has indirect effects and ramifications that over time result in less liberty overall (Klein and Clark 2010, 2012). Many of Smith's exceptions have an indirect reduction-in-liberty element to their justification (Clark 2010).

- Liberty enjoys a presumption, but so does something else, the status quo. The two presumptions are in tension for liberty-augmenting policy reforms, and they must moderate one another. The matter of how much of a presumption to give to the status quo makes another contextualization for a meaning of *conservative*; this "conservative" *in policy reform* relates to but should be distinguished from "conservative" *in polity reformation*. Hume, Smith, and Burke were conservative in polity reformation, but I would not assess them to have been particularly conservative in policy reform. They were PLPC (policy liberal and polity conservative), not PCPC.

- The Smithian "science of a legislature" is one thing, the art of liberal politics (think Burke), another, and liberals cannot expect to set about both birds with one stone; discourse is situational and a prime aspect of a discourse situation is the audience; sometimes liberals bargain instead of challenge; sometimes they write between the lines; sometimes they engage in "practical advocacy" (Cowen 2007), promoting the 17th best because it is salient or politically practicable (thus, liberal reform on a particular policy issue is *directional*, not necessarily destinational; Munger 2018).

Authority must be acknowledged essential to liberty's very existence

That section heading comes directly from Hume (EMPL, 40).

Smith's jural dualism implies that our discourse is contextualized to a polity with an integrated and presumably stable jural system with a singular superior. There may be multiple levels of government, but they are integrated. Today we are accustomed to thinking of "*the* government," and Smith's presuppositions seem natural.

But jural integration and political stability are a relatively recent development (Plumb 1967). Jural integration and political stability constitute a major theme in Hume's *History of England*,[8] as noted by Andrew Sabl (2012, 65)

---

8. Jacob Hall and I (2020) present 142 passages from Hume's *History* on the theme of the fog of jural pluralism and the integrating of political and jural authority in Britain. Hume's *History* teaches us to appreciate stable integrated polity in Britain and its promise of a liberal nation-state (Asher 2021).

and Duncan Forbes (1975, 263). In the early modern period, which began, say, sometime in the late 15th century (when the printing press gets going) and ends, say, in 1648 (the Peace of Westphalia), jural authority was not so integrated or unified; the period was a jural mishmash. Extreme in German regions,[9] jural pluralism was significant throughout early modern Europe.

Notice that the terms "jural pluralism" and "jural dualism" refer to two different species of objects: The "pluralism" refers to plural *authorities* (or jural superiorities), while the "dualism" refers to dual *relationships*. The United States of America is a polity of jural integration (as opposed to pluralism), and it is a polity of jural dualism (as opposed, most importantly, to jural monism[10]).

In early modern Europe, many institutions *other than the crown*—empires and foreign powers, ecclesiastical institutions, lords and barons, manorial communities, families and clans, masters-over-slaves, and towns and boroughs—might assert coercive authority within "the realm." "The realm" itself was often hazy, as different powers contended for the crown and battled over the territorial boundaries of the crown's authority.

In such a jumble, what is "one's own" (*suum*)? How could people build a liberal civilization on the logic of *suum* when *suum* itself was no matter of common knowledge? The problem is epitomized by the word "slaveowner": Is the slave's person his own, or the master's own? Such problems abound in worlds of lords, clans, etc.

Without conventions concerning one's own and its grammar, the very notions of our two jural relationships, equal-equal and superior-inferior, would be unclear even conceptually, for they presuppose a configuration of ownership. The fog of jural pluralism foils not only the propounding of mere-liberty but the very *defining* of mere-liberty. For this reason, Hume makes a big theme of jural integration (Hall and Klein 2020). "Authority

---

9. On jural pluralism in German regions, see Pufendorf (1667; English translation 1690, 1696); see (2007), 159, 174–7.

10. Jural monism would be a society such as a hunter-gatherer band in which the leaders are but firsts among equals, and so there is no superior-inferior jural relationship; one does voluntarily agree to the rules of the band. Social-democratic political philosophies sometimes see the governor-government relationship in a modern democratic polity as an equal-equal jural relationship, by seeing that relationship as a matter of voluntary agreement, and thusly see the modern democratic polity as jural monism, not dualism (see ch. 8 here).

must be acknowledged essential to its very existence," wrote Hume (EMPL 40). Smith and Burke likewise appreciated the long path to established integrated jural authority.

Liberal in policy reform

When it came to policy reform, Smith, Hume, and Burke were liberal. I remark briefly on Smith and Hume and at greater length on Burke.

Adam Smith

Dugald Stewart (EPS, 311) wrote that works such as Smith's WN "have aimed at the improvement of society,—not by delineating plans of new constitutions, but by enlightening the policy of actual legislators."[11] Although some of the policy issues covered in WN would lean toward polity reformation, for the most part they can be thought of as policy issues in our narrowed sense. As shown above in Chapter 2, many scholars write explicitly of Smith's pro-liberty "presumption" or "burden of proof." Smith's presumption of liberty in policy reform is variously tempered and qualified, as already noted, and, when it comes to liberty-augmenting reforms, moderated by a presumption of the status quo.

Here I offer further observations about apprehending the presumption of liberty in Smith:

1. The original political meaning of "liberal" emerged in Britain in the 1770s. Smith was crucial in the semantic emergence, by repeated use of the adjective "liberal," e.g., "the liberal system...this liberal system," (538–539.39) and "the liberal plan of equality, liberty, and justice," which he summarized as "allowing every man to pursue his own interest his own way" (WN 664.3), used also in "the system of natural liberty" (687.51), noting there that "his own way" must

---

11. Emma Rothschild (2001, 57f) suggests that Stewart's remarks do not soundly represent Smith, and perhaps that Stewart is being somewhat insincere. Rothschild helps us understand why Stewart made the remarks, but I think Stewart's remarks are sound enough.

be within the bounds of commutative justice.

2. Smith's lectures covering domestic policy from his jurisprudence course in 1763–64 (LJ(B)) are remarkably consistent in propounding liberal policy attitudes, with nary an
exception, save tax-supported night-watchman functions.

3. Regarding the exceptions found in WN,[12] keep in mind: (1)
On small-denomination bank notes, he explicitly acknowledges that the restriction he endorses "is a violation of natural liberty," and he takes up the burden of proof (WN 324). (2)
Almost all of the exceptions are endorsements of status-quo
policy; he scarcely ever affirms a liberty-reducing reform to
the status quo (Clark 2021). (3) On schooling, Scott Drylie
(2021) explains that many have misread and misrepresented
Smith.[13] (4) Smith had cause to avoid appearing too rationalistic about the liberty maxim, and cause to hold back and
fudge, for example, on usury, perhaps.[14]

David Hume

Hume had a liberal orientation on policy reform. Matson and I in Chapter
3 here expound on mere-liberty in Hume, beginning with the *Treatise*, in
which we see language that suggests that the flipside of commutative justice is "liberty" (T 2.1.10.1), and in which Hume says that after "fixing and
observing" the rules of commutative justice "there remains little or nothing
to be done towards settling a perfect harmony and concord" (T 3.2.2.12).

12. As for judgments on particular policy issues in TMS, there are perhaps: the slave-trade/slavery
(206-207.9), suicide (287.34), and perhaps capital punishment (100.4).

13. On the schooling of children, never forget Smith's final words on the issue: "This expence, however, might perhaps with equal propriety, and even with some advantage, be defrayed altogether by
those who receive the immediate benefit of such education and [religious] instruction, or by the *voluntary* contribution of those who think they have occasion for either the one or the other" (WN 815.5;
italics added).

14. Most notable here is Smith on usury, where he endorses the status-quo policy, but in his description of how things work under that policy gives a feature that runs directly contrary to the reasoning
he gives for why, under laissez-faire, capital would be squandered on harebrained projectors (Diesel
2021).

Hume was not dogmatic, and for example acknowledged domestic beneficiaries of taxes on linen and brandy and the need for raising taxes somehow (EMPL 324); thus Roger Emerson (2008) says that Hume's "*laissez
faire* was one with qualifications" (28). John Stewart (1992, 181) says that
Hume's general favor for free markets "is a hallmark of classic liberalism"
(see also Hardin 2007, 200).

Nightwatchman functions aside, there is but one issue[15] on which
Hume elaborates a policy judgment that runs against the liberty principle
and an associated opposition to the governmentalization of social affairs:
He endorses church establishment, which presumably implies tax-based
subsidization and privilege, if not restrictions on dissenting activities (H
III:135–6). But the exception almost proves the rule. Hume introduces it
as an exception to a general maxim: "Most of the arts and professions" are
such that "*the constant rule of the magistrate*, except, perhaps, on the first introduction of any art, is, *to leave the profession to itself, and trust its encouragement
to those who reap the benefit of it*" (ibid., italics added). Governmentalizing
religion is a way of ensuring against the dangers of contentious and fervent
religious sects. Hume's remarks are offered in the course of narrating the
times of Henry VIII; Hume advises the magistrate to bribe the indolence
of the clergy. For Hume, the issue is not one of mere policy reform. In "Idea
of a Perfect Commonwealth," Hume writes: "Without the dependence of
the clergy on the civil magistrates…it is in vain to think that any free government will ever have security or stability" (EMPL 525).

On church establishment, it is clear that Burke's views run along similar lines (see McBride 2012, 192). As for Smith, the matter is not entirely
clear, because his advocacy in WN, though seemingly counter to Hume,
proceeds upon the premise "if politicks had never called in the aid of religion" (WN 792.8). It makes sense to think that Smith is advocating in the
context of the Americas something like the First Amendment clause that
prevents the establishment of religion, but it does not follow that he is suggesting disestablishment for Britain, much less a First Amendment for Britain. And it is unclear whether Burke would have endorsed the First Amendment for America.

---

15. See, however, Livingston (1995, 160), suggesting some other issues, but upon sparse textual evidence.

Edmund Burke

> Burke accepts the mockery of his sophisticated opponents, even
> with relish, and dares to convert their contempt into an adorn-
> ment. He answers burlesque with burlesque... –Ralph Lerner
> 1994, 71

No such words could be said of Hume or Smith. Burke differs from
them most notably in being a politico and in being famous for his jolting
works from 1790 about polity reformation.

In policy reform, however, Burke too was a liberal. His posthumous
"Thoughts and Details on Scarcity," 11,400 words, released as a pamphlet
in 1800 by his executors, is his only work focused on political economy,
and it is plainly and strongly favorable to the presumption of liberty and
free markets. It bubbles with insights about the disjointedness of knowledge, benefits of middlemen, autocorrective market tendencies, problems
created by government restrictions, hazards of government data gathering,
the intervention dynamic, and political psychology concerning economic
issues. "The moment that Government appears at market, all the principles
of market will be subverted" (79).

Burke speaks of government intervention as "coercion" (1999c, 61, 70;
1992, 161), saying that beneficial "timely coercion" is something that government owes to the people. But the interventions considered in "Thoughts
and Details," having to do with wages and agricultural supply, are not beneficial, and Burke sketches the proper role of government:

> But the clearest line of distinction which I could draw, whilst I
> had my chalk to draw any line, was this: That the State ought
> to confine itself to what regards the State, or the creatures of
> the State, namely, the exterior establishment of its religion; its
> magistracy; its revenue; its military force by sea and land; the
> corporations that owe their existence to its fiat; in a word, to
> every thing that is *truly and properly* public, to the public peace,
> to the public safety, to the public order, to the public prosperity.
> In it's preventive police it ought to be sparing of its efforts, and
> to employ means, rather few, unfrequent, and strong, than many,

and frequent, and, of course, as they multiply their puny politic race, and dwindle, small and feeble. Statesmen who know themselves will, with the dignity which belongs to wisdom, proceed only in this the superior orb and first mover of their duty, steadily, vigilantly, severely, courageously: whatever remains will, in a manner, provide for itself. But as they descend from the state to a province, from a province to a parish, and from a parish to a private house, they go on accelerated in their fall. They *cannot* do the lower duty; and, in proportion as they try it, they will certainly fail in the higher. They ought to know the different departments of things; what belongs to laws, and what manners alone can regulate. To these, great politicians may give a leaning, but they cannot give a law. (Burke 1999c, 90)

In his *Speech on Economical Reform* in 1780, Burke said: "Commerce... flourishes most when it is left to itself. Interest, the great guide of commerce, is not a blind one. It is very well able to find its own way; and its necessities are its best laws" (quoted in Canavan 1995, 117). In *Regicide Peace* he said the less the government meddles in economic matters the better (1999b, 167). The chapter "Burke on Political Economy" by Richard Whatmore (2012) consistently indicates that the thinking represented by "Thoughts" was present throughout (starting with Burke and Burke 1757). Burke's description in *Reflections* of the "real" rights of men strongly suggests mere-liberty (1999a, 150–151).

Emma Rothschild (2001) says that "Burke's pamphlet was received as little more than an exposition of Smith's 'principles'" (64). But she offers a left-Smithian case for a wedge between Smith and Burke (Rothschild 2001, 53–54, 64, 151, 275n77, 279n117). Significant impasses are also suggested by Donald Winch (1996, 180–91, 198–220). Rothschild portrays Burke's pamphlet as "the simple prescription of economic freedom" (64). She writes: "Burke and Smith were no longer seen as opponents by the end of the century; they were equivalents, and economic conservatives" (64).

She neglects, however, to show anyone ever seeing them as opponents.[16] I find Winch and especially Rothschild unconvincing, and instead side with scholars who have long connected Burke and Smith.[17] One of Smith's biographers wrote: "Burke and Smith, always profound admirers of one another's writings, had grown warm friends," and had remained so, to Smith's final years (Rae 1895, 387).

When Burke explained in 1789 "what the freedom is that I love," he described it as follows:

> It is not solitary, unconnected, individual, selfish liberty, as if every man was to regulate the whole of his conduct by his own will. The liberty I mean is *social* freedom. It is that state of things in which liberty is secured by the equality of restraint. A constitution of things in which the liberty of no one man, and no body of men, and no number of men, can find means to trespass on the liberty of any person, or any description of persons, in the society. This kind of liberty is, indeed, but another name for justice; ascertained by wise laws, and secured by well-constructed institutions. (Burke 1992, 8)

Burke says that if the goings-on in France in fact lead to good arrangements, he will be well pleased. But he doubts that, in fact, the French citizen will find himself "in a perfect state of legal security, with regard to his life, to his property, to the uncontrolled disposal of his person, to the free use of his industry and his faculties" and able to "decently express his sentiments upon public affairs, without hazard to his life or safety, even though against a predominant and fashionable opinion" (1992, 8, 9). Burke saw the flipside relationship between liberty and commutative justice. In his *Appeal* of 1791, he suggests that traders prosper from, among other things, having "cultivated an habitual regard to commutative justice" (1992, 168). Pocock (1985) explains how Burke regarded Jacobin energy: "Burke saw

16. If Rothschild's portrayal of Burke is oversimplified, her portrayal of Smith is twisted; see Martin (2011).

17. E.g., Dunn (1941); Barrington (1954); Huntington (1957, 462–3); Canavan (1995, 117); Himmelfarb (2004, 73). Burke (1759) is a warm review of *The Theory of Moral Sentiments*.

the antithesis against which this energy was aimed as a liberal commercial state, the Whig order as ruled by Sir Robert Walpole and expounded by Adam Smith" (209).

Russell Kirk (1997) said that Burke "steadfastly opposed all policies calculated to reduce private liberties" (147), and he repeatedly calls Burke a "liberal" (161; Kirk 1960, 20, 22, 214). Samuel Huntington (1957) wrote: "[I]nsofar as Burke had views on the desirable organization of society, he was a liberal, a Whig, and a free trader" (461); "In Parliament Burke was consistently for laisser faire" (463). Yuval Levin explains that Burke the parliamentarian "was, above all, a reformer," and suggests that Burke represents what he calls "conservative liberalism" (2014, 9, 229; Levin 2019). Pocock (1985) writes: "Burke to the last was a man of his modern age, with little nostalgia in his make-up" (209).

On the word *liberal*, Burke joined in on the post-1776 Smithian "liberal" semantic practice. In the 1777 Letter to the Sheriffs of Bristol he spoke of "the liberal government of this free nation" (Burke 1904, 16). In a 1778 letter he writes that "the prosperity which arises from an enlarged and liberal system improves all its objects: and the participation of a trade with flourishing Countries is much better than a monopoly of want and penury" (Burke 1961, 426). In 1778 Burke speaks of the "liberality in the commercial system" (1999c, 33). In the *Reflections* he speaks significantly of "a liberal descent," (1999a, 123), a moment that Gertrude Himmelfarb aptly seizes as liberal in our sense (1986, 167–173). Burke declaims against the revolutionary assembly in France: "Their liberty is not liberal" (1999a, 174); and: "It is a vile illiberal school, this new French academy of the *sans culottes*" (1992, 299).

Whether Burke was a Smithian liberal in policy reform is a matter that would have to consider not only his discourse but all of his activity as a politician, issue by issue. I am no expert in Burke. I hope that those who are will correct and augment the catch-as-catch-can tyro smatterings in Table 5.1 and Table 5.2.

In Table 5.1 I begin a listing of *favorable* evidence of liberalism on issues that are amenable to parsing in terms of the liberty principle, even if the issue broaches on polity reformation. Especially for a practical politician, we judge such matters on the basis of the *direction* of reform, without carping about not going far enough or about holding his tongue or worse, in the compromising setting of politics.

TABLE 5.1: ISSUES ON WHICH BURKE SEEMS TO HAVE PUSHED IN THE LIBERTY-AUGMENTING DIRECTION

Slavery/slave-trade	Thomas Clarkson (1808, 1, 55–56) salutes Burke in his classical account of the anti-slavery movement, quoting Burke and William Burke's *Account of the European Settlements* (1757). David Brion Davis (1975, 356) speaks of Burke as among the "eloquent opponents of the slave trade." See Collins (2019a; 2020b, 56ff).
Free Port Act of 1766	See Collins (2017, 580; 2020b, 235ff).
Trade with Ireland	Burke "argued for easing the restrictions on Irish trade for the sake not only of justice, but also of the mutual benefit of the two countries" (Canavan 1995, 121–2). See also Collins 2017, 584f; 2020b, 299ff; Gregg 2019.
Liberalizing coercive restrictions on Catholics, Irish, dissenters	See Levin (2014, 73, 193).
Privatizing Crown lands	"In his *Speech on Economical Reform* in 1780, Burke advocated selling the smaller landed estates of the Crown to private owners" (Canavan 1995, 119).
Speenhamland system of rural wage support	Burke vociferously denounces the system and related interventions in rural wage and sustenance markets; see "Thoughts and Details" ([1800]).
Poor Removals Bill (related to Settlement Act)	In 1774, Burke approved a measure that "would have circumscribed the ability of magistrates to return indigent immigrants back to their parish of origin" (Collins 2020b, 102). Burke: "The laws of settlement and removals are the essence of slavery...—if you will not let me live where I please, which necessarily implies, where I can best maintain and support myself, I am a slave" (quoted in Canavan 1995, 118).
Forestalling, regrating, and engrossing	"In 1772 Burke led efforts in Parliament to repeal statutes that proscribed these trading practices" (Collins 2017, 582; see also Collins 2020b, 70ff).
Linen bounties bill	1770, Burke opposed (Collins 2020b, 84–5).
Butcher's meat bill	In 1776 Burke opposed a bill that would have "mandated that livestock, upon reaching the market, be slaughtered only after a certain period of time in order to ensure high quality meat" (Collins 2020b, 138).
Homosexuality	"Burke rose in the House of Commons to protest the treatment of two homosexuals" (Kramnick 1977, 84). One hostile commenter at the time wrote: "We therefore see him come forward as the advocate of the guilty, and displaying his talents to obtain mercy for *sodomites!*" (reproduced in Norton 2014).

Table 5.2 itemizes—again, very tyro—areas in which Burke seems to have defended incursions on liberty or advocated reductions in liberty.

TABLE 5.2: ISSUES ON WHICH BURKE DEPARTED (OR MAY HAVE DEPARTED) FROM THE LIBERTY PRINCIPLE

Church establishment	"Burke was a vigorous supporter of the state-backed Church of England" (Collins 2019c); cf. Winch (1996, 181–184). E.g., Burke (1999a, 188; 1992, 190).
Primogeniture and entail	Whatmore (2012, 81) and Collins (2019c; 2020b, 3, 110, 129, 499) speak of Burke's defense of primogeniture and entail; see also Winch (1996, 181–184). See Burke 1992, 150, 214. However, "entail" is not found in the Burke works at Liberty Fund site, except as a metaphor in *Reflections*.
Anglo-French Treaty of 1787 (Eden Treaty)	Burke (2015, 235–241) oppsed it, or at least certain provisions of it; see Collins (2020a; 2020b, 338ff); Bourke (2015, 601ff).
War posture on "regicides" —hot	Burke (1999b, 164–7) seems to call for a D-Day-like invasion of France.
War posture on "regicides" —cold	Burke (2015, 575–586). Burke "supported the Traitorous Correspondence Bill of 1793" (Collins 2019c; 2020a, 2020b, 507–8).
Pitt's "reign of alarm"	See Levin (2014, 37); Burke (1992, 189n; 1999b, 132). However, at 1992, 46–47, he seems to specifically refrain from advocating the restricting of speech/press.
Corn (grain) bounties	Burke "conveyed steady support throughout the eighteenth century for the corn bounty" (Collins 2019c). "[I]n 1773, Burke begrudgingly supported Pownall's Act, the bill that reformed, but still retained, British bounties on grain exports" (Collins 2020b, 141; see also 78ff, 276ff, 292ff).
Scottish weavers petition	In 1787 Burke "introduced a petition from Scottish weavers in the House of Commons that would have lengthened the years for apprentices to receive instruction in the weaver trade" (Collins 2020b, 476).
Navigation acts	Burke "defended the older system of the Navigation Acts" (Collins 2019c); cf. Collins (2017, 590–2; 2020b, 213ff).
East India Company charter	Collins (2019b) says Burke worked to preserve the Company's charter whereas Smith favored its annulment; see also Collins 2020b, Ch. 9.
1785 commercial propositions (Ireland)	See Collins (2017, 593–4).
Other	Passing remarks on: divorce (1999b, 128), suicide (147); suppressing Jacobin morals (132).

I should like to learn more about such items and others that could be added: How did the policies or reform proposals actually work? How might we reasonably parse them in terms of the liberty principle?[18] What did Burke say or do on the issue? Would Hume or Smith disagree? Were

---

18. Collins (2020b) treats Burke on a number of issues that are about the rules of ownership or of legal sanction once commutative justice has been violated, including enclosure (88–92), the Shipwreck Bill (326–327), and the Insolvent Debtors Bill (85).

Burke's exceptions based on considerations of polity reformation?

Gregory Collins (2020a) discusses two of Burke's exceptions to the liberty principle, namely the 1787 speech opposing the Eden Commercial Treaty with France, and the 1793 speech on the Traitorous Correspondence Bill.[19] In both cases, Burke's argumentation is based on polity considerations (including, for the Eden Treaty, *plus doux* integration with Ireland; see Burke 2015, 236) and plausibly, if only implicitly, overall liberty. Collins (2019c) writes: "[T]he idea that trade can, and should, be used as an instrument of leverage and power against hostile foreign countries…was not anathema to Burke's economic thought."

Conservative liberalism allows for some variance of opinion. Even if Smith would have disapproved of Burke's conduct on these and a few other issues—which is not obvious to me[20]—that by itself would not imply that they were not both conservative liberals.

Conservatism in polity reformation

Burke gave warm expression to polity conservatism in an undelivered speech of 1782, championing "a presumption in favour of any settled scheme of government against any untried project, that a nation has long existed and flourished under it" (1999c, 21).

The stark contrast to polity conservatism is polity radicalism. Burke in his last years saw polity radicalism run amok in France and surge as "*armed doctrine*. . . in every country." "To us it is a Colossus which bestrides our channel,"[21] "a sect aiming at universal empire, and beginning with the conquest of France" (1999b, 76, 157). In attacking polity radicalism —which makes men "little better than the flies of summer" (1999a, 191)—

---

19. Reporting of the 1787 speech is on pages 235-241 and of the 1793 speech is on pages 575–586 of Burke 2015.

20. I think of Smith's exceptionally praiseful remarks about the Duke of Marlborough (TMS 251–252.28).

21. Burke repeatedly expresses a concern within Britain itself, for example: "If ever a party adverse to the Crown should be in a condition here [in Britain] publickly to declare itself, and to divide, however unequally, the natural force of the kingdom, they are sure of an aid of fifty thousand men, at ten days warning, from the opposite coast of France" (1999b, 393).

he expounded the virtues of polity conservativism. This conservatism, in *Reflections, Appeal, Regicide Peace*, and lesser works (Burke 1992), is well noted. "The burden of proof lies heavily on those who tear to pieces the whole frame and contexture of their country" (1992, 90; cf. 196; 1999a, 153). Burke declares for "the great body" of the British people: "We are resolved to keep an established church, an established monarchy, an established aristocracy, and an established democracy, each in the degree it exists, and in no greater" (1999a, 187). As for Hume and Smith, I think that polity conservatism can be said to go for them, too. "New courts and new laws are...great evils," says Smith in LJ (287).

There are general arguments for polity conservatism:

1. Established ways have been through a historical process of selection and survival and adaptation, a process that reflects, albeit highly imperfectly, functional goodness. "Our patience will atchieve more than our force" (Burke 1999a, 275; see also 1999c, 21).

2. To some extent goodness is historistic; to some extent established ways are good because they are established. Burke laments that "everything is to be discussed...as if the constitution of our country were to be always a subject rather of altercation than enjoyment" (1999a, 187). Polity conservatism operates from a disposition to appreciate the political functionality we do have. "I know there is an order, that keeps things fast in their place; it is made to us, and we are made to it. Why not ask another wife, other children, another body, another mind?" (Burke 1999c, 27).

3. The citizen's knowledge is slight, as is that of the social theorist or reformer, and such knowledge is highly conditioned by experience and practice; the consequences of a proposed polity innovation, or even its true nature, are scarcely known. Political projectors are subject to "innumerable delusions" (WN 687.51). Rampant delusion throws politics into the hazards of collective foolishness and opportunistic abuse.

4. Happiness depends on tranquility, which depends on confidence. Confidence in living depends on the certainty and stability of rules. Every reformation excuses, arouses, and inspires a next reformation, reducing certainty, stability, confidence, and the quality of life. "By this unprincipled facility of changing the state as often, and as much, and in as many ways, as there are floating fancies or fashions, the whole chain and continuity of the commonwealth would be broken" (Burke 1999a, 191).

5. Bad reformations are not easily corrected: Their badness enjoys plausible deniability and is stubbornly denied (Burke 1992, 92–93). Also, they breed interest groups who stoutly defend them.

Prefer the devil you know to the devil you don't know. The foregoing points speak in favor of *any* polity's established ways.

But another facet of the troika's polity conservatism is that *they were British*, writing in English, with the Anglosphere particularly in mind. Burke writes: "Personal liberty…which in other European countries has rather arisen from the system of manners and the habitudes of life, than from the laws of the state, (in which it flourished more from neglect than attention) in England has been a direct object of Government" (1999b, 181). Burke in 1782 wrote of living under the British constitution:

In that Constitution I know, and exultingly I feel, both that I am free, and that I am not free dangerously to myself or to others. I know that no power on earth, acting as I ought to do, can touch my life, my liberty, or my property. I have that inward and dignified consciousness of my own security and independence, which constitutes, and is the only thing, which does constitute, the proud and comfortable sentiment of freedom in the human breast. (1999c, 27)

Burke (1999a) goes so far as to say that in France in 1790, "The triumph of the victorious party was over the principles of a British constitution" (237). Hume and Smith would concur that England had "the best system of liberty that a nation ever enjoyed" (Burke 1999b, 352), and thus they were especially wary of polity reformation.

Full of all such wariness, the troika were, nonetheless, ready to take up the burden of proof and espouse reformations. Again Burke is most elaborate, explaining that preservation depends on flexible adaptation. Brittleness awaits a shattering stress; rigidity loses touch with the sublime, and is a sort of death (1999a, 108). All three are imbued with a sense of the polity as a becoming, an emergence amenable in whatever small way to guidance and influence. And none ruled out outright revolution and political overthrow. But in the regular course of things the changes are conceived as adaptations and improvements, not transformations, to be undertaken with caution, preferably a bit at a time. "I would make the reparation as nearly as possible in the style of the building" (Burke 1999a, 363).

Polity conservatism has its starkest contrast in polity radicalism. But another contrast might be called *polity loutishness*. In former days, as a libertarian, I did not think enough about the dependence of liberty and liberalism on stable and functional polity; I did not much consider the polity-reformation dimension. Faced with polity recklessness, mischief, or radicalism, polity loutishness might tend toward inappositeness, indifference, denial, dupedom, or appeasement, when what is called for is often confrontation and sometimes forthright opposition. Burke excels in calling out polity louts.[22] In promoting polity conservatism, Burke says that it "made power gentle, and obedience liberal" (1999a, 170).[23] Polity loutishness and polity radicalism are not liberal in the sense of the word *liberal* that long pre-dates any political sense.

On polity reformation, one might be a polity conservative, a polity radical, or a polity lout. But can one be a polity liberal? I say the troika were polity conservatives. Why not see them as polity liberals? Seeing them as polity liberals requires, first, trying to separate out a pure (or neutral) polity conservatism from the character of the polity that is being conserved,

---

22. E.g., Burke (1999a, 156): "Finding their schemes of politics not adapted to the state of the world in which they live, they often come to think lightly of all public principle; and are ready, on their part, to abandon for a very trivial interest what they find of very trivial value."

23. "I must bear with infirmities until they fester into crimes" (Burke 1999a, 247).

and then identifying the concern for each in their thought: If the polity that one tries to conserve is quite liberal in character, then that person's being a polity conservative might look and sound the same as that person's being a polity liberal. Furthermore, even for a polity *like 1788 France*, it might be that what polity liberalism recommends pretty much coincides with what pure polity conservatism recommends—on the grounds that any signficant departure from polity conservatism will tend to conduce to making the character of that polity *less liberal*. I conclude that, as a concept, polity liberalism would not necessarily be meaningless, but it would be a category that is hard to contradistinguish conceptually and hard to operationalize empirically. There would not be much point in contending that, in addition to being policy liberals, the troika were polity liberals *as opposed to* polity conservatives.

Policy liberalism as polity reformation

Didn't Hume, Smith, and Burke see policy liberalism as polity reformation? Indeed, Hume and Smith saw that the liberal plan carried with it changes that conduce to polity reformation. And Burke, too: "The world on the whole will gain by a liberty, without which virtue cannot exist" (1999a, 201). Augmentations in liberty tend to serve as affirmations of the liberty maxim, and of the dignity and responsibility of the individual. Imagine if the government today repealed restrictions on payments for human kidneys. That would most likely nudge the culture to be a little more accustomed to liberty; it would tend to make the character of the polity a little more liberal.

So here we have a bit of a twist. Liberal policy is often not easily separable from polity considerations, and the troika's polity conservatism would not be *simply* conservative, in the sense of neutral with respect to prospective polity reformations. They favored overall liberty in prospective polity reformation.[24] In the expression "conservative liberalism," *liberalism* is a noun, and it is primary. It is modified by the adjective *conservative*.

Polity conservatism moderates and loosens policy liberalism, but does

---

24. Even when it comes to the *overall*-liberty principle, there is no reason to suppose that any of the troika would think that it coincides perfectly with his sense of the desirable. But it would coincide better than the direct-liberty principle.

not undo it. On issues for which the polity-reformation dimension is very pertinent, that pertinence can bolster the case for sticking to the liberty principle. For example, the 19th and 20th century expansions of government into schooling, and the concomitant liberty reductions (higher taxes, compulsory attendance, restrictions on private and home schooling), indeed brought reformations to the polity—and might indeed have justly *bolstered* opposition to many of those expansions.

Smith contrasted grammar-like or "precise and accurate" rules with "loose, vague, and indeterminate" rules—*rules*! A lack of precision and accuracy does not imply utter unruliness; it does not preclude "ruliness." There is still a spine of commutative justice and liberty within the whale of political ethics, though the whole whale is not grammar-like.[25] Hume, Smith, and Burke wrote as artists, and art is not arbitrary. Their political artistry I call conservative liberalism.

In this chapter I have indicated several ways in which conservative liberalism is bound to be somewhat loose and vague. I acknowledge one more: What polity does "polity conservatism" seek to conserve? What is the benchmark? Burke's take on 1688–89 is a case in point: He strives to paint the "revolution" as a rehabilitation of the polity, a correction (*Appeal*, in Burke 1992, 119–46). As for the United States today: Is the spirit of the polity the vision of the Declaration, the Constitution, and the Founding Fathers, or is it the current status quo? Suppose we were to roll back Social Security significantly: Is that a changing of the polity, against the presumption of polity conservatism, or a *cancellation of a change to it*, consonant with polity conservatism? Is James Madison still a leading spirit of the polity? Here again it is important to acknowledge the non-neutrality of the troika's polity conservatism. And, however the benchmark problem is handled, it remains true that policy liberalism and polity conservatism combine to place a double burden of proof on new reforms that would reduce liberty.

25. On political ethics not being grammar-like, see Smith's LJ 311, 325, 326, 433 and Burke's 1992, 91; 1999a, 107ff; 1999b, 69.

A basis for friendship

Hume, Smith, and Burke differed in activity, social role, personality, and siren pitch. Yet as regards political sensibilities I agree with the likeness that David Miller (1981, 196), noted above, offers in his three-sided comparison ("a belief in economic freedom, a belief in social hierarchy, and a commitment to the political establishment of eighteenth-century Britain").

Several scholars have suggested wedges between Hume and Smith in moral theory. Smith's works should be seen as development on, not departure from, Hume.[26] As for Burke, I think that he scarcely saw himself as out of step with Hume or Smith, save in small ways—for example, thinking Hume too agnostic and sassy toward organized religion.

Alexis de Tocqueville (1955, 145) noted: "In England writers on the theory of government and those who actually governed co-operated with each other, the former setting forth their new theories, the latter amending or circumscribing these in the light of practical experience." It is enchanting to think of Hume, Smith, and Burke as teammates, as a troika. If I over-homogenize, it is from indulging in such enchantment, and from a self-flattering passion to assume a coherence. Thank goodness for frank and open engagement to keep us on the straight and narrow.

---

26. With regard to TMS Part IV, see Matson, Doran, and Klein (2019); Burke's "just prejudice" (1999a, 182) fits that reading.

CHAPTER 6

Adam Smith on Reputation, Commutative Justice, and Defamation Laws

By Mark J. Bonica and Daniel Klein

The libertarians Murray Rothbard (1982, 126–7) and Walter Block (2008, 49) say that insofar as one's reputation exists as a coherent thing, it exists in the minds of other people. Since one cannot have property in other people's minds, one cannot have property in what they think. Similar thinking was articulated by Samuel Pufendorf, Gershom Carmichael, and Francis Hutcheson.

In Adam Smith, reputation is crucial to the confidence, cooperation, and correction mechanisms of the market economy. And it is central in sympathy and moral approval. We are concerned with our own reputation, the reputation of our trading partners, of our associates, and of moral authorities. Our conscience involves our own reputation in the eyes of the man within our breast.

Yet it is unclear whether Smith sees reputation as something that is covered by "mere justice," or commutative justice, or, rather, as something in the realm of beneficence, or distributive justice. Also unclear is his support for legal rules aimed at protecting one's reputation, that is, laws against defamation (libel and slander).

On these matters, Smith is equivocal; he leaves us with contrarieties. Reputation is absent from the "most sacred laws of justice" passage in *The Theory of Moral Sentiments* (TMS 84.2), which lists duties to guard your neighbor's (1) person or life, (2) his property, and (3) the promises due to him. Yet other passages do feature reputation alongside those staples of commutative justice.

Smith says that the rules of commutative justice are "precise and accurate." Does reputation fit that? Consider the following bit of gossip: "Steve's work stinks." Or: "I think Steve's work stinks." Or: "I heard Steve's work stinks." The matters of truth, intent, and meaning ("work," "stinks") do not seem to be precise and accurate. They would seem to belong to duties of distributive justice, whose rules are "loose, vague, and indeterminate" (TMS 175.11, 327.1).

On the matter of defamation laws, it sometimes seems that Smith regards them as unnecessary, even undesirable, because they stifle or distort mechanisms of social accountability and correction. Such laws, however, were a feature of Smith's society, and traditions of natural jurisprudence had typically associated at least some issues of reputation with commutative justice. Numerous passages in TMS and the *Lectures on Jurisprudence* (LJ) seem to stay within those conventional grooves and seem to endorse defamation laws.

In this chapter, we offer a reading that involves a distinction that goes back at least to Pufendorf between "simple" and "intensive" esteem or reputation.[1] We use "simple reputation" when describing verbal communication that attacks a person on the grounds that would potentially lead to arrest, assault, and so on, such as, "Steve steals horses." Refraining from attacking someone's simple reputation is in the spirit of the Ninth Commandment against bearing false witness. Simple-reputation detractions are likely to incite invasion of person, property, and promises due, the three staples of commutative justice. In contrast, intensive reputation—"Steve's work stinks" —pertains to communication that does *not* put the estimated party in jeopardy of invasion of person, property, and promises due.[2] Intensive-reputa-

---

1. Most of the Pufendorf, Carmichael, and Hutcheson texts used in this chapter were originally published in Latin (the one exception being Hutcheson 1755). In the English-language versions, the word esteem in the expressions "simple esteem" and "intensive esteem" means reputation. We here use "reputation" when talking "simple" and "intensive."

2. The first staple, person, can be viewed as property owned by the soul, in which case the three staples reduce to just two, property and promises due/consent. But we proceed by keeping person separate, thus three staples.

tion slights may well jeopardize one's career and social standing, but not by invading the three staples.

We aim to attribute to Smith—who surely knew the simple/intensive terminology but nowhere employed it—a projection that does not see intensive reputation as something covered by commutative justice, instead seeing it in terms of distributive justice. The projection flows most importantly from the hardy fact that intensive reputation does not fit commutative justice.

Figure 6.1 lists the three staples of commutative justice. Hovering around them is a penumbra against incitement, abetting, conspiring, endangering, etc.—activities that might bring on invasions of the three staples. Detractions against one's simple reputation are something that commutative justice guards against, just as it does against the inciting of a riot or the intention to steal one's car. The formulation here suggests that, although simple-reputation detractions are covered by commutative justice, they do not constitute *a staple* of commutative justice. Commutative justice covers the staples *and the penumbra around the staples.*

FIGURE 6.1: COMMUTATIVE JUSTICE COVERS THE THREE STAPLES AND THEIR PENUMBRA

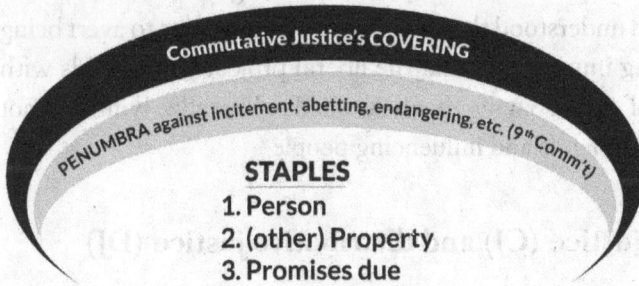

Commutative Justice's COVERING

PENUMBRA against incitement, abetting, endangering, etc. (9ᵗʰ Comm't)

STAPLES
1. Person
2. (other) Property
3. Promises due

As for *intensive*-reputation detractions, we suggest that Smith did not see them as covered by commutative justice at all. To go around saying of Steve, "His work stinks," especially when malicious and untrue, is certainly bad for Steve and unbecoming of the gossiper. Smith shared and inculcated sensibilities about the deep wrongness of such "attacks" on Steve. It would have made sense, however, for Smith to have been reluctant to expound a careful parsing. We speculate about Smith's equivocation, but we stoutly advance that Smith knew very well that intensive reputation does not fit commutative justice.

On laws against intensive-reputation detraction, our contention is looser. Smith endorsed certain exceptions to the liberty principle. Perhaps Smith endorsed intensive-reputation defamation laws, while quietly seeing them as an exception to the liberty principle. But we suggest that Smith was at most half-hearted in his support of them and, plausibly, inclined against them. On the assumption that he opposed such laws, it makes sense that he would *not* have been candid and straightforward about it: He took pains to assure us that he was not rationalistic about the liberty principle. If he thought that government should liberalize laws against spreading lies ("Steve's work stinks"), he would not have made that judgment plain.

We are familiar with the unfortunate attitudinal syndrome about an interventionist law ostensibly designed and intended to reduce perceived social evil X such as malicious gossip, homelessness, poverty, drunkenness, drug use, prostitution, child pornography, illegal immigration, terrorism, etc. The syndrome suggests that anyone who opposes such a law must be callously indifferent about X, or even in favor of X. This attitude flows partly from shallowness in thinking and partly from misrepresentation of the liberal ethos, which maintains a presumption against such interventionist laws. Smith understood the syndrome and took pains to avert being attacked for giving impressions that the liberal project was at odds with traditional ways of virtue. Saying that he wished to liberalize lying was not his path to making friends and influencing people.

Commutative justice (CJ) and distributive justice (DJ)

Smith distinguished, affirmed, and copiously spoke three senses of *justice*, as discussed in Chapter 1. These are:

> *commutative justice* (CJ): Not messing with other people's stuff, or "abstaining from what is another's" (TMS 269.10). The context of this precept concerns the *initiation* of messing, not what to do about thieves, etc. after they have initiated messing.
>
> *distributive justice* (DJ): "proper beneficence, ...the becoming use

of what is our own" (TMS 270.10)

estimative justice (EJ): Estimating objects properly (TMS 270.10)

Whereas CJ and DJ are defined by Smith at TMS 269–270, estimative justice is there exposited but not labeled; the "estimative"is our own appellation for it. Although EJ always looms in the background, the focus here is on CJ versus DJ.

Smith wrote: "The general rules of almost all the virtues" are "loose, vague, and indeterminate" (174.9, 175.11), and that includes the "social virtues" of distributive justice (270.10). "There is, however, one virtue, of which the general rules determine, with the greatest exactness, every external action which it requires. This virtue is [commutative] justice" (175.10). The rules of CJ are "precise and accurate," like the rules of grammar (327.1; 175.11). In this respect CJ is unique among the virtues.

Let us articulate how we view things. The question will then be whether Smith viewed things similarly.

Suppose you meet a friend for lunch, and you say about a colleague: "Steve's work stinks." Is that a "messing" with Steve's "stuff," as understood by CJ? Are you violating the CJ duties you owe to Steve?

The present authors, like Rothbard and Block, say no, it is not (assuming that it does not violate a promise you've made). The remark violates none of the three staples of commutative justice—person, property and promises due. And we go further: On said assumption, even if you were to publish in a newspaper or website "Steve's works stinks," it would violate none of Steve's three staples. And even further, an outright lie: "Last night on Broad Street I saw Steve lying in the gutter in a drunken stupor." If you publish that in a newspaper, perhaps you violate one of the *newspaper's* three staples, namely, a promise you made to the newspaper not to lie in your writing. But, irrespective of the legality or illegality of your issuing such communications, they do not violate any of Steve's three staples—that is, they do not tend to bring down coercion upon him.

Steve cannot claim a CJ right to having you refrain from issuing such statements, but it would be reasonable of him to claim a DJ or "metaphoricall" right (LJ 9).[3] Surely he may claim a DJ right in protesting the gutter lie. The DJ violation calls for rebuke. Further, Steve might be able to claim a legal right, depending on the law, but that would not make it a CJ right.

Having allied ourselves with the libertarians Rothbard and Block on the parsing of such matters, we hasten to add that we should not be understood to be allied to their definite libertarian position on what government law should be. We follow, rather, Smith's looser sensibilities: Perhaps such outright lies about Steve should be illegal; or perhaps the laws against defamation are estimatively just. Smith made liberty a central maxim of his policy outlook, not an axiom as do Rothbard and Block. We happily confess, however, that our inclination is to lean in the libertarian direction on such matters.

Simple reputation and intensive reputation

We, the present authors, hereby define "simple reputation" to signify communication—such as "Steve steals horses"—that might incite a three-staple violation against Steve. Note that a three-staple violation may be triggered by reports of Steve simply violating government law. "Steve pays under the table" and "Steve sells cocaine" too can bring down coercion upon him. Also, "Dr. Steve's malpractice has killed some of his patients" could bring down coercion upon Dr. Steve in a civil suit on grounds of malpractice.

By contrast, we define "intensive reputation" to signify communication—such as "Steve's work stinks"—that, however detrimental to Steve, does not tend to incite any such three-staple violation. We suggest, along the lines of

---

3. Besides "metaphoricall" at LJ 9, in the "Fragment on Justice" Smith says that beneficence informed by circumstances is "by a metaphor" also denominated a kind of justice, which he then identifies as DJ, in distinction to CJ, using those terms. See TMS App. II, 389-90.

As for the language of "perfect" and "imperfect" rights: Although they are sometimes understood to correspond to what we've here called "CJ rights" and "DJ rights" (agreeable to Smith in LJ[A]), 5, 7), they are also associated with (1) what is or is not necessary, (2) what is and what is not enforced by force (whether governmental or among jural equals), or (3), what should be and what should not be enforced by force. Each of these three categories correlates with, yet is nonetheless conceptually distinct from, our way of distinguishing CJ rights and DJ rights (namely, whether the rules are precise and accurate). See for example Pufendorf 1729, 81; 2009, 92; 2003, 50n; Carmichael 2002, 44, 51, 72, 76, 214-215; Hutcheson 1755, Vol. I, 257-258; [1747], 11-14; Smith LJ 9, 326-27, 545. Smith's LJ(B) dispenses entirely with perfect/imperfect except for a single "perfect right" in passing at 545.

Figure 6.1, that when Smith does include reputation as something covered by CJ, simple reputation is what he had in mind, in which case CJ remains confined to the three staples. We recognize, however, that CJ's basic precept against messing with the three staples naturally suggests an injunctive penumbra against incitement, intent, conspiracy, aiding and abetting any such messing. It is true that things become less than precise and accurate within that penumbra, but that is true of the like penumbra pertaining to assault, robbery, etc. The key is that such penumbras pertain to activity, actual or potential, that has the character of precise-and-accurate violation. Simple reputation, then, is simply adjunctive to the securing of the three staples.

Again, Smith surely knew the simple/intensive terminology but nowhere employed it. Nor does Smith set out such a distinction under other terms. But the terms do appear in Pufendorf, Carmichael, and Hutcheson. We treat those important predecessors to show that our delineation of simple esteem is really quite aligned to how they used the term, and to present an arc concerning reputation as society continued to evolve away from older customs of "honor."

Our strategy is to set out our own definitions—Bonica-Klein definitions, as it were—and then to explore how well our definitions can be read into Smith's textual muddle. We conclude: Pretty well!

The ninth commandment, against bearing false witness

Several passages of the Mosaic code censure defamatory statements (*Exodus* XXII 28; XXIII 1; *Leviticus* XIX 16; see Carter-Ruck 1972, 34–5), but we highlight the Decalogue's Ninth Commandment. Smith's religious upbringing is treated by Gavin Kennedy (2013, 465): "Sunday sermons in his local kirk…instructed him on repeating the Calvinist Catechism." Kennedy cites Ian Ross (2010,18) saying that in adulthood Smith was able to repeat the catechism. The catechism, written in 1647, includes the following:

> Quest. 76. What is the ninth commandment? Ans. 76. The ninth commandment is, Thou shalt not bear false witness against thy neighbour.

Quest. 77. What is required in the ninth commandment?
Ans. 77. The ninth commandment requireth the maintaining
and promoting of truth between man and man, and of our own
and our neighbour's good name, especially in witness-bearing.

Quest. 78. What is forbidden in the ninth commandment?
Ans. 78. The ninth commandment forbiddeth whatsoever is prej-
udicial to truth, or injurious to our own or our neighbour's good
name.

Here we see "false witness" and "especially in witness-bearing." Twice
appears "our neighbour's good name," and perhaps that means especially
his *simple* good name.

Study of Pufendorf, Carmichael, Hutcheson, and Hume helps us see
the natural jurisprudence tradition that Smith continued, and supports the
aptness of our explorative strategy.

Pufendorf, Carmichael, Hutcheson, and Hume

Simple searches at Google's Ngram Viewer and the Liberty Fund website
turn up nothing of significance in English for simple/intensive esteem/rep-
utation prior to Pufendorf. We pick up with Pufendorf.[4]

Samuel Pufendorf (1632-1694)

In his earliest work on jurisprudence (1660), apparently not much consulted by the Scots, Pufendorf treats simple and intensive esteem (or reputation).[5] He notes the "extremely copious crop" of titles that have "sprung

---

4. As for Grotius (2005): In Smith's long paragraph on the three senses of justice (TMS 269.10), he
associates commutative justice with Grotius's expletive justice. When speaking of expletive justice
(142–47, 403, 406, 408, 581, 584, 599, 889, 951–55), however, Grotius (2005) does not much specify
its constituents; elsewhere Grotius recognizes reputation and honor as part of one's own (885; see
also Barbeyrac's note 88n7), writes briefly of punishment and reparation due for damages done to
them (897, 407), and remarks briefly on slander (362–63). Grotius does not speak of simple/intensive
esteem and does not make any distinction along such lines.

5. On the translating of *existimato*, see Haakonssen 2010, esp. 7.

up in this present age" (86). Intensive esteem pertains to ascending titles, whereas simple esteem belongs to:

> a complete member of the state, or as one who has not been declared a defective member of the state according to laws and statutes. And any and all free men and respected, or those who have not been branded by disgrace in process of law, rejoice in that esteem… This esteem is lost as a result of antecedent misdeed, when some one, in accordance with the laws, because of a definite kind of misdeed (for not all misdeeds extinguish esteem in a civil sense)… (Pufendorf 1660, 95)

As Pufendorf turns to intensive esteem, the treatment seems to give it more generalization than the initial association with titles may have led us to expect:

> That is intensive esteem, in accordance with which persons equally honourable in civil capacity are preferred one above another, in proportion as one has a larger share than another of those things whereby the minds of others are commonly moved to show honour. Now honour, which corresponds to the intensification of esteem, is properly the signification of our judgement concerning the superiority of another; and therefore, in truth, honour is not in the person honoured *but in the person who shows honour,* although by a certain kind of metonymy, esteem also itself, or that which deserves honour, is denoted by this word, and, in a special sense, definite statuses which honour is wont to accompany, are called honours, because in due course these statuses are bestowed only upon those who surpass others in some point of superiority. (Pufendorf 1660, 96, italics added)

It is but a species of metonymy to say that Jim's honor is something of Jim's, for that honor is actually in "the person who shows honor" (see likewise Pufendorf 1729, 805). Later in the book, in his observations on right reason in private ethics, Pufendorf briefly urges: "*Let no one detract from the good name of a second person, or lessen the esteem in which he is held"* (351–52).

Pufendorf's very large work *On the Law of Nature and Nations* lacks a modern edition; we have consulted the English version printed in 1729 (799f) and find that on the matters at hand it runs along the lines of his subsequent famous textbook *The Whole Duty of Man, According to the Law of Nature* (1673, first English translation 1691), so we focus on *Whole Duty*. Pufendorf says that intensive esteem "redounds from such worthy Actions as are conformable to Right Reason" (2003, 75), and later in the book it is called *accumulative*. Thus, reputation "is divided into *Simple*, and *Accumulative*" (233). "Simple Reputation...under Civil Government, is that Sort of Esteem, by which a Man is looked on at the lowest, as a common but a sound Member of the State: Or when a Man hath not been declar'd a corrupt Member, according to the Laws and Customs of the State, but is supposed to be a good Subject" (234; see likewise 1729, 801f). It *"perishes*, either by Reason *of the Course of a Man's Life* [e.g., *"Slaves...Panders, Whores"*] or *in Consequence of some Crime...* By *Crimes* Men utterly lose their Reputation" (234).

Accumulative reputation, meanwhile, "we call *that*, by which Persons, reciprocally equal as to their Natural Dignity, come to be preferr'd to one another according to those Accomplishments, which use to move the Minds of People to pay them Honour: For *Honour* is properly, the Signification of our Judgment concerning the Excellency of another Person" (235). Such honor may flow from "Acuteness and Readiness of Wit, a Capacity to understand several Arts and Sciences, a sound Judgment in Business, a steddy Spirit, immoveable by outward Occurrences, and equally superiour to Flatteries and Terrours: Eloquence, Beauty, Riches; but, more especially the Performing of good and brave Actions" (235).

Is accumulative reputation a matter of commutative justice? Pufendorf writes:

> All these Things together, produce a Capacity to receive Honour, *not a Right*. So that if any Person should decline the Payment of his Veneration to them, he may deserve to be taken Notice of for his Incivility, but not for an Injury. For a *perfect Right* to be honoured by others, that bear the Ensigns thereof, proceeds either from an Authority over them; or from some mutual Agreement;

or from a Law that is made and approved by one Common Lord and Master. (235; see likewise 1729, 808–810)

Knud Haakonssen (2010) characterizes Pufendorf's simple esteem as meaning that the individual is presumed innocent (8); Haakonssen says the expression suggested "the Ciceronian idea that mere justice, as distinct from benevolence, made a man 'good'" (7; see also Zurbuchen 2019, 160-1). We believe that Haakonssen rightly captures Pufendorf's drift,[6] but it must be acknowledged that, according to the text, certain peaceful individuals including "slaves," "panders," "whores" by such conduct forfeit simple esteem.

But in the matter of accumulative or intensive esteem, Pufendorf seems to indicate that it would become a perfect right only by some special condition, such as a private contract, a legal recognition, or a special standing of "Authority." Haakonssen (2010, 8–9) says: "We may conclude that the graduated 'intensive' *existimato* that may be due as a consequence of our actual performance in life cannot be claimed as a perfect right, properly speaking." And: "Only civil authority or contractual arrangements can turn these claims into proper, *perfect* rights" (8). Merely *deserving* some intensive level of estimation does not make for any CJ right to such estimation.

On the matter of laws against defamation, libel, and slander, Pufendorf only considers the following scenario:

> You have been maliciously slandered, you have been insulted. Will your first move be to seek satisfaction through the magistrate, satisfaction which often you may not need? If your reputation is sound, if you have nothing with which to reproach yourself, the offender's barbs will fall back on him alone. The best means of revenge, if revenge were permitted, is scorn. It will at least spare you anxiety and disturbance of mind on account of a harm that in fact is imaginary, when it entails no real damage. (Pufendorf 2003, 355)

---

6. Especially noteworthy for seeing Pufendorf's drift as liberal is a passage at Pufendorf 1729, 809, where he writes of the importance of intensive esteem being left to "*Liberty.*"

Here we see an anti-litigious attitude, which continues in Carmichael, Hutcheson, and Smith.

Gershom Carmichael (1672-1729)

"It was Gershom Carmichael…who introduced the natural rights tradition [of Grotius, Pufendorf, and Locke] to the universities of Scotland" (Moore and Silverthorne in Carmichael 2002, x). In his commentaries on Pufendorf, Carmichael said that reputation "is nothing but *the opinion* of one's excellence *on the part of other men*," and that it cannot be won and kept among "good and sensible men" "except by doing good and deserving well of human society; and that it cannot be weakened by insults, except so far as they raise a suspicion that one deserved to be so badly treated; hence reputation can only be restored and renewed by measures which altogether remove that suspicion." As for dueling, "No one but a madman could convince himself that violence leveled by private assault against the author of the insult would contribute to this one little bit" (2002, 68, italics added).

On simple reputation, Carmichael writes:

> Every man should take the greatest care to preserve, so far as he can, his simple reputation, that is, the character and report of being *an honest man*. If it should be assailed by slander, he should do everything he can to restore its luster. But if, after every effort, an unfavorable opinion prevails with the public, a good man may be satisfied with the consciousness of his own innocence, whose witness is God. (Carmichael 2002, 68)

Carmichael says natural rights are those endowed by nature, and among them is the perfect "right of *simple reputation*" (78). Carmichael takes exception to Pufendorf only to object to denying simple reputation to slaves: "It is inhuman and contrary to reason that simple reputation in civil society should be thought lacking in anyone on account of a condition [slavery] which contains no moral turpitude" (194).

As for intensive reputation, Carmichael makes quite clear that it does not fit the precise and accurate rules of CJ, saying:

A wise man should not seek an intensive reputation, which is founded in special honors and marks of honor, except so far as it arises from a distinguished ancestry or opens a wider field to illustrious action by which he will deserve well of the human race... And if we should not win honors equal to our merits, our spirit should not be cast down, nor the zeal for doing well abandoned. (62)

And later he explains that titles and official "civil" honors are often at variance with true merit, about which men "inevitably disagree with each other, and from that disagreement more serious evils would arise to disturb human society more than if precedence were completely neglected" (195).

Francis Hutcheson (1694-1746)

Two works by Hutcheson deal with jurisprudence, one published near the end of his life and the other posthumously. In the first, *A Short Introduction to Moral Philosophy* ([1747]), he sprinkles remarks in line with the predecessors treated above. He says that "natural honour" is "the good opinion others entertain of our moral excellencies," whereas "[c]ivil honours" are "external indications of deference which are appointed by law"— "often conferred injudiciously" (Hutcheson 2007, 272-3). He distinguishes simple and intensive:

> The *simple estimation*, or character of common honesty, is so much every man's right, that no governors can deprive one of it at pleasure, without a cause determined in judgment. The higher estimation, or intensive, as some call it, is not a matter of perfect right; as no man can at the command of others form high opinions of any person, without he is persuaded of his merit. (Hutcheson 272; see also 129)

Here we once again get the feeling that intensive reputation is a matter of distributive justice, and suggests only loose metaphorical rights ("imperfect"). Such rights, he says, "are sometimes indeed of the greatest consequence to the happiness and ornament of society, and our obligation to maintain them, and to perform to others what they thus claim, may be very sacred: yet they are of such a nature that *greater evils would ensue in society from making them matters of compulsion, than from leaving them free to each one's honour and conscience to comply with them or not*" (113, italics added).

A System of Moral Philosophy, edited by Hutcheson's son (also named Francis), was published in 1755, nine years after Hutcheson's demise. This work is fuller than the *Short Introduction*, but on the matters at hand runs along the same lines. He speaks of "the simple character of integrity, honesty, and purity of manners, or the reputation of a good honest man" and associates that with "a perfect right" (II, 39; see also I, 257): To simple esteem, "every one who has not forfeited it by some crime of a more atrocious nature than is readily incident to men in the main good, has a natural perfect right" (329). As regards "the degree of eminent praises," "each one is some way judge for himself," and "the right of others in this matter is only of the imperfect kind" (II, 39; see also 330). As Hutcheson goes on to discuss what one should do when one has learned of another's "crime," he advises private admonition and repair of damages, in secrecy, although once that proves ineffectual then "publick censure...is prudent and just" (40–41).

Hutcheson denounces dueling and speaks of the need for law to provide for "proper vindication" for some kind of calumnies, in order to deter dueling. However, the remedies are not specified and, again, the calumnies he has in mind might be principally of the simple-esteem variety (1755 II, 97-101; see also [1747], 203-204).

Our review of Pufendorf, Carmichael, and Hutcheson suggests that their thought shows an idea of simple esteem that pertains chiefly to threats to CJ's three staples, while intensive esteem corresponds to matters beyond any threats thereto. Thus, we see that it is well before Smith's time that his forerunners were projecting a liberal way of seeing matters of reputation.

David Hume (1711-1776)

We supply a few words on David Hume, even though Hume nowhere talked simple/intensive esteem nor wrote (or lectured) on jurisprudence in quite the same mode. But since Smith evolves in ways that, in our judgment, remain so concordant with Hume we remark briefly on features in Hume.

In *A Treatise of Human Nature* Hume makes a large point of (commutative) justice evolving to be precise and accurate in its basic injunction or precept against messing with other people's stuff; thus, the rules of CJ are such that that precept "admits not of degrees" (Treatise 3.2.6.8; see also Hume's EPM 3.2.34-45). Hume remarks on reputation—in fact saying that reputation is a major motive to complying with CJ (T 3.2.2.27)—but never as a constituent of CJ. In discussing justice, Hume speaks of "the three fundamental laws of nature, *that of the stability of possession, of its transference by consent, and of the performance of promises*" (T 3.2.6.1). He examines at length the principles that establish ownership of property and the obligation of promises, but never gives the slightest suggestion of a CJ right or obligation in regard to reputation.[7] And that goes also for the second *Enquiry* and indeed all of Hume's writings. CJ is central in Hume's moral and political thought, and *nowhere* does he mention reputation as a constituent of CJ.

Smith's threefold "most sacred laws" passage (TMS 84.2) corresponds to Hume's threefold "fundamental laws" passage better than it might at first appear, because Hume says that the logic of property builds upon a notion of self-ownership: "they must seek for a remedy, by putting these goods, as far as possible, on the same footing with the fix'd and constant advantages of the mind and body" (T 3.2.2.9).[8] Reputation is absent from both signal passages. In our view, Pufendorf, Carmichael, Hutcheson, Hume, and Smith all belong to a tradition that was easing reputation (intensive, especially) out of CJ, without being candid and open about doing so.

---

7. In Hume's *Treatise*, there are no occurrences of "defam" ["defamation"?], "libel," or "slander," nor of "intensive."

8. See the discussion of self-ownership in Hume in Klein and Matson (ch. 4 of the present book); the key passages in Hume's *Treatise* are at 3.2.2.7-9. In the *History*, Hume (1983, III, 323-4, 391) discusses Henry VIII's laws against talking, and even not talking (in the sense of not affirming), of the status of the king's wives and heirs, highlighting the inconsistency and incoherence of the laws: "no regard was paid to the safety or liberty of the subjects" (323).

Reading Smith on CJ and reputation

What did Smith consider to be the constituents of CJ? Was reputation a constituent? To treat the matter, we proceed as follows: (1) We make a complete inventory of pertinent passages from TMS and WN, and assess that material; (2) we explain that, as Smith well knew, intensive reputation does not fit CJ; (3) we sketch out the case for saying that when Smith does include reputation, he means simple reputation; (4) we then acknowledge other passages in the *Lectures on Jurisprudence* and admit that the waters remain somewhat muddy.

TMS and WN passages on the constituents of CJ

Here collected are seven passages—six from TMS and one from WN—on the constituents of "one's own" covered by CJ to make a complete inventory (no such in EPS, LRBL, or Corr.). The label "TMS-Q1" means the first quotation from TMS. We put some words in boldface.

TMS-Q1:

Mere justice is, upon most occasions, but a negative virtue, and only hinders us from hurting our neighbour. The man who barely abstains from violating either the person, or the **estate**, or the **reputation** of his neighbours, has surely very little positive merit. He fulfills, however, all the rules of what is peculiarly called **justice**, and does every thing which his equals can with propriety force him to do, or which they can punish him for not doing. (TMS 82.9)

TMS-Q2:

Murder, therefore, is the most atrocious of all crimes… To be deprived of that which we are possessed of, is a greater evil than to be disappointed of what we have only the expectation. Breach of property, therefore, theft and robbery, which take from us what we are possessed of, are greater crimes than breach of contract, which only disappoints us of what we expected. **The most sacred laws of justice**, therefore, those whose violation seems to call loudest for vengeance and punishment, are the laws which guard the life and person of our neighbour; the next are those which guard his property and possessions; and **last of all** come those which guard what are called his personal rights, or what is due to him from the promises of others. (TMS 84.2)

TMS-Q3:

[T]he situations which call forth the noblest exertions of self-command, by imposing the necessity of violating sometimes the property, and sometimes the life of our neighbour, always tend to diminish, and too often to extinguish altogether, that sacred regard to both, which is the foundation of **justice** and humanity. (TMS 153.37)

TMS-Q4:

In one sense we are said to do **justice** to our neighbour when we abstain from doing him any positive harm, and do not directly hurt him, either in his person, or in his **estate**, or in his **reputation**. This is that justice which I have treated of above, the observance of which may be extorted by force, and the violation of which exposes to punishment. (TMS 269.10)

TMS-Q5:

It is the same case with **justice**. To abstain from what is another's was not desirable on its own account, and it could not surely be better for you that I should possess what is my own than that you should possess it. You ought, however, to abstain from whatever belongs to me, because by doing otherwise you will provoke the resentment and indignation of mankind. (TMS 297.11)

TMS-Q6:

The chief subjects of the works of the casuists, therefore, were the conscientious regard that is due to the rules of **justice**; how far we ought to respect the life and property of our neighbour; the duty of restitution; the laws of chastity and modesty, and wherein consisted what in their language are called the sins of concupiscence; the rules of veracity, and the obligation of oaths, promises, and contracts of all kinds. (TMS 339.32)

WN-Q1:

The second duty of the sovereign, that of protecting, as far as possible, every member of the society from the **injustice** or oppression of every other member of it, or the duty of establishing an exact administration of **justice** requires too very different degrees of expence in the different periods of society.

Among nations of hunters, as there is scarce any property, or at least none that exceeds the value of two or three days labour; so there is seldom any established magistrate or any regular administration of justice. Men who have no property can injure one another only in their persons or **reputations**. But when one man kills, wounds, beats, or **defames** another, though he to whom the injury is done suffers, he who does it receives no benefit. It is otherwise with the injuries to property. The benefit of the person who does the injury is often equal to the loss of him who suffers it. Envy, malice, or resentment, are the only passions which can prompt one man to injure another in his person or **reputation**. (WN 708–9.1–2)

These seven passages can be assimilated to our reading without difficulty, if not conclusively. The fullest and most deliberative account of the constituents of CJ is TMS-Q2, "The most sacred laws of justice," which lists three constituents in descending order: person, property, promises due. Reputation is not listed at all—again, just as it is not in Hume's "three fundamental laws." The third constituent, promises due, is introduced as "last of all." Were reputation to be covered by CJ, it would trail somewhere behind promises due.

Smith uses the morpheme "sacred" 23 times in TMS, eight of which are in reference to the rules or laws of justice (84.2; 84.3, 175.10, 216.15; 241.11; 330.8, 330.9, 330.11). Of those eight, the passages variously refer to murder, theft, and violation of promises—none to the violation of reputation. Of the remaining 15 uses of "sacred,"[9] none refers explicitly to reputation. The repeated use of "sacred" without reference to reputation suggests that reputation's absence in the "most sacred laws" hierarchy was no casual omission. In relation to the penumbra shown in Figure 6.1, we might say that it is the sacredness of the three staples that gives rise to the penumbra: The staples are so sacred that we naturally punish even endangerment or incitation of violation of them. The sacredness emanates the penumbra.

But in three of the other passages reputation is treated as a constituent of CJ: TMS-Q1, TMS-Q4, and WN-Q1. Is it reasonable to understand it as only "simple"? For the first two passages, there is no clear indication that reputation is so confined, but neither is there indication to the contrary. We saw that Hutcheson seemed to want to limit perfect-right reputation to simple reputation (though, admittedly, perhaps not strictly to our *narrowed* signification of "simple reputation"). That would suggest that Hutcheson would limit CJ's covering to simple reputation only. We think it reasonable to suppose that Smith was like Hutcheson in that respect: That he too would limit CJ's covering to simple reputation. That would be one way to make Smith consistent throughout all of the relevant "reputation" TMS passages. Realize, however, that Smith never says that government should be strictly confined by CJ—that is, he does, of course, make exceptions to the liberty principle, including his endorsement of taxation. The question of what the government law regarding reputation should be is a separate question; it is the second of the two major questions to be discussed in this chapter.

As for the WN-Q1 passage, it is contextualized to nations of hunters. In such context—the first stage of the four-stage theory—society is small, simple, and familiar. Detracting someone's intensive reputation—"Steve's work stinks"—would make little sense because, as in a family household, others would know whether Steve's works stinks. So it seems likely that reputation here would be only simple—"Steve took more than his share of the mammoth" or "It was Steve who killed Ælfwig." Also, something like "Steve betrayed the tribe to our enemies" would arguably speak of a CJ violation:

---

9. The other 15 "sacred" occurrences are at TMS 71.5, 89.8, 138.6, 153.37, 159.8, 161.12, 163.2, 170.12, 174.9, 218.2, 225.18, 274.18, 280.25, 331.11, 332.12.

Betraying the tribe might be regarded (by us modern analysts) as breaking a contract. Prior to the propertization of land and other modern developments, however, belonging to such a primitive group might be regarded as a voluntary contractual arrangement, and not betraying the group a term of the agreement, if only tacit.

In simpler society, even traditional society, intensive reputation would pose less difficulty than in more complex society. As society complexifies, people need to learn how to cope with intensive reputation: Should they try to capture it within CJ, or should they learn to leave it to DJ? Smith belonged to a tradition that understood that intensive reputation in modern society defies any precise and accurate rules. That tradition therefore guided society toward the DJ approach to intensive reputation, even if that tradition favored some intensive-reputation defamation laws for extreme cases.

Another thing to note about the seven passages is that "promises due" is specified in only the "sacred laws" passage, TMS-Q2. That might be because the other passages illustrate it more elliptically. Also, two use "estate," which plausibly subsumes promises due (LJ 9, 399–401).[10] Indeed, "property" itself might loosely serve to subsume promises due.

Intensive reputation cannot be precise and accurate

Why does Smith not include reputation in his hierarchy of most sacred laws of justice? Again, the rules of CJ are precise and accurate, like those of grammar, at least by comparison to those of all other virtues, which are "loose, vague, and indeterminate." There are several other ways in which CJ is special among the virtues, but those other ways depend on its defining feature: Its precept has rules that are precise and accurate.

But can rules governing intensive reputation be precise and accurate? Does intensive reputation fit CJ?

Consider "Steve's work stinks." To attempt to assimilate that to messing with Steve's stuff, we would want to consider the following facets of the matter:

---

10. The *Oxford English Dictionary* gives as the 12th definition of the noun estate, "Property, possessions, fortune, capital," supported by quotations back to 1600.

1. What is the criterion for "stinks"? What does it mean for Steve's work to stink? Compared to what? Is the criterion for "stinks" a shared understanding?

2. What does the speaker refer to with "Steve's work"?

3. What was the tenor or humor of the remark? Was it made in jest? Did it carry conviction?

4. What was the intent or motivation of the remark? Did Steve do something to provoke the remark? Is the remark part of an ongoing feud?

5. *Is it true?* Does Steve's work stink? If it is true, we might have a DJ duty to warn people. That is how reputational mechanisms serve universal benevolence.

6. If we can say that it is *not* true, was the utterer simply misinformed? Was it an honest mistake? Should the remark be understood as "I *think* Steve's work stinks"?—which might have been true even if Steve's work does not stink.

7. Does the remark matter much? Does it make Steve worse off in any significant way? Who heeded the remark and was influenced by it?

These facets spell looseness, vagueness, and indeterminacy. Attempting to ascribe precision and accuracy to intensive reputation would exemplify Smith's critique of what he identified as casuistry:

> It may be said in general of the works of the casuists, that they attempted, to no purpose, to direct, by precise rules, what it belongs to feeling and sentiment only to judge of… When it is that secrecy and reserve begin to grow into dissimulation? How far an agreeable irony may be carried, and at what precise point it begins to degenerate into a detestable lie? (TMS 339.33)

Indeed, a theme introduced early in TMS is that people's estimations vary and that we can coolly tolerate such variation provided that we do not feel affected by others' estimations:

> Though you despise that picture, or that poem, or even that system of philosophy which I admire, there is little danger of our quarrelling upon that account. Neither of us can reasonably be much interested about them. They ought all of them to be matters of great indifference to us both... (TMS 21.5)

Another notable moment is his discussion of how literary figures fret over their reputation and scheme to pump it up (123–4.19, 125–6.23). Another is how propriety depends on such particulars as age and occupation (200ff). Indeed, we are so unsure of our *own* merits that we require social feedback simply to correct our own self-estimations (126.24). Another important theme is that wisdom and virtue are lonely,[11] and that theme broadcasts the idea that intensive reputation cannot have the strictures of CJ behind it, for people do not judge wisely.

The following passage shows a degree of variation in Smith's regard for how we approve of the response to detraction:

> We often esteem a young man the more, when he resents, though with some degree of violence, any unjust reproach that may have been thrown upon his character or his honour... Persons of an advanced age, whom long experience of the folly and injustice of the world, has taught to pay little regard, either to its censure or to its applause, neglect and despise obloquy, and do not even deign to honour its futile authors with any serious resentment. This indifference, which is founded altogether on a firm confidence in their own well-tried and well-established characters, would be disagreeable in young people, who neither can nor ought to have any such confidence. (144-5.19)

Here Smith approves of two dramatically different responses to detraction. The lack of precision concerning the appropriate response conflicts with the idea that reputation can be governed by precise rules.

---

11. For passages suggesting that wisdom and virtue are lonely, see TMS 62.2, 77.8, 77.9, 155.43, 162-3.1, 192.11, 253.30–31, 285.31, 307.5, 335–6.23; WN 617.66; Corr. 382.

Smith seems to mean simple reputation

Among the special features of CJ is that "we feel ourselves under a stricter obligation" to it (TMS 80.5), so much so that it may be enforced by force among equals (TMS 79.5, 175.10, 269.10). Those features depend on the precision and accuracy of its rules. Precision and accuracy afford a high degree of certainty, so society can establish consistency in assessment and reaction.

The precision of the rules relates to the tangibility of possession and certainty of past experience, making more definite the objects in question and terms of agreement. Smith establishes a hierarchy of justice with those things which we have the most control over (see TMS-Q2 above and LJ 87). Promises due come last in this hierarchy because we have the least certainty about them. When we have to rely on someone else delivering us a good or service, we can never be as confident as if we had possession or experienced performance. In fact, the delivery helps to complete a mutual idea of what had been promised.

Smith's way of doing ethics gives centrality to sympathizing with expectations. That would naturally extend to matters of reputation. But expectations surrounding one's reputation lack context, moment, and focus. The expectations and standards upon which they would be based are even less clear than for promises due, because there are not even promises broken when one's reputation is damaged. From lack of precise and accurate rules, perhaps it is best to simply count reputation out of CJ, except for detraction that amounts to possible threats to the three staples of CJ. We think that Smith's reasoning points this way.

We now turn to important passages in the *Lectures on Jurisprudence* (LJ). Here it must be borne in mind that the text is the words that a student notetaker thought Smith said, or meant to say, in his circa-1763 oral presentation to a classroom of students, mostly teenagers.

In the LJ Smith says plainly that reputation is one of the "respects" in which a man may be injured (8, 399). And his initial elaboration does not make for a neat fit with our preferred reading:

> A man is injured in his reputation when one endeavours to bring
> his character below what is the common standard amongst men.
> If one calls another a fool, a knave, or a rogue he injures him in his

reputation, as he does not then give him that share of good fame which is common to almost all men, to perhaps 99 of 100. (LJ 9)

Simply calling someone a fool hardly poses a physical threat; Smith speaks of bringing one's character below "the common standard." However, he then, effectively, defines "common" to mean, not "average," but rather the bar separating the lowest percentile from the other 99. Maybe he means a grave accusation after all; maybe reputed criminals constitute about 1 percent of the population.

In the second set of lecture notes (LJ(B)), the parallel passage reads as follows:

> [a man may be injured] in his reputation, either by falsely representing him as a proper object of resentment or punishment as by calling him a thief or robber, or by depreciating his real worth, and endeavouring to degrade him below the level of his profession. A physician's character is injured when we endeavour to perswade the world he kills his patients instead of curing them, for by such a report he loses his business. (LJ 399)

If one is falsely accused of being a thief or robber, the accusation may subject one to a formal action by the legal system. The next sentence, however, is where perhaps the greatest challenge to our interpretation comes. A physician accused of killing his patients could again have coercion brought down upon him by civil suit for negligence or malpractice. But the challenge comes in the final clause. Smith says "*for* by such a report he loses his business" (italics added), and in that way Smith seems to go outside the neat interpretation that we wish to make primary. Smith is pointing out not only that the physician loses business. The "for" suggests that *that is why* his "character is injured." We admit that this does not fit our take. A physician loses business when a competing physician starts a practice nearby, but surely Smith would not consider that a violation of CJ.

In response we say the following points: (1) As for "injured," we commonly speak of injuries without their involving CJ violations, and perhaps Smith is speaking of reputation being "injured" in a sense that is not narrowed to CJ violations (thus, the competing physician injures or hurts the other's business). (2) Perhaps Smith is communicating to his teenagers how the matter is understood by others—part of his purpose in the course is to teach what the law is and how it is understood. (3) The text says that the physician "loses *his* business" (italics added) which might suggest that civil action brought against the physician for killing patients leads to the loss not just of *some of* his customers but *his entire business*, perhaps because he is legally barred from practicing as a physician. (4) The bit of text is of highly problematic provenance, and just one piece in the whole constellation of textual passages and our wider understanding of Smith's thought.

Smith then distinguishes real injury (CJ) from failing to give people all the esteem they deserve (DJ):

> We do not however injure a man when we do not give him all the praise that is due to his merit. We do not injure Sir Isaac Newton or Mr. Pope, when we say that Sir Isaac was no better philosopher than Descartes or that Mr. Pope was no better poet than the ordinary ones of his own time. By these expressions we do not bestow on them all the praise that they deserve, yet we do them no injury, for we do not throw them below the ordinary rank of men in their own professions. (LJ 399)

Whereas CJ generally represents a negative obligation (TMS 82.9), Smith clearly sees reputation as involving both negative and positive obligation:

> In another sense we are said not to do justice to our neighbour unless we conceive for him all that love, respect, and esteem, which his character, his situation, and his connexion with ourselves, render suitable and proper for us to feel, and unless we act accordingly. It is in this sense that we are said to do injustice to a man of merit who is connected with us, though we abstain from hurting him in every respect, if we do not exert ourselves to serve him and to place him in that situation in which the impartial spectator would be pleased to see him. (TMS 269.10)

Justice in this sense obliges us to render "love, respect, and esteem" to worthy people. This conception of obligation requires us to "exert ourselves," rather than merely abstain from another's stuff. This justice is DJ. And in LJ(A) (9) Smith distinguishes CJ and DJ, along with perfect and imperfect rights, citing Pufendorf and Hutcheson, but he does not make perfectly clear how reputation fits in.

In a discussion that leads into the topic of dueling, Smith gives several paragraphs to "injuries" "to a fair character," by action, by words, and by writing (LJ 122–126). These paragraphs come when Smith is describing actual historical bodies of law; only sometimes does he give an indication of what such laws *should* be, or how we should think about such matters.

In speaking of affronts, Smith mentions physical acts or threats: "A blow, or the shaking of ones fist at one, or the spitting in ones face...pulling ones nose" (122). Smith says that modern law has made the mistake of making the punishment or sanction for such affronts too small—based too narrowly on the physical aspect (e.g., spittle landing on one's face)—and not enough on the larger moral and reputational significance. Unless one faces one's detractor in a duel or combat, one is "for ever after despised and contemned as a poor, mean-spirited, faint-hearted wretch by those of his own rank, from whose company he will be ever afterwards excluded" (123). Here we perhaps come to understand that call by Smith's teacher, Francis Hutcheson, for "proper vindication" by law.

In this way modern law "is to be accounted a deficientia juris," a legal deficiency, and is one of the reasons that people felt the need to challenge their detractors to a duel: "For when the law do [*sic*] not give satisfaction somewhat adequate to the injury, men will think themselves intitled to take it at their own hand" (124). How this fits into our issue is tricky: The grounds for counting these affronts as matters of CJ is that they are injuries to the staples (your spittle impinged on my face), but the issue Smith is raising concerns the punishment or sanction for such a violation. At any rate, Smith indicates that the punishment for such affronts should be greater. It is not entirely clear, however, whether he is saying that higher punishment is recommended by some logic of CJ or simply broader considerations like the problem of dueling. When Smith says that "[t]he small pecuniary punishment is not sufficient recompense for such an affront," it is unclear

We have argued that Smith regarded intensive reputation as too nebulous and uncertain to be governed by CJ, and that the "reputation" that he would make a constituent of CJ seems to be principally simple reputation, which is itself adjunctive to the staples of person, property, and promises, but which might also result in other troubles such as a loss of business.

What was Smith's attitude about intensive-reputation defamation laws?

In the previous section we contended that Smith was highly sympathetic to not including intensive reputation as a constituent of CJ. That whole first matter is related but distinct from our second: What was Smith's attitude about intensive-reputation defamation laws? Table 1 shows the two issues and the possible combination of answers. The bottom row of Figure 6.2 corresponds to our contention that Smith did not genuinely regard intensive reputation as a constituent of CJ. The two columns speak to the second matter.

FIGURE 6.2. SMITH WAS MOSTLY IN CELL 4.

		Are intensive-reputation defamation laws desirable?	
		Yes	No
Is intensive reputation covered by commutative justice?	Yes	**Cell 1** Intensive reputation is part of one's CJ "stuff"— intensive-reputation defamation laws do not initiate coercion. Defamation laws are like laws against robbery and are desirable.	**Cell 2** (which is not sensible or pertinent): Intensive reputation is part of one's CJ "stuff," but laws to protect it are undesirable.
	No	**Cell 3** Intensive reputation is not part of one's CJ "stuff"—intensive-reputation defamation laws initiate coercion, like restrictions on issuing small-denomination notes, and are desirable.	**Cell 4** Intensive reputation is not part of one's CJ "stuff"— intensive-reputation defamation laws are coercive, like minimum wage laws, and are undesirable.

The two matters, whether intensive reputation is part of CJ and whether defamation laws should protect intensive reputation, are certainly related. If our reading of Smith on the first matter is correct, then Smith regarded intensive-reputation defamation laws as initiating coercion, and to endorse another public-policy exception to CJ and its flipside liberty would be to weaken CJ and liberty as guiding principles in lawmaking. But Smith certainly did make exceptions; he upheld liberty as a maxim, not a 100% axiom. In the TMS paragraph about the jural superior, Smith said he may "command mutual good offices to a certain degree" while cautioning against pushing it "too far" (81.8). So maybe Smith favored some intensive-reputation defamation laws.

Nowhere does Smith take a clear position for or against intensive-reputation defamation laws. We must assess his writings on the whole and discern his attitudes in a general way. We suggest that Smith is a little bit in Cell 3 but mostly Cell 4.

Smith says that "of all the external misfortunes which can affect an innocent man immediately and directly, the undeserved loss of reputation is certainly the greatest" (TMS 144.19). He says that our success "must very much depend upon the good or bad opinion which is commonly entertained of us" (TMS 298.13).

But as surely as Smith emphasizes the importance of reputation, he pervasively emphasizes the healthy workings of reputation. Our success also depends "upon the general disposition of those we live with, either to assist or to oppose us," and they are the ones who know us best (TMS 298.13). He continues:

> But the best, the surest, the easiest, and the readiest way of obtaining the advantageous and of avoiding the unfavourable judgments of others, is, undoubtedly, to render ourselves the proper objects of the former and not of the latter. 'Do you desire,' said Socrates, 'the reputation of a good musician?—The only sure way of obtaining it is to become a good musician. Would you desire, in the same manner, to be thought capable of serving your country either as a general or as a statesman?—The best way in this case too is really to acquire the art and experience of war and government, and to become really fit to be a general or a statesman. And, in the same manner, if you would be reckoned sober, temperate, just, and equitable, the best way of acquiring this reputation is

to become sober, temperate, just, and equitable. If you can really render yourself amiable, respectable, and the proper object of
esteem, there is no fear of your not soon acquiring the love, the
respect, and esteem of those you live with.' (TMS 298.13)

Smith's qualified optimism about the workings of reputation is pervasive and unmistakable:

- In the middling and inferior stations of life, private morals
  show a strong tendency toward self-correction, and honesty is the best policy (TMS 63.5; see also 213.7).

- When people move to an urban area and need self-disci-
  pline, they may join a sect so as to develop "a character to
  lose" (WN 795.12).

- Making 20 deals a day a merchant vigilantly guards his reputation, making probity and punctuality the principal virtues of a commercial nation (LJ 538–539).

- Curriculum "improvements were more easily introduced
  into some of the poorer universities, in which the teachers, depending upon their reputation for the greater part
  of their subsistence, were obliged to pay more attention to
  the current opinions of the world" (WN 772-3.34). "In modern times, the diligence of publick teachers is more or less
  corrupted by the circumstances, which render them more
  or less independent of their success and reputation in their
  particular professions" (WN 780.45; for likewise on clergy
  see 790.2).

- Smith showed general disapproval of restrictions that supposedly would protect consumers from frauds, believing
  rather that the "real and effectual discipline which is exercised over a workman, is not that of his corporation, but that
  of his customers. It is the fear of losing their employment
  which restrains his frauds and corrects his negligence… If
  you would have your work tolerably executed, it must be

done in the suburbs, where the workmen having no exclusive privilege, have nothing but their character to depend
upon, and you must then smuggle it into the town as well
as you can" (WN 146.31; see also 762.10-11; LJ 84–85, 472,
497, 529; the 1774 letter to Cullen in Corr. 241–5).

The pattern here is that Smith explicitly and consistently inclines
against calling in government restrictions to do the job of reputational
mechanisms and private virtue. Indeed, intensive-reputation defamation
laws might promote evil by helping people conceal their bad deeds, and by
reducing the incentive to refrain from evil. A matter of distributive justice,
intensive reputation is best left to free and voluntary action.

Smith saw reputation as built on character, "the usual and customary
disposition of the person" (TMS 271.13), or a pattern of conduct. If we have
a character for virtuous conduct, unjust detraction is unlikely to be effective: "A person may be very easily misrepresented with regard to a particular action; but it is scarce possible that he should be so with regard to the
general tenor of his conduct" (TMS 167.8). There is a social momentum
behind reputation. Likewise, a person of bad character may get away with
one bad action, but time wounds all heels: "A knave...may escape censure,
or even meet with applause, for a particular knavery, in which his conduct
is not understood. But no man was ever habitually such, without being
almost universally known to be so" (TMS 167.8).

Smith thought that most people are able to sort out true statements
from false statements: "Men of the most ordinary constancy, indeed, easily learn to despise those foolish tales which are so frequently circulated in
society, and which, from their own absurdity and falsehood, never fail to
die away in the course of a few weeks, or of a few days" (TMS 119.11). "In
general people of circumstances take no notice of such lybels, unless it be
absolutely necessary to clear themselves of some crime" (LJ 194). Smith
advised us to ignore most detraction: "Smaller offences are always better
neglected; nor is there any thing more despicable than that forward and
captious humour which takes fire upon every slight occasion of quarrel"
(TMS 38.8). "[I]t is most prudent to despise and not to raise prosecutions
on such libell, unless the accusation be particularly marked with circumstances as to make it probable, and be of such a nature as to hurt consid-

somewhat modest figure except that 91 had fatal consequences" (Schneider 2004). At any rate, Smith's example of Socrates evokes the wisdom associated with ancient Greece. Socrates' Athens is not a primitive society; the men Socrates conversed with were wealthy citizens and political leaders, and they ignored his behavior. Smith is suggesting that a developed society might have social standards that guide individuals to ignore and disdain detraction, rather than respond with violence, and that such a society did indeed exist. Then something in society changes, and he notes a "new notion of honour" becomes the social standard (what Smith says comports with Peltonen 2003). Smith uses the example of Socrates to show us that Western civilization had indeed advanced to that point, and had fallen back. Verbal injuries became regarded as grounds for dueling—which Hume (H I, 359) called a "great absurdity." The historical accuracy of all this—whether Greeks actually ignored detraction, the origin of dueling—is secondary. What matters here is that Smith seemed to be suggesting that violent response to intensive-reputation detractions is something to put behind us.

Patent and copyright: A parallel

Patent and copyright provide a useful parallel. The way that Smith consistently speaks of them as "priviledges," even "exclusive priviledges," and "monopolies" (LJ 11, 83f, 400, 472, WN 754.30) suggests that he would not count such rights as constitutive of CJ, just as he would not count other exclusive privileges as constitutive of CJ. Such rights do not fit the jural logic of one's own: If our neighbor Bob tried to claim and enforce a "patent" for a device and physically threatened others who, without breaking any contract, implemented the same design, Bob would be regarded as initiating coercion; by the jural logic of one's own it is therefore initiation of coercion when a patent is established by the government. The logic of person, property, and contract among Bob and his jural equals simply has no place for patent or copyright. As with intensive reputation, it would be impossible to evolve precise and accurate rules for patenting and copyrighting. If the government cannot invoke a commutative justice counterpart in equal-equal jural relationship (E-E), it is initiating coercion.

Smith says "they are all creatures of the civil law in each country" (LJ

11), and, by such law, rights are conferred, which Smith calls "real rights" because they are good against the world (as opposed to specific persons). And he does at one point refer to them as "property" (LJ 11). Still, it seems to us that Smith is saying that they are not constitutive of CJ but rather privilege created by certain rights against others' using their property in certain voluntary ways.

The CJ issue is one thing, the desirability issue another. Smith is only glancing and lukewarm on status quo patents and copyright policy. He propounds a strong presumption against exclusive privileges (e.g., LJ 83-84), but makes something of an exception for patents and copyrights: "These two priviledges therefore, as they can do no harm and may do some good, are not to be altogether condemned"; he says they are "harmless enough" (LJ 83). In LJ(B) the impression is a bit more favorable: "The priviledge however of vending a new book or a new machine for 14 years has not so bad a tendency. It is a proper and adequate reward for merit" (LJ 472), and in WN Smith says that, in some situations, "a temporary monopoly" "to establish a new trade with some remote and barbarous nation…may not be unreasonable" "upon the same principles upon which a like monopoly of a new machine is granted to its inventor, or that of a new book to its author" (WN 754.30). Remarks like "may not be unreasonable" and "harmless enough" are words of non-condemnation made in passing.

We see a parallel between patent/copyright and intensive-reputation defamation laws. We think that Smith regarded both as not constitutive of CJ, but was perhaps willing to support them nonetheless. Any support he had for intensive-reputation defamation laws was probably more reluctant than that for patent and copyright.

Conclusion

A thorough examination of Smith's texts casts doubt on the notion that Smith supported the idea that intensive reputation was covered by commutative justice and on the notion that he whole-heartedly favored intensive-reputation defamation laws. Smith's "most sacred laws of justice" passage leaves out "reputation" entirely, and when Smith does indicate "reputation" as a constituent of CJ it is plausible that he means simple repu-

tation (the kind that keeps one safe from physical invasion). Smith's friend
Hume nowhere mentions reputation as constitutive of CJ. And the natural jurisprudence of Pufendorf, Carmichael, and Hutcheson seems to have
been oriented toward easing intensive reputation out of CJ.

Smith saw far too much vagueness in intensive reputation for it to be
governed by CJ. The inherent uncertainty that exists both within the self
about the self's virtue as well as the uncertainty about the virtue of the self
to external observers leaves a high degree of indeterminacy about what
behavior is owed to an individual. Furthermore, the obligations due a person are highly situation-dependent, leaving even greater indeterminacy
and lack of precision. In terms of Figure 6.2, we believe that Smith leaned
toward Cell 4.

If Smith were inclined toward such views and positions, why did he not
simply say, in polite terms, that he thought intensive reputation was nothing
more than "the thoughts of others," as Pufendorf, Carmichael, and Hutcheson had done? Why did he not condemn intensive-reputation defamation
laws as unnecessary and even harmful? Perhaps his way was to ensure his
continued prominence in the establishment, the mainstream, and posterity,
to not come across as a rigid man of system, a man of rationalistic reasoning, yet all the while trying to shift mainstream belief in the right direction.

CHAPTER 7

Instilling Duties above Instilling Rights: Two Features of Adam Smith's Talk of Justice and Liberty

I suggest that two features of Adam Smith's talk of justice and liberty reflect a priority on instilling duties, as opposed to instilling rights. The first feature has to do with his manner of talking "justice"; I distinguish between calling loudly and proffering coolly. The second feature is Smith's refraining in his two great works from using "liberty" in expansive senses of the term. I treat each feature in turn.

Calling loudly

In TMS, Adam Smith writes of "loud" calls and objections (TMS 71.5, 73.2, 74.4, 84.2, 105.2, and 131.33). Loudness constitutes a disturbance, a demand on other people's attention. In the opening pages, he writes: "If we hear a person loudly lamenting his misfortunes, which, however, upon bringing the case home to ourselves, we feel, can produce no such violent effect upon us, we are shocked at his grief; and, because we cannot enter into it, call it pusillanimity and weakness" (TMS 16.6). Already in the second chapter he insinuates pusillanimity and weakness for those who neglect duties.

But Smith clearly sees a place for loudness. In the "most sacred laws" passage about justice among equals, he says violations of person, property, and promises due "call loudest for vengeance and punishment" (TMS 84.2).

In policy matters, Smith sometimes calls loudly, or somewhat loudly, as when he writes of:

- "an evident violation of natural liberty and justice" (*Wealth of Nations* (WN) 157.59), "an act of such violent injustice"

(WN 326.100),

- "evident violations of natural liberty, and therefore unjust" (WN 530.16),

- "contrary to all the ordinary principles of justice" (WN 826.6),

- "In both regulations the sacred rights of private property are sacrificed to the supposed interests of public revenue" (WN 188.27),

- "a plain violation of this most sacred property" (WN 138.12),

- "the most sacred rights of mankind" (WN 582.44),

- the rebuke of the slave trade in TMS (206-207.9).

These cases speak of violations of person, property, or promises due. There are other moments where Smith's sentiment is warm, if not loud, such as the famous "equity, besides" passage (WN 96.36). That passage says that all people, including those "who feed, cloath, and lodge the whole body of the people," are to be accorded equal dignity, equal rights, and equal moral worth in an accounting of the common good. As Christopher Martin (2015, 2021) shows, Smith's policy orientation toward the poor was quite consistently[1] along the lines of the liberal plan of allowing every man to pursue his own interest his own way (WN 664.3).

Proffering coolly

Fonna Forman-Barzilai writes: "[I]mpartiality requires a sort of cool distance." In TMS, Smith abundantly used "cool" to signify calm or composed, as when he speaks of "the sentiments of the cool and impartial spectator" or of "the cool hours" (2010, 159).[2]

I beg pardon for mixing metaphors: The "loud" decibels metaphor

---

1. One possible exception is Smith's endorsement of a law to require (enforce?) payment in cash, as opposed to payment in-kind (WN 158.61).

2. The "cool and impartial spectator" is at 38.8; "cool hours" is at 88.7, 161.12, 163.2, 237.1, and 268.5; for other "cool" moments, see 84.3, 105.2, 118.9, 147.26, 156.44, 157.4, 167.9, 215.12, 217.16, 241.11, 242.12, 251.28, 252.30, 263.3, 311.10, and 316.2.

would suggest an opposite in *quiet*, while the "cool" temperature metaphor of would suggest an opposite in *warm*, *fervent*, or *ardent*. However, to echo Smith's verbalisms, I propose: *calling loudly* versus *proffering coolly*. *Proffer* means to propose something, and connotes calmness and quietness, as opposed to the verb *to call*, which connotes loudness. The proffering we mean is proposing an idea or an estimation of an object, such as a position on an issue of government policy.

In WN, whenever Smith's justice talk does not involve his objecting to a violation of "mere" justice (TMS 82.9), he proffers coolly (e.g., WN 815.4-5, 827.7, 834.20, 944.88, 946.92). Smith seems to suggest that when we talk about what is "just" in government policy and we are not protesting violations of "mere" justice, we should proffer coolly. It is a duty not to call loudly. That duty is elevated over the assertion of supposed rights that supposedly call for redress. That is the first of the two features of Smith's talk. Now we turn toward the second.

An asymmetry

A group of scholars has elaborated a tri-layered understanding of justice in Smith: commutative, distributive, and estimative.[3] Commutative (or "mere") justice is not messing with other people's stuff, namely, their person, property, and the promises due to them as by consent and contract. Distributive justice "consists in proper beneficence, in the becoming use of what is our own" (270.10). Estimative justice is estimating objects properly, including pursuing them and treating them with corresponding ardor. Smith explained that the rules of commutative justice are like grammar, in that they are "precise and accurate," whereas the rules of distributive and estimative justice are "loose, vague, and indeterminate," like the rules of criticism or aesthetics (175-176.11, 327.1-2).

As shown in the first chapter of the present book, Smith talks justice beyond commutative justice. In the governor–governed relationship, commutative justice has a flipside, called liberty. Now we come to the second

---

3. For research beyond the present book elaborating Smith's tri-layered justice, see Hall and Shera 2020; Diesel 2020.

feature of Smith's talk. It is natural to ask: If Smith practices beyond-gram-mar-like justice talk, does he also practice beyond-grammar-like liberty talk?

The question makes sense insofar as, beyond commutative justice, we consider distributive justice. Justice concerns duties. In the cases of com-mutative justice and distributive justice, duties involve obligations—bear-ing on our man Jim, say—to particular sets of people. A duty on Jim's side implies a kind of right on their side, however loose or vague that right might be. In the *Lectures on Jurisprudence* (9), Smith opens by acknowledging how the correlative notions of duty and right can, in "a metaphoricall sense," be loosely construed in matters of distributive justice.

And rights can be fashioned, however vaguely, into a kind of liberty. As Richard Tuck puts it: "[I]f active rights are paradigmatic, then to attribute rights to someone is to attribute some kind of liberty to them" (1979, 7). If one's rights are violated, one experiences a sort of unfreedom, a reduction in liberty.

Try to imagine a super-knowledgeable God-like beholder of all the rules of all the virtues, for whom the rules of even our becoming virtues were precise and accurate. Try to imagine that that beholder was able to extend the grammar of commutative justice into all social matters, and that *for her* there would be, as Francis Bacon put it, "a true coincidence between commutative and distributive justice" ([1605], 190).[4] *For her*, the distinction between commutative and distributive would dissolve. However, to main-tain a living societal meaning of these notions of justice and of the correla-tive duties and rights, Bacon's "true coincidence between commutative and distributive justice" must be, not only for her, but also for all the members of society. We are trying to imagine a *complete circuitry* of the correlative individual duties and individual rights as we mere mortals understand such duties and rights on the ground. Thus, we must take the fantasy yet much further. To do that, our God-like beholder must also *communicate* the duties and rights to us mere humans on the ground. Furthermore, the communi-cation must be intelligible, credible, and compelling: We must heed them

---

4. On the ideal correlative relationship between the justices in the thought of Samuel von Cocceji (as well as his father Heinrich), and a comparison to Smith, see Haakonssen 1996, 143–48. For parallel thoughts in terms of "perfect" and "imperfect" rights, see Stewart 1854, 176–77.

and take them to heart. The God-like beholder must be a quarterback of Team Society, making the duties and rights something like common knowledge in the technical sense (everyone knows them; everyone knows that everyone knows them; etc.). Thus, we might try to imagine how a complex society might, in a fantastic allegory, have a complete circuitry of correlative duties and rights. The only way to join social complexity and complete circuitry is to dream up a God-like quarterback of Team Society.

But there is no God-like quarterback of Team Society. Even if one believes in God and books of revelation, one should agree that there is no God-like quarterback issuing play-by-play communications that make for common knowledge of a complete circuitry of precise and accurate duties and rights. Scripture may speak to our daily lives, but the counsels it offers for moment-by-moment action are wide open to interpretation ("loose, vague, and indeterminate," not "precise and accurate") and far from being common knowledge.

Our genes are not so unlike those of our ancestors of 10,000 B.C. In a very small, simple, intimate society, like the primeval band of forty people, where interpretation is quite static and quite common and there was a strong and meaningful sense of Team Society, the notion of a complete circuitry between commutative and distributive justice may not be so far-fetched. Drop societal complexity and you can imagine something closer to complete circuitry. The primeval band enjoyed something closer to a complete circuitry of correlative duties and rights. But we aren't in the band anymore.

The logic appropriate to band-like existence or a God-like quarterback is reflected in the idiom *I take the liberty*, an idiom that Smith often used in correspondence (Corr. 21, 22, 72, 247, 250, 253, 260, 267, 289, 294, 306, 316, 324, 414). For example, Smith wrote to William Robertson a short letter of introduction, begging Robertson to receive three visitors from Spain: "You are, I imagine, by far the best modern linguist among us, and I therefore, have taken the liberty to give you this trouble; which I hope, you will forgive me" (Corr. 316). The logic of the idiom works as follows: Smith presumes that, were his correspondent to know as much about the situation as Smith knows, the correspondent would recognize his duty to serve the interest in question; and correlative to such duty are rights, or liberty, which

Smith presumes to exercise.

But Smith's use of the idiom is an exception that proves the rule against talking liberty in that extended sense.[5] Indeed, when he speaks of *taking the liberty*, he strikes an apologetic note. The idiom is a sort of apology for presuming to know the "imperfect" rights so well. In his published works, Smith in fact did not much talk "liberty" in matters of distributive justice.

The third sense of justice is estimative justice, that is, estimating objects properly. Smith used the example of a poem or a picture. In that case, a question arises: One's duty is *to whom*, or *to what*?

The duty would seem to be to the poem, the picture, or whatever is the object of estimation. But to speak of a poem or a picture having rights and an associated liberty would be awkward, indeed.

The duties of estimative justice, even in the matter of a poem or a picture, however, are not unattached to the common good. The attachment is abstract or general. So perhaps, even here, our super-knowledgeable God-like quarterback could see rights and liberty. The idea here would be to the effect that people's liberty involves the right to live in a world *free from others' bad estimations of objects*.

Smith refrains from such extended use of *liberty*. In his two great works, his "liberty" talk is chiefly the grammar-like liberty; the few exceptions are *not* the sort that would suggest any corresponding duty.[6] Figure 7.1 expresses the asymmetry in Smith's semantic practice: On the duties side, he talks justice beyond the grammar-like but he keeps it cool. Thus, figure 7.1 exhibits the first feature, discussed at the outset, by placing Smith in row 3 rather than row 4.

---

5. It is interesting that since Smith's time usage of the "take the liberty" idiom has declined vastly, as one can see at Google's Ngram Viewer.

6. With the help of Jacob Hall, I have collected all occurrences of "liberty" in TMS and WN into an Excel sheet. There are ninety occurrences of "liberty" in which the mere-liberty sense (others not messing with one's stuff) is central. There are eleven other occurrences: The first one in WN is about a boy devising a string to open the valve automatically, "leav[ing] him at liberty to divert himself with his play-fellows" (WN 20.8). That "liberty" means unoccupied. That is not a "liberty" to which duties of others are correlative. The eleven occurrences that are not mere-liberty are as follows: TMS 32.2, 51.1, 57.7 150.31, 151.3, 205.8, 280.25; WN 9, 20.8, 50.7, 912.12.

FIGURE 7.1: AN ASYMMETRY IN TALKING JUSTICE/LIBERTY BEYOND THE GRAMMAR-LIKE

		LIBERTY TALK Beyond precise and accurate:			
		Avoid all liberty talk	Allow yourself only the precise and accurate concept	Allow yourself only proffering coolly	Allow yourself calling loudly (and proffering coolly)
JUSTICE TALK — Beyond precise and accurate:	Avoid all justice talk	(A1)	(B1)	(C1)	(D1)
	Allow yourself only the precise and accurate concept	(A2)	(B2)	(C2)	(D2)
	Allow yourself only proffering coolly	(A3)	(B3) **SMITH**	(C3)	(D3)
	Allow yourself calling loudly (and proffering coolly)	(A4)	(B4)	(C4)	(D4)

On the rights side, Smith does not talk liberty beyond the grammar-like, putting him in the B column. Istvan Hont and Michael Ignatieff say it clearly:

> Natural jurisprudence—particularly its distinction between 'strict' and 'distributive' justice—provided Smith with the language in which his theory of the functions of government in a market society took shape. In this tradition, liberty was defined primarily in the passive sense, as the perfect right to enjoy and improve one's property free from the encroachments of others. (1983, 43)

If Smith's practice were symmetric, he would be in a cell along the diagonal, but he is not. In TMS and WN, Smith's "liberty" talk was confined to the precise and accurate, but his "justice" talk was not. He allowed himself to talk "justice" beyond the precise and accurate; when he did so he proffered coolly.

Why the asymmetry and why the unwillingness to call loudly when talking justice beyond commutative?

Smith's justice talk necessarily entails identification of the actor—whether the action concerns messing with other people's stuff (commutative justice), distributing one's social resources (distributive justice), or estimating some object (estimative justice). Justice talk then speaks of that actor's duties. Mindfulness of duty is something to be promoted.

On the other side of things, the *rights* side, we have someone claiming rights, which, according to the claim, are to be enjoyed unencumbered and uninvaded. But do the claimed rights clearly hook up to correlative duties? That is, is it clear who bears those duties, and what the duties are?

The right of property is a grammar-like claim not to be messed with. As for who bears the don't-mess duty, it is everyone and anyone—the claim is "against the world." Though nonpersonal in that respect, the right of property works because it is grammar-like. We all can interact peaceably enough, even as strangers, by complying with the basic social grammar.

But if we proceed to talk rights[7] and liberty beyond the grammar-like, the result is extensive assertions of entitlements but without clear responsibility in the correlative duties and on whom those duties bear.

Again, in a very small, simple society, such as a primeval band, we might be able to approach a more complete circuitry of correlative duties and rights. But in a complex, disjointed society, that is utterly impossible. People tend to overstate their rights and understate their duties, and everyone knows that. That is one reason for the asymmetry. Furthermore, there's more danger in asserting supposed rights than in assiduously minding one's duties. When the asserting of rights is unleashed, we will face a chaos of correlative duties, often imposed on others selfishly, opportunistically, and maliciously—in a word, *illiberally*. In the political arena, when liberal norms break down, we have a Hobbesian state of nature, a war of illiberal (and anti-

7. Figure 7.1 addresses Smith's "liberty" talk. The reader may wonder: What about Smith's "rights" talk? It is my impression that Smith does not much talk "rights" beyond jural matters (by which I mean, roughly, matters of commutative justice and "positive" or legal law), but I have not made a systematic study. One problem in trying to study "rights" in the fashion that "justice" and "liberty" are studied here is that no clear corresponding noun suggests itself, something like "righthood"—the whole of one's rights (perhaps the Latin would be something like *suum*). In Smith's time, the word *property* perhaps had something of such a meaning, among other meanings.

liberal) factions against all. Smith himself indicated as much. Of becoming virtues, such as civility and hospitality, Smith writes: "[U]pon the tolerable observance of these duties depends the very existence of human society, which would crumble into nothing if mankind were not generally impressed with a reverence for those important rules of conduct" (163.2).

It is wise to refrain from talking liberty in political discourse when the grammar-like notion of liberty is not the essence of the matter. Liberal civilization strives to keep a lid on asserting rights and liberties. The result is something of an asymmetry, such that we think of ourselves bearing duties to which no distinct rights correlate. The feeling of duty arises not from a respecting of certain distinct rights of other human beings, but from *right*. As Smith emphasized (e.g., 20.3-4, 137.4, 163.2, 166-7.8, 189.7, 209.13, 238.5, 253.31, 258.42, 335.22, 337.27, 338.30), we have, as it were, duties to truth, to importance, to wisdom, to beauty, to right, to the well-being of humankind, to good, to God.

There are no distinct rights without correlative duties, but *there are duties without correlative distinct rights of other human beings*. This insight helps us see why "Big Gods" were vital in sustaining humankind beyond the band: New duties corresponded to rights of the Bigger Gods—duties that could not cogently correspond to rights of human beings. The bigger the social whole, the more needful is God. In Chapter 10 below, I discuss gratefulness and resentfulness, again arguing for a virtuous asymmetry, namely, favor for generalized gratefulness but disfavor for generalized resentfulness, and again see God as smoothing the way for that needful asymmetry. But I do not mean to argue against theism; God's existence is of course compatible with the evolutionary story suggested here. Indeed, the needfulness might have been a way to ensure that His creatures would find Him.

"a poem, or a picture, or a system of philosophy"

In the early pages of TMS Smith explains that our judging of Jim's sentiments regarding some objects can be considered upon two different sorts of occasions: (1) "when the objects…are considered without any particular relation, either to ourselves or to [Jim]"; and (2) "when they are considered as peculiarly affecting one or other of us" (TMS 19.1). In the latter case, "it is at once more difficult to preserve this harmony and correspondence, and at the same time, vastly more important…We do not view them *from the same station, as we do a picture, or a poem, or a system of philosophy*, and are, therefore, apt to be very differently affected by them" (20-21.5, italics added).

Smith says that a *system of philosophy* is something that we view from the same station. Today, when it comes to political viewpoints, it hardly seems so!

On those early pages, Smith also makes remarks that, rather, seem to fit so much of the political discourse today:

> But it is quite otherwise with regard to those objects *by which either you or I are particularly affected.* [I]f you have either no fellow-feeling for the misfortunes I have met with, or none that bears any proportion to the grief which distracts me; or if you have either no indignation at the injuries I have suffered, or none that bears any proportion to the resentment which transports me, *we can no longer converse upon these subjects. We become intolerable to one another. I can neither support your company, nor you mine.* (TMS 21.5, italics added)

Smith also uses a picture and a poem as examples in the discussion of estimative justice in the major paragraph on the three senses of justice (269-270.10). It is remarkable that he suggests (at 21.5) that "a system of philosophy" ought likewise to be a matter of such cool and distant sentiment. In fact, Smith brings these together twice, as he then soon says: "Though you despise that picture, or that poem, or even that system of philosophy, which I admire, there is little danger of our quarrelling upon that account" (21.5). The remarkable connection between the two moments (that is, 21.5 and 270.10) supports an estimative-justice interpretation of political discourse. After all, Smith's science of a legislator is a system of philosophy, one that Smith presumably deems "just, and reasonable, and practicable" (TMS 187.11). The connection shows that Smith quietly suggests refraining from calling loudly in matters beyond commutative justice.

Interpretations of the good are expansive.

Interpretations of what serves it are expansive.

People disagree vastly.

They always will. A circuitry of duties and rights will never be
closed and commonly beheld. Curb enthusiasm for complete
circuitry ("integralism"?).

In espousing government intervention, it is but propriety to proffer coolly.

Besides instilling civility in our discoursing about politics, Smith's treatment of estimative justice prompts us to ask: What governmental policies
conduce to coolness—and, hence, harmony? To this question, answers are
proffered by Paul Mueller (2021).

Finally, what of instilling in the individual a sense of *her* rights? Certainly, Smith did aim to instill his reader with an understanding of her rights,
notably those associated with ownership and freedom of association. But
the main reason for his doing that was to make her more willing and better able to do her *duty* of defending those rights. Once again, the instilling
of duty seems to be foremost. Liberty is like a public good or even a com-
mon-pool resource ripe for depletion. The individual's sense of her own
duty checks her free-riding and free-loading on the common good.

CHAPTER 8

A Call to Embrace Jural Dualism

By Jonathon Diesel and Daniel Klein

B lack's Law Dictionary gives as the first definition of the word *jural*: "Pertaining to natural or positive right, or to the doctrines of rights and obligations," as in "jural relations" (1983). William Whewell (1845, 1853) wrote significantly of "jural," as did Wesley N. Hohfeld in expositing jural relations in the *Yale Law Journal* (1913, 1917). The "jural" talk offered in the present article runs along the lines of the jural thinking of David Hume and Adam Smith—who did not use the word *jural*—but our usage does not seem to be at odds with that of Whewell or Hohfeld. Figure 8.1 shows an Ngram plot for "jural." Whewell belonged to the rise from 1833 and Hohfeld to that from 1906.

FIGURE 8.1: GOOGLE NGRAM PLOT FOR "JURAL," 1730-2019.

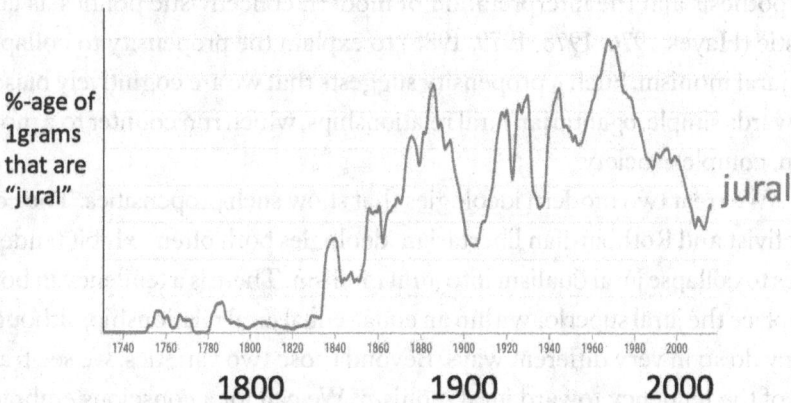

This chapter treats the jural relationships, equal-equal and superior-inferior, suitable to the conventional notion of the modern nation-state. The two jural relationships make for a framework of jural dualism. Such concepts are not novelties that we have dreamed up. Up to and including Adam Smith, the terminology of "superior" and "equal" were commonly used by writers in a "jural" sense in discourses in jurisprudence, political theory, and early political economy.

In the 1830s Alexis de Tocqueville aptly wrote of "the democratic centuries that we are entering" (1835, 419). Into the democratic age, "superior" talk—that is, talk differentiating between jural relationships—fell out of modern discourse. The decline of "superior" talk is unfortunate, because "superior" talk creates a set of semantics and establishes certain presumptions that better serve a liberal outlook. "Superior" talk brings the coercive nature of government to the forefront and therefore calls on us to restrain governmental coercion with a presumption of liberty, in order to stave off the nightmare warned of by Tocqueville, namely, the nightmare of big, smothering, tutelary government, whose cultural centricity displaces traditional religions.

As a byproduct of our evolutionary journey, humans developed propensities pushing us to revert back, notionally, to jural monism, meaning a single jural relationship. These propensities have been aroused and celebrated in the age of the democratic nation-state. The democratic age has been uncomfortable with jural dualism. We use Hayek's two-worlds hypothesis and the interpretation of modern collectivistic politics as atavistic (Hayek 1976, 1978, 1979, 1988) to explain the propensity to collapse to jural monism. Such a propensity suggests that we are cognitively biased towards simple, egalitarian jural relationships, which run counter to a modern, complex society.

We treat two modern ideologies that show such propensities. The collectivist and Rothbardian libertarian ideologies both often exhibit tendencies to collapse jural dualism into jural monism. There is a tendency in both to place the jural superior within an equal-equal jural relationship, although they do so in very different ways. Beyond those two varieties, we see traces of the tendency toward jural monism. We call for a conscious embrace of jural dualism. By embracing jural dualism we clarify the specialness of government and develop appropriate presumptions for avoiding the Tocquevillian nightmare. Embracing jural dualism involves recognizing terms

distinctive to each jural relationship—taxation, for example, is a term specific to the superior-inferior relationship; it is neither theft nor voluntary
payment.

What is "jural"?

Our thinking about "jural" is in the spirit of an arc that extends through
Grotius, Pufendorf, Hume, and Smith, as in Stephen Buckle's book *Natural Law and the Theory of Property: Grotius to Hume* (1991). Humankind is
constituted in a way that impels recognition of individual organisms, as
each organism enjoys unique advantages in knowledge and control over
the mind and organs that come to be recognized as his or her own mind
and organs (Hume 1740, 487). Notions of "one's own," or (in Latin) *suum*,
become focal, and there emerge rules clarifying the duty of not messing
with another's *suum*, or stuff. Cultural evolution selects for groups with such
rules, and for precision and accuracy in such rules. *Suum* or "one's own"
itself comes into sharper focus with integration and stability of a governing authority; universality clarifies individuation (as with monotheisms;
Siedentop 2014). With individuation come individual rights or liberty. The
"natural property" focal points (Friedman 1994) start in one's own person
and, as Hume indicated (1740, 489) and Smith said in his jurisprudence lectures (1763, 20, 460), get *extended*, first to immediate possession and then
outward to advanced propertization of objects, according to conventions
that are partly historistic, like the conventions of a grammar. Bart Wilson
aptly calls humankind *The Property Species* (2020). *Suum* comes to also subsume promises due, or what is due by consent or contract, a related system
of focal points, alongside those of ownership of property (Hume 1740, 516,
522ff; Haakonssen 1996, 117).

   In what follows, we suppose an integrated nation-state.

   We follow Smith in calling the duty of not messing with other people's
stuff *commutative justice*, the rules of which evolve to be precise and accurate,
or grammar-like. The grammar-like rules enable a sort of jural grammar of
jural correlatives—the jural rights of one person are the flipside of certain
jural duties (or obligations) of other persons. The flipside of commutative
justice (not messing with other people's stuff) is others not messing with

one's stuff. Among jural equals, one steadfastly claims the security of such rights. In the citizen's relationship with government (the jural superior), the situation is much trickier, even paradoxical. In the superior-inferior jural relationship, the flipside became one important meaning of the word *liberty*.[1]

"Jural" suggests a way of seeing social relations—a lens. That lens looks to make a complete account of the parties involved and the correlative jural rights and jural duties of each party, in those relations. The jural lens aspires for a complete parsing, in such fashion. The lens is not apt when parties ("stakeholders," some might say) grow diffuse and the rules behind the notional rights and duties grow loose, vague, and indeterminate. Thus, the lens tends to be apt only for certain sets of rules, which we here term "jural rules." One may try, however, to apply the jural lens to one's looser ethical or aesthetic claims or duties, in the hope of making one's actions more becoming by making them less far from being grammar-like.

The word "jural," then, suggests itself for certain sets of rules. In Figure 8.2 the symbol ⊂ means "is a proper subset of":

FIGURE 8.2: JURAL AND NON-JURAL RULES

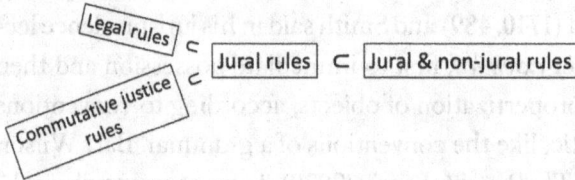

Legal rules are the rules instituted by government law (or "positive" law). Jural rules subsume legal rules, but jural theory also recognizes the rules of commutative justice, even when legal rules conflict with those rules.[2] Legal rules that restrict liberty piggyback on the rules of commu-

---

1. For a discussion of that meaning of *liberty* in Smith, Benjamin Constant ("modern liberty"), Isaiah Berlin ("negative liberty"), and Raymond Aron ("liberal" liberty), see Klein 2023, ch. 17.

2. Whewell presents Grotius (treating here only the law of nature, not the law of nations) as saying: "A Jural Claim, belonging to any one, the jurists call *suum*, his own thing... A Jural Claim, or Right proper, belongs to Expletory Justice, or Justice proper" (Whewell 1853, 2–3). Expletory justice corresponds to Smith's commutative justice (see TMS 269). Thus, Grotius says that, in natural law, "jural" corresponds to commutative justice. Our usage of "jural" is highly Whewellian.

tative justice, by specifying the attenuations[3] of ownership or free association. The last sentence of David Friedman's 1994 article is: "Legal rules are in large part a superstructure erected upon an underlying structure of self-enforcing rights" (16)—by which Friedman means the rights of commutative justice within equal-equal jural relationships, and he means only that such rights *tend* to be self-enforcing.

"Jural" deals with the grammar-like rules of commutative justice and with the legal rules of government, which also aspire to be grammar-like (though they so often fail in that respect, as in others).[4] A likeness to grammar, that is, precision and accuracy, in the rules attends a number of the features that Smith identified as special to the virtue of commutative justice, such as a stronger allegiance to the precept, a one-sidedness to sanction (only negative or blame, no positive or praise), and a more definite sanction or punishment of violation. "Jural" concerns the systems of rules that ought to aspire to serve as social grammars.

Smith, however, did not confine "rules" to what is precise and accurate. Other moral or ethical sensibilities also are termed "rules," even though "loose, vague, and indeterminate" (1759, 175, 327). Beyond the set of jural rules, then, is a larger set, which includes non-jural rules.

The jural "superior" in Smith and others

The term jural dualism refers to two jural relationships, superior-inferior and equal-equal. The superior-inferior relationship implies that the inferior acquiesces to the jural superior, who exercises some degree of overt, institutionalized coercion. The jural superior creates and enforces government laws and regulations. Such actions would be violations of justice among equals (Diesel 2021, 107-10). We are referring to the normal tasks and expectations of a jural superior in executing its role. Taking an equal's money is a crime, yet as done by a jural superior, collecting taxes is official practice.

---

3. Here, instead of "attenuations," Richard Epstein (2011) uses "takings."

4. In LJ (287), Smith says: "New courts and new laws are…great evils. Every court is bound only by its own practise. It takes time and repeated practise to ascertain the precise meaning of a law or to have precedents enough to determine the practise of a court. [A new court's] proceedings will be altogether loose and inaccurate."

"The jural superior" should not be thought of as coextensive with the public or government sector. Once a city or national government or governmental department has taken ownership of a park, road, university, or monument, rules are made governing the use of such resources, rather as a private owner would set rules for the use of her property. Thus, a large part of government-sector rulemaking and activity ("public administration") should be seen along the lines of equal-equal, not superior-inferior—although the government-sector qua jural equal is, in other respects, peculiar, among equals. When we speak of "the jural superior" we should not think of the provost of a university or the head of the highway department. The quintessential feature of the jural superior is its moral and cultural standing to institutionalize overt initiations of coercion—something which a university provost never does (save when deputized to enforce wider legal restrictions).

"Superior" talk, referring to the jural superior, was quite common among authors of the Scottish enlightenment and their precursors. We have traced the use of "superior."[5] Hugo Grotius, Samuel von Pufendorf, John Locke, Gershom Carmichael, Francis Hutcheson, David Hume, and Adam Smith all talked of the jural "superior" (Gregg 2009, 88-90 & 101).[6]

In TMS, Smith discusses commutative justice among jural equals, and then turns out to speak of the jural superior: "A superior may, indeed, sometime, with universal approbation, oblige those under his jurisdiction to behave, in this respect, with a certain degree of propriety to one another" (81). In this "superior" paragraph Smith lays out some expectations of the jural superior such as enforcing justice and "mutual good offices." Within the "superior" paragraph, Smith uses "the laws," "magistrate", "law-giver",

---

5. Diesel's search is not exhaustive, but rather demonstrates sufficient evidence that Smith was not alone. He was engaging in superior talk consistent with both predecessors and peers. Diesel's methodology consists of performing a keyword search using the Online Library of Liberty to find examples of the author's use of "superior," as in the jural superior.

6. For examples from each author see: Grotius 2005 [1877], 83, 136-7, 302, 336, 354, 500, 528, 622, 792, 1553; Pufendorf 2003 [1673], 44n, 85, 159; Locke 1764, 407; Carmichael 2002 [1707], x, 162-3, 170; Hutcheson [1747], 113, 164, 244, 269; Hume EMPL xlviii–xlix, 10-11, 14–31, 40; Smith WN 179, 188; TMS 81. It should be noted that we utilize English translations of Grotius and Pufendorf. It is possible that the use of superior is a product of the translator's interpretation and not the author's intent. We did not consult the Latin texts. We feel confident in our claims, given the number of examples found and the context in which "superior" is used.

and "sovereign," to clarify that he means jural superior, not a comparative superior in some non-jural aspect (Diesel 2020), such as Isaac Newton in science, Novak Djokovic in tennis, or the CEO of a corporation in that organizational hierarchy.[7] Smith's jural dualism extends throughout his works. For example, in WN he says that "civil government supposes a certain subordination" (710.3) and in LJ he says, "A conquered country in a manner only changes masters" (550).

"Jural relations," the particular relations between parties, discussed by Hohfeld (1913, 1917), may be distinguished from "jural relationship," a conceptual category. The CEO of a corporation might be said to enjoy a sort of superiority within the organization's jural relations, but she is not a jural superior. Rather, she is a jural equal, just as Isaac Newton was a jural equal to other natural philosophers. Newton was a superior in scientific standing, and the CEO is a superior in organizational standing, but neither was a superior in jural standing.

Associated with jural dualism, historically speaking, was a burden of proof on the proponent of policies that reduce liberty. As the "liberal plan" or "liberal system" advanced, the proponent of a restriction or intervention was expected to demonstrate why the situation should not be left to free equal-equal jural relationships, "allowing every man to pursue his own interest his own way" (WN 664).

Using loose language to refer to the special nature of the jural superior, or ignoring coercion altogether, changes presumptions. Language may be used, instead, to place the burden of proof on the opponent of the status quo, or even on the opponents of proposed new interventions. Looser language often obscures or elides the jural superior's initiation of coercion.

The human's predisposition towards jural monism

We humans have spent most of our time organized in egalitarian hunter-gatherer bands (Boehm 1999, 198; Rubin 2003, 161). Likening the small simple band to a voluntary organization, we would say that the equal-equal

---

7. It is useful to distinguish at least three categories of "superior": (1) a comparative superior, like Djokovic in tennis—and here we mean a human superior; (2) a jural superior; (3) an ontological superior, such as a god or a god-like being.

jural relationship was the only jural relationship that existed. There was no alternative to the equal-equal jural relationship, so there was monism by default. The superior-inferior jural relationship emerged as private property and commercial exchange became more prevalent. Our social structure has evolved to include jural dualism; however, our lengthy development period as hunter-gatherers created certain predispositions that run counter to commercial society (Lucas 2010, 7).

In small, simple bands our ancestors carried their property with them as they followed food sources. What property did exist was a combination of communal and private. The small amounts of private property included their persons, clothes, or weapons. Spoils were divided amongst the group (Boehm 2012, 37). Our ancestors emerged from hunting and gathering only in the last 10,000 years (Tuschman 2013, 205), but our genes have not changed fundamentally since when our ancestors lived in small bands.

Did our ancestors in the primeval band enjoy liberty? They lived without jural superiors messing with their stuff, so, in that sense, yes. On the other hand, they lived without jural superiors. Saying that they enjoyed liberty is a bit like saying that a stone, enduring no illnesses or ailments, enjoys good health. We are inclined to see liberty as a concept contextualized to jural dualism, and hence not to describe our primeval ancestors as having enjoyed liberty.

Hayek was concerned with how our genetic evolution meshed with our social world today. The Hayekian narrative, or "two-worlds hypothesis," characterizes Hayek's thoughts on cultural evolution and modern politics (Hayek 1976, 1978, 1979, 1988). It illuminates our penchant for jural monism. His two-worlds hypothesis captures a conflict between modern society and man's predispositions based on his genetic development.

During humans' formative years as hunter-gatherers, decisions were made through consensus (Boehm 1999, 65-9; Cronk 1999, 128; Rubin 2003, 161; de Waal 2009, 184; Boehm 2012, 35; Brewer 2008, 11-2). People were punished for doing things detrimental to the survival of the collective such as eating more than their share or shirking their duties (Sober & Wilson 1998, 142-9; Boehm 2012, 152-3). But there was no magistrate to speak of. Leaders were firsts among equals.

A key concept in pondering jural outlooks is a notional underlying configuration of ownership. Today, it is natural for us to think in terms of territorial polities, and in terms of extensive propertization. It is also natural for us to project such thinking onto earlier epochs. For the ancestral band, we do so as follows: The band collectively owned, for the time being, the grounds it occupied and inhabited. Our attributing a notional ownership of such sort—ownership in the occupied grounds—is a way for us to assimilate band existence to territorial polities and to ground (no pun intended) our jural concepts in notional configurations of ownership. The band, then, collectively owned the grounds, and each band member was, therefore, by dwelling on those grounds, enmeshed in a contract with the collective owner of the grounds, namely the band, the source of our instinctual mold for a sense of "the people".

The possessions of a band member were enveloped within the norms of the band. As mankind moves from bands towards more complex forms of social organization, knowledge became more disjointed and private property expanded. The rise of agriculture and the Neolithic age sees increasing propertization of land and sedentary existence. Agricultural surplus allowed for more extensive divisions of labor and specialization. Jural rights and duties become more clearly defined and institutions of law developed.

There emerged the ruler or king. The rule of the ruler no longer felt like a voluntary, equal-equal relationship. One might nonetheless construe it as a sort of contractual relationship if one interprets the realm as the king's property. By dwelling upon the king's property one consents to his rules. In the Western tradition, many came to resist the notion of an ownership of the territory (or of a substratum of the territory) by the ruler, and within that tradition we get the concept of the jural superior, and hence jural dualism. The Smithian liberalism that emerged saw the jural superior not as a great landlord but as a special player in commercial civilization, a player who institutionalized initiations of coercion. Seeing the jural superior as such brought with it certain semantics, which carried certain presumptions.

Living in a commercial society with genes developed in egalitarian bands creates conflicting fancies. Accepting jural dualism has become especially hard to do as modern politics has tapped our band instincts and appealed to our yearnings for jural monism. Such is the crux of Hayek's narrative. Band-man can be described as egalitarian, and driven toward consensus by a desire for encompassment within the band, now transferred to the imagined community of the top polity, the nation-state. A sense of encompassment motivates members to conform to collectivist decisions. Uniformity of experience and behavior reinforces what are thought of as the collectivity's decisions and institutions.

Ideological collapsing of dualism into monism

What is meant by collapsing the jural relationships is folding the jural superior, and thereby the superior-inferior relationship, into the equal-equal jural relationship. The tendency to collapse the jural relationships is shaped by ideologies. The tendency is seen in traces quite widely, but makes itself especially clear in certain modes of thought. We treat Rothbardian libertarianism and collectivism. Their ways of collapsing to jural monism are archetypical, but seeing those archetypes help us to see wider, if fainter or inchoate, tendencies along similar lines.

Rothbardian libertarian collapsing: A thief among equals

> [T]he libertarian refuses to give the State the moral sanction to commit actions that almost everyone agrees would be immoral, illegal, and criminal if committed by any person or group in society. The libertarian, in short, insists on applying the general moral law to everyone, and *makes no special exemptions* for any person or group.

> If anyone but the government proceeded to 'tax,' this would clearly be considered coercion and thinly disguised banditry. Yet *the mystical trappings of 'sovereignty'* have so veiled the process that only libertarians are prepared to call taxation what it is: *legalized and organized theft* on a grand scale.

> Murray Rothbard, *For a New Liberty* (1978, 28, 30, italics added)

Rothbard proposes that we view the agents of the state (jural superior) like anyone else: "police must be treated in precisely the same way as any-one else; in a libertarian world, every man has equal liberty, equal rights under the libertarian law" (Rothbard 1998, 82-3). There is no jural differ-ence between the income tax and getting mugged on the street. Rothbard urged libertarians to view taxation as theft, war as murder, and conscrip-tion as slavery. The libertarian collapsing of jural dualism to monism occurs by placing the jural superior into the equal-equal jural relationship. The magistrate and tax collector are expected to behave in ways similar to the butcher and brewer, and to be discussed in similar terms.

In the Smithian view, by contrast, the rules of commutative justice remain pertinent when viewing the jural superior; the initiation of coercion is still recognized for what it is. But the jural superior is recognized as a special player—its coercions are overt and institutionalized, specified on an official public website, accessible by all. The recognition of the jural supe-rior's special status affords two changes in seeing things through the lens of commutative justice. First, the precept, "Don't mess with other people's stuff," is significantly relaxed. Second, a different set of terminology is used. Taxation is taxation, not theft; intervention is intervention, not assault; etc.

Rothbard's flattening of the semantics of government action down to criminality obstructs useful political discourse. Calling all government action criminal closes off further discussion. Suppose that beauticians cur-rently have to be licensed by a state board, and that a legislator proposes that, instead, the state mandates only that beauticians be insured. The proposed policy still regulates beauticians, but in a less oppressive manner. Rothbard-ian libertarians would approach both policies using the same semantics. Licensure and verified insurance both threaten the use of force towards beauticians trying to work without satisfying the state. Shall the libertari-an endorse the liberalization as "less criminal"? In contrast, jural dualism acknowledges the state as the jural superior without engaging in such "crim-inal" talk. The jural dualist approaches the policies with semantics that keep the coercive nature of the government in mind, but accepts the reality and the special nature of the jural superior. Mandatory insurance is preferable to the status quo of licensure in terms of liberty, even if it is still undue reg-ulation. From the jural dualists' point of view a burden of proof is on propo-nents of the status quo since the reform would increase individual liberty.

Further, the jural dualist recognizes that the status quo, too, enjoys a certain presumption, so the two presumptions (of liberty, of the status quo) moderate one another for liberalization. The Rothbardian, by contrasts, recognizes no presumption of the status quo, at least not for anything regarded as institutionalized criminality.

Now imagine a similar case where the status quo is licensure and the proposed policy is to augment the licensing requirements, for example by also requiring insurance. Libertarian monism again has a problem, for in combatting the reform it would seem to be defending the existing criminality. The opposite case remains for jural dualism. The burden of proof rests on proponents of reform, because the reform reduces liberty relative to the status quo. Here the two presumptions (of liberty, of the status quo) stand shoulder to shoulder against the reform.

Traces of Rothbardian collapsing in other libertarians

In *The Problem of Political Authority* (2013), Michael Huemer explains that one aspect of political authority is "*Political legitimacy*: the right, on the part of a government, to make certain sorts of laws and enforce them by coercion against the members of its society—in short, the right to rule" (4). From "common sense" moral intuitions against coercion, he maintains that no such legitimacy exists. But he neglects that the "common sense" that has developed and that prevails today acknowledges jural dualism, and that taxation is thereby distinguished from extortion. In the first chapter, Huemer writes:

> I shall ultimately conclude that political authority is an illusion: no one has the right to rule…The failure to find any satisfactory account of political authority may therefore lead one to give up the belief in authority, rather than to give up common sense moral beliefs…. [P]olitical authority is a moral illusion. (Huemer, 2013, 16, 17)

Just as Rothbard's approach is ineffective in discriminating between two government interventions condemned as "criminal," Huemer seems to leave no place for arguing that some governments are more legitimate than others.[8] Abandoning the concern for more-versus-less legitimate government belongs to a wider vice, namely, shirking the civic duty to help stave off greater evils. Our call to embrace jural dualism is not so much an argument about the desirability of government as opposed to no-government as it is a call to appreciate and promote better versus worse politics. Like it or not, we are political animals, if only in the sense that we bear a responsibility to help make politics better rather than worse. The embrace of jural dualism is less a matter of justifying the existence of government as it is a matter of apprehending our fate and stewarding the realities. Fateful matters—death, taxes, inflation—are matters to be coped with, evils to be mitigated, not matters for justification.

A great admirer of Huemer is Bryan Caplan, who also tends toward jural monism, for example, by holding that "taxation is theft" (2009a) and propounding anarcho-capitalism (2009b). Politics is a matter of lesser evil, and there is a civic duty to help stave off greater evils. Libertarians too often shrug off or even undercut that duty (consider Caplan 2020). Huemer and Caplan leave little place for public affection for traditions, institutions, and public figures that help stave off greater evils. As Edmund Burke (1790, 171) wrote: "These public affections, combined with manners, are required sometimes as supplements, sometimes as correctives, always as aids to law."

Many libertarian writers exhibit traces of the sort of collapsing to jural monism that Rothbard, Huemer, and Caplan make explicit. Deirdre McCloskey often accepts political authority and at times endorses welfare-state programs, yet at other times she writes as though liberalism leaves no place for the institutionalization of coercion—that is, for the jural superior:

> Liberalism, that is, was the theory of a society consisting entirely, if ideally, of free people...No masters. No kings. No popes... Equality of status...No pushing people around by physical coercion...No messing with other people's stuff or persons or businesses. (McCloskey 2020, 1)

---

8. We shared a draft of this article with Professor Huemer, who kindly confirmed that he is a jural monist, adding that he doubles-down on jural monism in his new book *Justice before the Law* (2021) (we write this with his approval).

McCloskey then says that her description is what Smith meant by "the liberal plan" and "the obvious and simple system of natural liberty." But clearly Smith accepted and sometimes even recommend governmental initiations of coercion; he apprehended the inexorability of the jural superior. Smith strove to establish recognition that such coercion was coercion and a presumption against such measures.

We do not mean to suggest that the "libertarian" identity necessarily implies a regrettable tendency toward jural monism; one may embrace jural dualism and still reasonably identify as "libertarian." We, the present authors, are not averse to identifying as "libertarian," though more inclined to identify as "classical liberal." That said, those who do identify as libertarian quite often show undue tinctures of jural monism.

Collectivist collapsing: Us taking care of us

Collectivists also show a tendency to collapse the jural relationships. At the heart of collectivism's notional jural monism is a collectivist configuration of ownership—"Hotel USA" or "Club USA." It is as though the collectivist imagines a substratum of earth below the territory, a substratum collectively owned by the citizens (or residents). The government is, notionally, a voluntarily appointed set of club officers (Klein 2011, 166). The myriad objects that are privately owned are enveloped within a framework which the club defines by its territorial domain. As when one checks into a hotel, each of us owns our own property, but underneath the individual's ownership rests an enveloping contract with terms and conditions that limit or constrain what a person can do with his or her property while in the "hotel."

Imagine extending the social organization of the band to a much larger and diverse social setting. The band makes rules for acceptable uses of that property while in the band. When the government redefines the conditions of the contract, it is redefining the terms under which each member of the group, a part of the "Us," can use his or her possessions.

An analogous description is the government as the owner of an apartment building and the individual as the tenant. The tenant has some degree of freedom in what he or she can do within the apartment, but it is always subject to the agreement between the owner and the tenant. Under the collectivist configuration the tenant's actions are voluntarily circumscribed by the rules of the polity. The relationship is voluntary because one has voluntarily entered into the contract (by being on the substratum), and one is free to leave. But as long as one's property, ranging from one's person and, if one owns real estate, one's topsoil, is on the collective property (the substratum of earth), one is bound by the rules voluntarily agreed to—a notion often celebrated as "social contract."

There was a time when such collectivist jural notions were rather explicit. The following quotations from the website *Lost Language, Lost Liberalism* date from 1882 to 1914 and are arranged chronologically:

George Harwood, *The Coming Democracy (1882)*: "As no man gave the land, so no man can be allowed to take it away, for the nation has rights over it which no private titles can ever annul. The Coming Democracy will unflinchingly assert these rights" (171-172).

William Galbraith Miller, *Lectures on the Philosophy of Law (1884)*: "[The state] recognizes the individual, and gives him rights. It formulates the duties of the paterfamilias. When once the law has given a name to the family group, it lays down the duties and rights of all the members, as members not of the family but of the state" (177-178).

Joseph Alden, *The Science of Government (1886)*: "The relation of individuals in the State to the sovereign power may be illustrated by a joint-stock company...[T]he whole power of the State belongs to the members of the State—the individuals composing the State; but this power is not divisible among those individuals, to be wielded separately by each" (14).

Ernest Belfort Bax, *Outlooks from the New Standpoint* (1891): "Liberty, in any society, is inseparable from property. Good, but this does not say it is inseparable from private property... No! liberty may be inseparable from property, but nowadays it is assuredly inseparable from the common holding of property by the community" (81).

Frank Sargent Hoffman, *The Sphere of the State* (1894): "No individual can take any of the materials of wealth without the consent of the State, and by his labor make them his property, and the State can never rightly give this consent except with the limitation that the ultimate ownership and control of all property is with itself...The natural right to property, therefore, is ultimately resolvable into a State right. The people, as an organic brotherhood, are to decide what disposition is to be made of all property...The supreme ownership of all the natural sources of property is with the State. The land, the water, and the air, and all that they contain are the common possession of the race. They are under the supreme control of the whole people in their organic capacity as a State" (56-58).

James Ramsay Macdonald, "The People in Power" (1900): "During the brief reign of democracy we have noticed the rise of new conceptions of state activity which have been disturbing to old ideas of individual liberty" (75).

John Atkinson Hobson, *The Crisis of Liberalism* (1909): "Once grasp the idea of the public as a Social Organism, or even as a Corporation administering a property corporately made, it becomes clear that no right appertains to any individual to administer any portion of his property, because as an individual he has made no part of it. But while he has no right as an individual, he has a duty as a member of Society to contribute as best he can to the administration of the common property for the common good" (80).

Leonard T. Hobhouse, "Contending Forces" (1910): "[T]he Progressive 'trend' is setting strongly towards making England the

property of the English nation, not by any wholesale expropri-
ation of individuals, still less by any high-handed disregard of
prescriptive right, but rather by the moderate and cautious but
resolute and many-sided application of the principle of public
overlordship" (359).

Leonard T. Hobhouse, *Liberalism and other Essays* (1911): "I would,
however, strongly maintain that the general conception of the
State as Over-parent is quite truly Liberal as Socialistic" (19). "[T]
he State is vested with certain overlordship over property in general and a supervisory power over industry in general" (209-210).

Paul Vinogradoff, *Common-Sense in Law* (1914): "[T]he right of
ownership is, strictly speaking, quite as much a personal right—
the right of one person against other persons—as a right to service, or a lease" (68).

Nowadays, voices on the political left are less explicit. But the jural-mo-
nist tendency is nonetheless pervasive. One concrete illustration comes
from a survey of signatories of a petition to raise the minimum wage: A
large majority rejected the idea that the minimum wage restricts liberty in
any significant sense (Klein and Dompe 2007, 152). We suggest that, if only
in an inchoate way, they regard the minimum-wage law as being like a rule
of a hotel or club where one has voluntarily checked in.

The collectivist configuration of ownership, then, differs profoundly from that held by the Smithian or the Rothbardian. The Smithian joins
with Rothbard in rejecting claims that taxation "is in some sense really 'voluntary'" (Rothbard 1978, 30). But, though the Smithian joins Rothbard in
rejecting the "Club USA" configuration of ownership, the Smithian embraces jural dualism and accords a special role to government.

In the collectivist jural understanding, the government manages the
"club rules" attaching to the substratum. When, for example, redistributive
policies are enacted the policy is not considered coercive. Rather, it is a matter of "Us" taking care of "Us". The takings that are to be redistributed are
not the jural superior coercing the inferior. Instead, the people, as an equal,

makes use of what is "Our" own. Thus we often hear of the "generosity" of the welfare state. On the collectivist configuration, a notional generosity makes a sort of sense. But on the Smithian configuration of ownership, one scrutinizes the apparatus from top to toe and finds not a speck of generosity—neither the politician, the voter, the taxpayer, nor the civil servant is making a generous use of what is his or her own. In fact, the system in inherently devoid of generosity.

Where Rothbardians collapse to the equal-equal jural relationship and apply the same standards of commutative justice to government, the left collapses to the equal-equal jural relationship and assumes the government is acting like the leader of a band upon a collective configuration of ownership of the substratum. Now, government rules like minimum-wage laws are not violations of commutative justice, but rather are issues of how "We" make a becoming use of what is "Our" own—or what Smith called distributive justice (TMS 269-70). The collectivist jural monism allows the collectivist to seemingly avoid the problem of coercion.

Smith rejected the collectivist configuration

Smith rejected the collectivist configuration, for example where he writes of "the violence of law" and related expressions in *The Wealth of Nations* (525-526, 248, 285, 342, 372, 422, 586, 653) and of "fortunate violence" in *The Theory of Moral Sentiments* (253). Knud Haakonssen (1981, 96) notes that Smith recognized that taxation "involved forcible infringement of liberty, privacy, and property of individuals." Smith was explicit about the flipside relationship between commutative justice and liberty (WN 530). He often declared duly enacted laws to be violation of commutative justice/liberty (for example WN 145, 157, 326, 539, 582, 826). In this connection Smith even grows sarcastic, as when he writes about Englishmen's "boasted liberty" and how they "pretended to be free" (WN 660, 326). He says, "civil government supposes a certain subordination" (710.3), and, in LJ, "A conquered country in a manner only changes masters" (550).

Smith's distributive justice is focused on the individual and the individual's property. Smith defines distributive justice as "proper beneficence, in the becoming use of what is our own" (TMS 270). One might point at

Smith's use of "our" and read it as plural and political. That would be a mis-reading of Smith. Smith differentiates his meaning of distributive justice from that of Aristotle's in a footnote. Aristotle's conception of distributive justice, he says, specifically means "the proper distribution of rewards from the public stock of a community" (TMS 269n). As Peter Minowitz notes, "Smith's decision here to employ a footnote, especially given the paucity of footnotes in *The Theory of Moral Sentiments*, suggest the distance he wishes to put between his own position and a more political approach to justice'" (Minowitz 1993, 50). Smith's distributive justice focuses on what the indi-vidual should do with his or her property while Aristotle focuses on what the community should do with its property.

Accepting jural dualism

"Superior" talk attended the rise of classical liberalism up to Adam Smith, yet it has fallen out of favor. Perhaps explicit recognition of a superior is too jarring for modern vernacular. Perhaps we find it uncomfortable to address the jural relationships directly, because we would have to admit the coer-cive nature of policies we prefer. We are doing ourselves a disservice by avoiding superior talk. The jural superior is still there. Failing to address the jural superior openly and directly forces us to talk around it through flattened semantics and unclear presumptions. The collectivist approach effaces liberty.

Meanwhile, Rothbardian libertarianism flattens the jural relationships down to one, the equal-equal jural relationship, by treating government as an equal who happens to be criminal. The Rothbardian approach aims to efface government. Since both ways of collapsing to jural monism, the Rothbardian and the collectivist, are throwbacks to penchants suited to conditions that no longer fit the modern world, both are atavistic.

We implore readers to accept jural dualism. Accepting jural dualism does not imply accepting any specific policy positions. It advances a pre-sumption of liberty and it recognizes the unique role that is the jural supe-rior. Agreeing on the existence of a jural superior is a first step in facilitat-ing the discussion about what the proper roles of government is, so we can better address the question of preferred policy.

One aspect of accepting jural dualism is recognizing the jural superior as a special sort of actor. The same rules do not apply to the jural superior, so we must use a separate set of criteria when judging the jural superior's actions. Holding the jural superior to a different set of expectations and using terminology that recognizes that superiority are key steps in establishing and maintaining recognition of jural dualism.

Accepting jural dualism provides a commonality from which we can depart: Under jural dualism the actions of the jural superior are coercive. Such coercion is out in the open and, as a general principle, it is accepted. The focus of debate can turn to whether specific policies are appropriate, and to what degree. We should be addressing what the government should be coercing us to do or not do. Further, we must agree on what property is and who owns what. Jural dualism serves these needs, without imposing a rigidity in judging the desirability of particular policies.

CHAPTER 9

Four Sets of Nonconflicting Rules

The previous chapter discussed jural theory. This chapter extends that discussion. It formulates seven sets of rules. Of those seven, four are sets of nonconflicting rules. One could list other sets of nonconflicting rules, for example, those of the Major League Baseball or of the Roman Catholic Church. I submit, however, that the four sets here are the only ones that are focal and central for moral theory, political theory, and jural theory. (If there were a set #5, what would it be?) The formulations might help us define natural jurisprudence.

Why should you take an interest in how I—someone with no formal training in law—make sense of "law," "jural theory," "commutative justice," and "natural jurisprudence"?

The needed training is, in part, training in navigating and overcoming taboos. Taboo surrounds commutative justice; taboo has prevented moderns from doing commutative justice justice. Because commutative justice (CJ) has not been done justice, neither has jural theory. You need to see CJ to see jural theory. The failures to do CJ justice sunk what Smith called natural jurisprudence.

In the previous chapter on jural dualism, there is a figure called Figure 8.2. I now expand on it, in Figure 9.1, which has two panels. The two panels overlap at box 5. In your mind you can staple the two panels together there.

The symbol ⊂ means "is a proper subset of", hence, A ⊂ B means that A is a proper subset of B. You can turn the symbol around and say the same thing as B ⊃ A (just as A < B is the same as B > A).

FIGURE 9.1: SETS OF RULES/LAWS

Panel A: Boxes 1–5 of the schema.

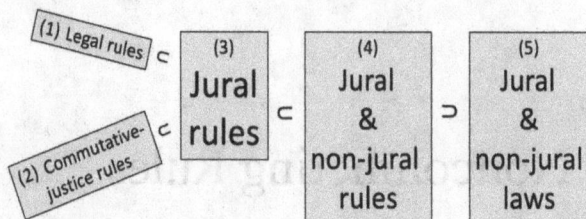

Panel B: Boxes 5–7 of the schema.

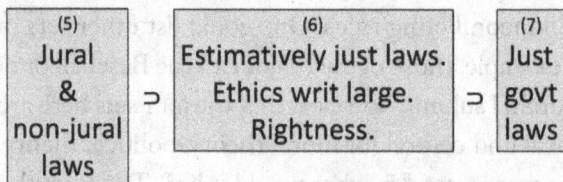

Boxes 1, 2, 3, and 4 are the same as appeared in the jural-dualism chapter. Recall that the diagram presupposes a jurally-integrated polity. New are boxes 5, 6, and 7, as well as the blue and pink coloring (for those reading a black-and-white version of this chapter: boxes 1, 2, 6, and 7 are blue, while boxes 3, 4, and 5 are pink).

Notice that boxes 1, 2, 3, and 4 say "rules," while the new boxes 5, 6, and 7 say "laws." I will speak to the distinction between a rule and a law, as well as to the coloring.

Notice that box 1 and box 7 have something in common, namely, rules of the government. Box 1 is legal rules, positive law, and box 7 is "Just government laws." It's quite a distance between them. In between is ethics.

Let's start with "rule." The concept involves a precept, for example: Take an umbrella if you're going out in the rain. A precept takes the form of an imperative. The broad precept of commutative-justice rules is: Don't mess with other people's stuff. The precept can be broken down into its particularities, getting into the parsing of "stuff," "other people's," and "messing with."

Now, when is a rule a law? Is "Take an umbrella if you're going out in the rain" a law?

Seeing a rule as a law is a lens. It might make sense in some discourse contexts to speak of the umbrella precept as a law. So, what is the "law" lens? What is involved in seeing a rule as a law?

First, according to Samuel Pufendorf, Gershom Carmichael, Francis Hutcheson and others, a law involves a precept and a sanction:

> In every law there are two parts, the *precept and the sanction*. The precept shews what is required or forbidden; and the sanctions contain the rewards or punishments abiding the subjects, as they observe or violate the precept. (Hutcheson 2007, 106)

Thus, a law involves not only an imperative "Do/Don't do X", but also an "Or else!" The "or else" can take the form of reward for observing or punishment for violating the precept, or both.

Second, in the same tradition of thinkers, there is another feature of "law": Law is a rule laid down by a superior. And it is the superior or his agents who apply the sanctions. Michael Zuckert (1994, 189) writes: "Only if one can find in nature the will of a superior can there be said to be a law of nature, as opposed, say, to a natural good. Obligation, and thus law, can ensue only when there is an antecedent superior/subordinate relationship."

What counts as a "superior"?

In my view, even within the moral ecology of the stable, jurally-integrated polity—for example, a stable, jurally-integrated nation-state—there are multiple superiors, and their laws sometimes, even often, conflict. The laws in box 5 are not all compatible. In particular, the laws of the jural superior (variously called the sovereign, the ruler, the lawmaker, the governor, the government, etc.) often conflict with the laws of the supremely superior spectator, God/Joy, and of our shared characterizations of such a spirit. As for the other two boxes in Figure 9.1 that feature the word "laws," namely boxes 6 and 7, in each case the laws there *are* compatible; there, within each box, are no conflicts between laws within the box.

It would usually be rather far-fetched to see "Take an umbrella..." as a law, but it is instructive to describe what it would take. We need a sanction, we need a superior, and we need the sanction to be the work of the superior or his agents. One way to get all this done is to believe in a providential

God—an ontological superior—who made a "ruly," as opposed to unruly, universe, with a law containing "Take an umbrella…" as a precept (contextualized in history, of course), and getting wet as the sanction.

Now, suppose you are not a theist. I cannot call myself one—rather, I call myself agnostic. Is there, then, a way to see "Take an umbrella…" as a law?

Yes, there is. Though allegorical, Joy can be fashioned a being. Joy has superhuman knowledge and superhuman benevolence. She subtly communicates to you: "Take an umbrella…" But since she is not the author of the wetness, the wetness does not work as the sanction. Rather, the sanction is: "Or else I will be disappointed and unhappy with you." Not only can Joy, along with her representatives, such as our conscience, be seen as a law-giving superior, but such disapproval can be seen as the sanction.

You might think that merely allegorical disapproval should not be taken serious and certainly should not serve as the basis for elevating a rule of thumb to the status of law. Here, I urge caution. For one think, notice this: If other people have a similar sense of Joy and thus take to heart sensibilities aligned to Joy, then her disapproval would tend to correspond to the disapproval of actual fellow human beings around—"You idiot! Why didn't you take an umbrella?!" That smarts, and it follows from violating the precept. I am not urging you to always think of norms as laws, but it is helpful to see how to see a norm as a law.

Some people seem to reserve the word "law" (at least in matters of rules for social interaction) for positive government law. Let's call it flat legal positivism. It strips non-legal or extra-legal moral thought and discourse of the word *law*, and all that it carries, including a sense of a superior and the superior's sanction. The *only* sort of superior that flat legal positivism recognizes in these matters is the jural superior, hence the only law, for the flat legal positivist, is government law. Such a view is especially characteristic of people who are irreligious to the point of being anti-religion and throwing the baby out with the bathwater. I think it is a mistake to never admit disapproval, notably that deriving from our own conscience, as a lawful sanction.

Government laws of any functional polity are and must be the creatures of norms and spirits, like God or Joy. The government law specifies both a precept and (however vaguely) a sanction that is to be carried out by government agents. Suppose Jim is some ordinary private citizen who violates the precept. It then falls to a government agent, Bob, to apply the sanction. Now, let us to suppose that there is a law for Bob to abide. For Bob, the precept is the applying of the sanction against Jim; but what is the sanction relating to *that* precept? Perhaps there is a specified sanction, and a specified sanctioner, named Ralph. But the problem recurs: What if Ralph shirks his (third-order) precept? Clearly, if this recurrence rolls back to anything redeeming, it rolls back, principally, if not wholly, to norms. And without such norms—Consciences! Spirits!—to see sanctions through, the law in the first instance will scarcely carry the sanction it entails, in which case it scarcely meets Hutcheson's definition of law. Empty verbalisms do not law make. Law only exists within human norms and consciences and spirits that give those norms meaning and coherence. I expect that any flat legal positivist would agree with all this. Yet he refuses the word "law" for that which sustains whatever decency and integrity is found in government law. Adam Smith said that the rules of *all* virtues "are justly regarded as the *Laws* of the Deity" (TMS 161, italics added). The semantic decision of the flat legal positivist breaks radically with our civilizational moral intuitions and cultural underpinnings, which are quasi-religious when they are not religious.

I imagine the flat legal positivist responding, "Oh, but those spirits aren't real." And I imagine C.S. Lewis replying: "Oh? I am inclined to see them as the realest things we know. After all, they underpin what you deem 'real.'"

So, getting back to Figure 9.1, our discussion of the meaning of law shows us that within any particular law there is a precept, and, for our purposes here, it is the precept that I wish to consider *the* rule within that particular law (in other words, leave aside rules that are entailed in the sanction). Thus, for any set of laws, we can also identify the corresponding set of precepts, and identify that set as a set of rules. Thus I speak of boxes 5, 6, and 7 as sets of rules, even though labeled "laws."

We thusly understand every one of the seven boxes as representing a set of rules. Those seven boxes can be divided into two categories: Sets of nonconflicting rules (blue), and sets of potentially-conflicting rules (pink).

Consider box 3, "Jural rules." As stated in the previous chapter, "jural" deals with the grammar-like rules of commutative justice and with the legal rules of government, which also aspire to be grammar-like. Among the rules within box 3 are the precepts within tax law, including for the Internal Revenue Service: "Forcibly take people's income as per the tax code." But also among the box-3 rules are CJ rules, including: "Don't forcibly take others' stuff." The precept of CJ is against the initiation of coercion; the government institutionalizes initiations of coercions. I could use as an example, instead of taxation, any of the government's 10,000 commandments that initiate coercion. Box 3 contains conflicting rules and hence is pink.

Sets of potentially-conflicting rules abound. What are special are the few touchstone sets of nonconflicting rules. I believe that the blue sets in the figure are *the* four very special sets of nonconflicting rules.

Four sets of nonconflicting rules

1. The actual current governmental law (in context)—in other words, legal rules or "positive" law. (I realize that, in fact, the rules may not fully nonconflicting, but they are supposed to be, and shall be, to the extent that our assumption of a jurally integrated polity holds.)

2. The grammar-like rules of commutative justice (CJ).

3. All laws (both precise and accurate, and loose, vague, and indeterminate) that delineate the rightness of any decision, made by anyone. Ethics writ large.

4. The would-be laws of government (in context) conformant to #3. Just government law, in the full sense of justice (think estimative justice, EJ).

By resuscitating CJ, we may resuscitate proper jural theory. Further, those resuscitations may then resuscitate an idea of natural jurisprudence. The definition ought to include the following feature as necessary or essential: *A study of rules and laws that duly recognizes CJ as one of the important sets of rules.* I'm not sure what else is necessary, or what set of things sufficient, for natural jurisprudence. But if a study does not recognize CJ as an important set of rules, then it is not natural jurisprudence.

The "natural" of natural jurisprudence is fitting, one reason being that CJ should be regarded as a system of natural conventions, and hence natural law, along the lines suggested in Chapter 4.

CHAPTER 10

Is It Just to Pursue Honest Income?

Morality and religion call constantly, imposing a constant duty: Serve the Greater Good! The constant duty is not: *Make a Buck!* Put differently, the constant duty is: *Please Universal Benevolence!* That is, please a universal beholder who is benevolent toward the whole.

We please universal benevolence when we benefit society. But benefiting others often involves neither a sense of duty nor a feeling of benevolence. The baker provides buns from the "mercenary exchange of good offices according to an agreed valuation" (86.2), as Adam Smith put it in *The Theory of Moral Sentiments.*

Bywords get blended in: Greed is good. The virtue of selfishness. The invisible hand. But, critics cry, greed is not good! The word greed has always had "not good" built in to it. Read the Bible. Rich men enter Heaven like camels pass through the eye of a needle (Matthew 19:24).

The profit motive, they continue, is at odds with social justice.

Some libertarians respond: "Social justice" is a mirage. Justice means not messing with other people's stuff. If you make money without messing with other people's stuff, there's no injustice—and that's that. Yes, others benefit too, but that's a bonus, separate from justice.

But, critics cry, justice is more than that! The word justice has always had more than that built in to it. Read the Bible: "The way of the just is uprightness"[1]—not merely not messing with other people's stuff.

Or read Smith.

Smith did indeed emphasize the virtue of not messing with other people's stuff, by saying that among jural equals—like you and the baker, or you

---

1. Isaiah 26:7 King James Bible.

and your neighbor—it is "indispensable" (175.11), by explaining the precision and accuracy of its rules, making it grammar-like, and by using its specialness to formulate key distinctions and arguments. Although Smith signifies that virtue often simply as "justice," he clarifies by calling it *commutative* justice (269.10). Think of commuting: The commuter travels *point-to-point*. Commutative justice looks at *part-to-part*. It asks: Has that fellow Jim messed with someone else's stuff? It does not otherwise ask how Jim affects larger wholes.

But Smith also affirmed "proper beneficence, ...the becoming use of what is our own" as another meaning of the word *justice* (270.10). Our man Jim is unjust when Jim makes an unbecoming use of what is Jim's own. This sense is identified by Smith as *distributive justice* (269.10).

Were Jim to make himself becoming, he would use—*distribute*—his resources in ways that serve the larger good, the larger whole—even the whole of humankind. The question no longer is part-to-part, but Jim in relation to the whole. No longer are things like grammar but, rather, aesthetics, "loose, vague, and indeterminate" (175.11, 327.1).

If Jim volunteers at a homeless shelter, we commend his generosity—distributive justice. There are many ways to work for the greater good which win one little in the way of income.

But should we commend Jim's day at the homeless shelter more than if he had distributed the day to his business or career?

Yet a third sense of justice affirmed by Smith is estimating objects properly (270.10). That third sense always looms in the background but here we focus on distributive justice.

I contend that we may indeed sustain a presumption of distributive justice in the pursuing of honest income. Honest income warrants presumptive, if only tepid, approval. Not every Jim is innocent, but the prosecution bears the burden of proof.

Making money is one thing, spending it another. Justice in spending is a great question, and not really fully separable from the question of making money justly. But the question of spending justly is not ours here. Let's assume that Jim's spending is ordinary and presumptively morally legitimate.

The whole entails me, myself, and I

Really? *Serve the Greater Good? Constantly?* It sounds so oppressive.

Yes, really. But it is not as oppressive as it sounds.

Jim's delighting in that brownie or the football game on TV might be his best way in the moment to serve the greater good, since his delight makes a part of the whole and presumably pleases the benevolent beholder. Maybe Jim wants to go with friends to the big game, and needs money for the expensive tickets, and pursues income.

In their expensive seats, people enjoy the spectacle on the field. Does the benevolent beholder enjoy the spectacle of their enjoyment? We always have to ask: *Compared to what?* We don't really know what Jim's alternatives are. Presumably Jim has a much better idea of what his practicable alternatives are. We're not in a good position to second-guess Jim about what's good for himself, his friends, and his family.

Adam Smith observed that man's attention, concern, and sympathy follow a pattern: "Every man... is first and principally recommended to his own care.... After himself, the members of his own family...are naturally the objects of his warmest affections" (219.1,2). At one point Smith identifies the wealth of nations with "the good cheer of private families" (WN 440.19).

And after family come other friends, including workmates: "Colleagues in office, partners in trade, call one another brothers, and frequently feel towards one another as if they really were so" (224.15). Concern for others recedes with social distance.

Why would providence have made us that way? If God loves the vast whole of humankind impartially, why would he have made us the morally near-sighted creatures that we are?

Smith's answer is that, though benevolence is agreeable, to be actualized as beneficence—actual benefit proceeding from benevolent impulse—it must be effective. We have "very limited powers of beneficence" (218.2). The effectiveness of our efforts depends on relationships and the relational knowledge that lives in relationships. It is a knowledge problem. Man's concerns have been directed to departments "suitable to the weakness of his powers, and to the narrowness of his comprehensions" (237.6):

That wisdom which contrived the system of human affections...

seems to have judged that the interest of the great society of mankind would be best promoted by directing the principal attention of each individual to that particular portion of it which was
most within the sphere both of his abilities and of his understanding. (229.4)

Again, distributive justice consists in making a becoming use of what is
our own. If becomingness corresponds to advancing the whole, and if our
most effective way of advancing the whole is to focus on our small part of
it, then we do distributive justice by doing just that.

What's more, without profane rewards Jim might be unable to keep
up his program in life, or to keep it on a sensible track, or to be creative in
discovering new and better tracks. Jim structures his recreation in habits,
routines, rituals, or Sabbaths, using rules. His own rules help to constitute
that small part of the whole on which he focuses.

Which of the 8,000,000,000?

Focus deserves focus. People manage to coordinate sentiment and action
upon focal points, that is, focal features of the situation that guide mutual
understandings and expectations. Focal points regularly relied upon are
conventions. David Hume taught the importance of conventions, including those of commutative justice and of political authority, and Smith followed suit.

To perceive a focal point, we need to read each other's interests and
intentions. We figure that the other person cares firstly about himself and
his family, partly because that is what is focal: What other interests shall
we impute to him? Surely they exist, but not of our ken, and perhaps none
of our business.

And we recognize that others stand in a like position of unfamiliarity
as regards us: We often pursue our own narrow self-interest, like going first
through the intersection, simply because it is focal: It's what others expect
of us. In making a deal, we now drive a hard bargain because that is what
our trading partner expected of us when making an initial offer.

The pursuit of honest income provides a basis for focal points, mutual coordination, and the greater good. Such focal points may not be especially lovely but when critics condemn them— "People! Not profits!"— we ask: Compared to what? A profane focal point—making an honest buck—may be better than none at all. Does "People!" provide good focal points? Which of the world's eight billion people are we to help—and *are to expect* help from us? What kind of relationship will it be based on? Are we to befriend them? If we do not befriend them, our knowledge is poor. And if we do befriend them, are we back to moral near-sightedness, to helping our friends?

An attitude of benevolence toward humankind is surely just, shared by all of public spirit. But the attitude needs to get beyond platitude. Until we allow a lot of concessions to not-so-lovely practical constraints, it does not make for functional focal points. Indeed, the focal points emerge as much from the concessions as from the spirit.

As rivers are lost in the sea

La Rochefoucauld (1959, 64) wrote: "Virtues are swallowed up by self-interest as rivers are lost in the sea."

In *The Wealth of Nations*, Smith tells of people acting "from their regard to their own interest" (27.2), knowing that behind such interests are deep souls, pursuing lives built on deep moral purposes. Wells of selfhood, explored in *The Theory of Moral Sentiments*, partly of "divine extraction" (131.32), live behind the transactions of *The Wealth of Nations*. Virtues occur often only in the background and effectuate themselves in life choices which are then implemented in adopting practices that become routine, matters of day-to-day busyness, or business—immediate and readily identifiable interests, narrow, mundane, too often regarded as narrowminded, selfish, greedy, profane.

Man, also partly of "mortal extraction," so often "appears to act suitably, rather to the human, than to the divine, part of his origin" (131.32). The soul, represented by the conscience, has always found itself bound to and situated with that mortal portion, which is barraged by passions of the moment, great and small, unceasingly. That mortal portion is terribly presentist.

Jim-the-soul manages this presentist self in a constant relationship, prompted by the social world, "the great school of self-command" (145.22).

To direct the present focus, to keep himself on track, to fuel his daily deeds, Jim develops practices of reward and disappointment, merit and demerit, approval and disapproval.

What kind of track does Jim pursue?

A poor man's son, Jim, "whom heaven in its anger has visited with ambition, when he begins to look around him, admires the condition of the rich" (181.8).

He's tempted by ambition. Besides, there are few ways in which a man can be more innocently employed than in getting money—Dr. Johnson says so (1798, 182-3).

Jim toils long and hard, spends years building a great career, and accumulates magnificent wealth. He joins the ranks of the filthy rich.

Forty years later, however, "in the languor of disease and the weariness of old age, the pleasures of the vain and empty distinctions of greatness disappear." Jim's wealth and reputation, his projects and properties, now appear to be "enormous and operose machines...which must be kept in order with the most anxious attention, and which, in spite of all our care, are ready every moment to burst into pieces, and to crush in their ruins their unfortunate possessor" (182-3.8).

Smith tells us that Jim was deceived by nature, and "it is well that nature imposes upon us in this manner":

> It is this deception which rouses and keeps in continual motion the industry of mankind. It is this which first prompted them to cultivate the ground, to build houses, to found cities and commonwealths, and to invent and improve all the sciences and arts, which ennoble and embellish human life; which have entirely changed the whole face of the globe, have turned the rude forests of nature into agreeable and fertile plains, and made the trackless and barren ocean a new fund of subsistence, and the great high road of communication to the different nations of the earth. The earth, by these labours of mankind, has been obliged to redouble her natural fertility, and to maintain a greater multitude of inhabitants. (183-84.10)

Thus Jim has been "led by an invisible hand to...advance the interest of the society, and afford means to the multiplication of the species" (184-5.10).

The benevolent beholder is glad of the effects, but can Jim be said to be distributively just in his pursuit of honest income? Heeding Dr. Johnson, Jim understands himself innocent. But innocence hardly makes *becoming*. Innocence may be preserved "by sitting still and doing nothing" (82.9)—a far cry from praiseworthiness.

Distributive justice calls for a responsible regard for the larger whole. It entails proper motives and intentions—propriety. If Jim acts without much regard for the larger whole, he does not make himself becoming, irrespective of any social benefits that flow as byproduct.

But from Smith's parable flows a second. The second parable is left unstated by Smith; it is, as Erik Matson (2019) has explained, left for the reader to see for himself. The parable between the lines is no unintended byproduct. It is, I believe, the invisible aim of the visible parable.

It is a parable of a second Jim, born, let us say, after Smith had completed his works. This young Jim, when he begins to look around him, admires the condition of the rich, but also that of certain others. He begins to look around the library and finds books by Adam Smith. He reads them and learns very well that by laboring, inventing, and producing, even if he meets only one in a thousand of the beneficiaries of his industry, he may serve the greater good. He pursues a career or business now not only that he attain that condition of the rich. Now he understands that he subserves the greater good. In honest income that subservice has a measure, albeit imperfect. Learning the measure, and its imperfections, the subserver serves better.

A commercial humanism had been not unsuccessfully constructed

In this parable Adam Smith is among the dramatis personæ. That persona is surely center stage when the intellectual historian J. G. A. Pocock (1985, 50) writes: "A commercial humanism had been not unsuccessfully constructed" by 1790.

This Jim, a son of commercial humanism, whom Smith in his benignity visited with a taste of wisdom, is like a character in the 1954 film

Sabrina, Linus Larrabee, played by Humphrey Bogart. Linus is a hardworking industrialist. His playboy younger brother doesn't get it: "You've got all the money in the world!"

> *Linus*: Well, what's money got to do with it? If making money was all there was to business, it'd hardly be worthwhile going to the office. Money is a byproduct...

> *Playboy brother*: Well, then, what's the urge? You're going into plastics now. What will that prove?

> *Linus*: Prove? Nothing much. A new product has been found, something of use to the world, so a new industry moves into an undeveloped area. Factories go up. Machines are brought in. A harbor is dug, and you're in business. It's purely coincidental, of course, that people who never saw a dime before suddenly have a dollar. And barefooted kids wear shoes and have their teeth fixed and their faces washed. What's wrong with the kind of an urge that gives people libraries, hospitals, baseball diamonds and, uh, movies on a Saturday night?[2]

The remarks are wonderful, but, still, commercial humanism takes things further. If Linus makes money going into plastics, does it really prove nothing? Is money really just a byproduct?

The prudent shipmaster

Suppose $100,000 is at hand and Linus ponders how to distribute it. He sees opportunities in plastics with expected return of 15 percent, and in textiles 10 percent. Linus's character is genuine. He strives to be distributively just, that barefoot kids may wear shoes, and cares nothing about garnering more wealth for himself. What should he do?

---

2. The text is my own transcription of the film clip, keeping close to the script online here. The script was adapted for the screen by Billy Wilder (the film's director), Samuel A. Taylor, and Ernest Lehman, based on Taylor's play *Sabrina Fair*.

such rationing: They evoke *greater* supply. Would-be suppliers hear the call: High returns! People respond to the emergency, far and wide, as though to an alarm.

Much of the pulling together is utterly unwitting, reminding us that the "pulling together" is half allegorical, or more than half. Users in other areas simply face higher prices, reduce consumption of grain or plywood, and thereby let it flow instead to where the need is urgent.

Honest income is a way of "keeping score"—not in the invidious race against the Jones's, but in caring for all aboard. It offers reassurance—immediate, focal—to manage oneself: "How am I doing?" When Linus Larrabee sees returns of 15 percent he is reassured that barefooted kids now wear shoes. Linus then feels *justified* in allowing himself to find daily motivation and inspiration in garnering honest income. Confident in his subservice, he lets it grow avid. But his avidity is not a subservience—an *over*-willingness to service the purposes of a superior—for subservice is a purpose of *his own*, as rivers are lost in the sea.

Commercial humanism and the Great Enrichment

If one wishes to understand our civilization, one should see the importance of Adam Smith's moral authorization. As Glasgow University professor and author of *The Theory of Moral Sentiments*, he established himself a leading moralist. His Scottish circle of peers constituted a peak in Europe's cultural landscape, and Smith was first among his peers. He attained a position of cultural royalty. With *The Wealth of Nations* he gloriously effected two moral authorizations. One was the green light to the pursuit of honest income: "by directing that industry in such a manner as its produce may be of the greatest value, he intends only his own gain, and he is in this, as in many other cases, led by an invisible hand to promote an end which was no part of his intention" (WN 456.9). "Without any intervention of law, therefore, the private interests and passions of men naturally lead them to divide and distribute the stock of every society, among all the different employments carried on in it, as nearly as possible in the proportion which is most agreeable to the interest of the whole society" (WN 630.88).

The other was "the obvious and simple system of natural liberty... Every man, as long as he does not violate the laws of [commutative] justice, is left perfectly free to pursue his own interest his own way" (WN 687.51). Smith christened it "the liberal plan of equality, liberty and justice" (WN 664.3) and "the liberal system" (538-9.39).

A commercial humanism had been not unsuccessfully constructed. And what was the consequence?

Bang!—The Great Enrichment—Barefooted kids now wore shoes. One reason it happened when it did was that, as Deirdre McCloskey (2016) explains, now commerce and industry—the market—was honorable. The pursuit of honest income had gained moral authorization.

FIGURE 10.1: THE GREAT ENRICHMENT

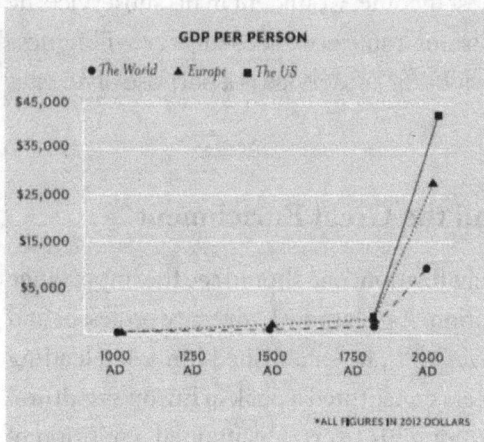

Figure reproduced from Noell, Smith, and Webb (2013, 7).

The green light and freeing of markets made societies rich. But did Adam Smith's new philosophy of commercial humanism sustain itself? The pursuer of honest income would invoke bywords such as "the invisible hand." But was he really distributively just? Who knows what lurks in the hearts of men?

Commercial humanism is a philosophy for the modern, complex world, some 12,000 years from the small band in which we evolved. In that small, simple society, the whole was visible, benefit moved with beneficence, and our instincts were formed accordingly. Now our small-band instincts are continually challenged, and, to manage ourselves, we make ourselves complicated. Commercial humanism teaches us to get used to that. Naturalize it. Be at one with it, and as friends we may approach at-one-ment.

We are out of our element and can never go back. Smith's moral theory involves regard for "agreement or disagreement of any action to an established rule" or convention (327.16), regard for expectations, so history plays a significant part *inside of* theory, reason, and justice. Our selfhood, our own theory of our justness, is complicated. Operose machines 'R' us.

Jim might accept the message and find good cheer in his life in modern society. But wisdom and virtue entail more than bywords. Their sustainability requires more. Liberalism was a bit of luck, and will always face a hostile environment.

Every maxim comes with many a "sometimes"

The green light to honest income is itself complicated. In fact, maybe the metaphor of a green traffic light is misleading.

First of all, it is only on the road of "honest income," the definition of which must reach beyond merely keeping to commutative justice. We'd want to extend the penumbra to not letting yourself mislead others, and so on, since not every instance of dishonesty is a violation of commutative justice. Furthermore, we may wish to cleave away income augmentation involving governments, not because it ought to be presumed dishonest—I myself am an employee of the Commonwealth of Virginia—but simply because the healthy tendencies toward self-correction characteristic of private markets are much weaker, sometimes perverted, when government is one of the players.

But even confined to said roads, the green light is merely presumptive. Sometimes the making of an additional honest dollar is *unbecoming*. Sometimes there is honest profit in serving folly—whether it be pernicious substances or pernicious art and discourse; sometimes real externalities appertain; sometimes the advantage can be had by the less worthy competitor; sometimes making *less* is becoming because nickel-and-diming is opportunistic, or because a dollar means less to a rich person than it does to a poor person, or because charging less means that more will enjoy a service with non-rivalrous benefits or very low marginal costs.

Sometimes honest income is over-pursued. People neglect other sides of life. No matter how honest, cupidity is unbecoming. Sometimes distributive justice lies in stepping back from honest dollars, in making *less*.

But every maxim comes with many a "sometimes." They make for exceptions and qualifications to a general green light on the road of honest income. Take a moderate pride in honest income. And once it has come in, try to distribute it justly.

CHAPTER 11

Gratefulness, Resentfulness, and Some Modern Slogans

I n "The Use of Knowledge in Society," Friedrich Hayek (1945) expounded on market mechanisms that promote the good of the whole without aiming at it. Twice he called the process a "marvel," and then insisted that the oddness that the reader may feel in finding an author in the *American Economic Review* express a sense of marvel illustrates the incapaciousness of our putative science of economics.

In the latter part of his career, Hayek ventured into moral and political psychology and one of the questions he addressed was: Why do we marvel at how the good of the whole can be promoted by humble focal interest? Why does Adam Smith's observation—that people acting with such focus nevertheless advance the interests of society—amaze us? Where does that feeling come from?

Hayek suggested an answer. We are still creatures of the small simple band of the Upper Paleolithic. Hayek came to that insight as he developed his theory that modern collectivist politics taps into corresponding mentalities, penchants, and yearnings (Hayek, 1976; 1978; 1979; 1988). He theorised modern collectivist politics as atavistic.

Evolution programmed us to assume design in processes that promote the good of the whole. When the whole was a mere 40 people, that was largely how its good was promoted. The concatenation of human activities was readily perceivable—as in Smith's pin factory, where the concatenation is "placed at once under the view of the spectator" (WN 14). But now our ethics identify the whole as something larger than the primeval band or the factory. Instead of 40 band members cooperating day in, day out, we are more than eight billion persons plus future generations.

Hayek suggested that the propagandistic power of the modern slogan of "social justice" is atavistic. In this article I draw on Smith, Hayek, and some modern research about gratefulness to suggest that the propagandistic power of the modern slogans of "inclusiveness" and "equity" is atavistic.

Distinguishing gratefulness and gratitude

Many researchers find positive effects of gratitude and gratefulness. Some of those findings are surveyed by Reuben Rusk, Dianne Vella-Brodrick, and Lea Waters in "Gratitude or Gratefulness? A Conceptual Review and Proposal of the System of Appreciative Functioning," published in *Journal of Happiness Studies* (2016). A main theme of Rusk et al. is that it is important to distinguish conceptually between gratitude and gratefulness. They write:

> [T]he term gratefulness is defined here as an appraisal of benefit that does not involve the perceived agency of any person or entity (e.g., "I am grateful for the warm sunshine.'). On the other hand, gratitude is defined as an appraisal of benefit that strictly concerns the perceived agency of another person or entity (e.g., "I am grateful to John because he helped with the chores.'). (Rusk et al., 2016, 2194)

The authors express the distinction concisely: "Unlike gratitude, gratefulness does not concern specific benefactors" (2203). One may be *grateful for* the warm sunshine without being grateful to anyone for it. Another way of putting the distinction is that gratefulness announces grateful for, while gratitude announces, furthermore, *grateful to*. The authors allow that gratitude normally involves gratefulness, but gratefulness does not imply gratitude.

Rusk et al. (2016, 2199) explain that the agency in gratitude involves a grey area:

> The nature of the perceived agency may fall anywhere on a continuum from very concrete, specific, and vivid perceptions (e.g., "Sarah baked this cake for me.') to more vague and abstract ideas

(e.g., "The police help to make the city safe.').

Perhaps it is best to see the existence of a benefactor as a continuum without sharp demarcation. If one can feel gratitude to the police for making the city safe, then one might feel gratitude to the farmers and truck drivers who helped produce one's lunch. And then there is God, who made the warm sunshine. Thus, one can always imagine agents to be grateful *to*. But the benefactors grow more abstract—less definite and concrete—as we move away from concrete human benefactors.

The authors discuss another nuance (2197), this one about assessing the benefit, the nuance being: "Compared to what?" What is the benchmark for saying that certain benefits have come to me? Is the benchmark what would be mere propriety, neither blameworthy nor praiseworthy? What is expected?

But concepts always involve grey areas. The distinction between gratitude and gratefulness is clear enough. Nor is it idiosyncratic to Rusk et al. The authors cite other researchers as maintaining the distinction (including Solomon, 1977; Walker, 1980; Adler & Fagley, 2005; McAleer, 2012). The distinction was made nicely by A.D.M. Walker (1980, 45): "[G]ratefulness need not always be 'focused' upon another person, does not always have to be gratefulness to *someone*, and hence…cases of gratefulness cannot always be cases of gratitude."

The benefits of gratefulness and gratitude

Feeling grateful is attended by positive attitudes towards life and pro-social conduct (Rusk et al., 2016, 2192, 2201–4). Gratitude prompts reciprocal benefit, returned upon the benefactor. But even mere gratefulness is attended by positive personal consequences, such as life satisfaction and stronger personal relationships. Thus, feelings of gratefulness are something to encourage. A propensity towards feeling grateful is a virtue.

In *The Theory of Moral Sentiments*, Adam Smith (94.2) writes of feeling grateful even towards inanimate objects:

We conceive… a sort of gratitude for those inanimated objects which have been the causes of great or frequent pleasure to us. The sailor, who, as soon as he got ashore, should mend his fire with the plank upon which he had just escaped from a shipwreck, would seem to be guilty of an unnatural action. We should expect that he would rather preserve it with care and affection, as a monument that was, in some measure, dear to him... The house which we have long lived in, the tree whose verdure and shade we have long enjoyed, are both looked upon with a sort of respect that seems due to such benefactors. The decay of the one, or the ruin of the other, affects us with a kind of melancholy, though we should sustain no loss by it. The Dryads and the Lares of the ancients, a sort of genii of trees and houses, were probably first suggested by this sort of affection which the authors of those superstitions felt for such objects, and which seemed unreasonable, if there was nothing animated about them. (94.2)

There is a sweetness about gratefulness; it is a "social" passion (38.1), a "double sympathy" like benevolence (301.4). In living somewhere, among familiars, gratefulness naturally merges with the affection, the love, and the attachment one feels for the familiar objects of life: "The sentiment of love is, in itself, agreeable to the person who feels it. It soothes and composes the breast, seems to favour the vital motions, and to promote the healthful state of the human constitution; and it is rendered still more delightful by the consciousness of the gratitude and satisfaction which it must excite in him who is the object of it" (39.2).

Gratitude and resentment

The opposite of gratitude is ingratitude, that is, not feeling grateful to a benefactor, returning neither thanks nor good offices. The opposite of gratefulness is ungratefulness, or not feeling glad for the benefits one enjoys. Ingratitude and ungratefulness do not necessarily involve bitterness; they may be merely thoughtless and negligent.

Ingratitude should be distinguished from resentment. Resentment is a negative feeling *for slights or harms* done and responding accordingly.

Resentment is a sort of inverse (not opposite) of gratitude. Resentment supposes a maleficence whereas gratitude supposes a beneficence.

Smith writes: "Gratitude and resentment...are in every respect, it is evident, counterparts to one another" (TMS 76.7). Smith says that we can feel resentment, if only for a moment, even at an inanimate object: "We are angry, for a moment, even at the stone that hurts us. A child beats it, a dog barks at it, a choleric man is apt to curse it" (94.1).

Our first distinction, between gratefulness and gratitude, suggests a similar distinction between resentfulness and resentment. The difference again is perceived agency: Resentment is directed at a malefactor, the perceived author of the harm; resentment is *resentful at*. Resentfulness does not necessarily involve a malefactor; it is *resentful for*.

Resentment can be virtuous

Resentment can be virtuous. It is proper to feel a certain antipathy toward malefactors, and to respond appropriately. Indeed, Smith writes that one can show positive virtue in resentment:

> [W]e admire that noble and generous resentment which governs its pursuit of the greatest injuries, not by the rage which they are apt to excite in the breast of the sufferer, but by the indignation which they naturally call forth in that of the impartial spectator; which allows no word, no gesture, to escape it beyond what this more equitable sentiment would dictate; which never, even in thought, attempts any greater vengeance, nor desires to inflict any greater punishment, than what every indifferent person would rejoice to see executed. (TMS 24.4)

Proper resentment for wrongs done by malefactors is a necessary part of any organic social system of morals. As part of a functional moral ecology, resentment serves to enforce the moral rules of the system; it is necessary to make the system self-enforcing. Smith says that feelings of resentment render "it dangerous to insult or injure"; they are "the guardians of justice" (TMS 35.3).

A modern and proper asymmetry

For a generalized resentfulness, however, there is no malefactor who has dealt a harm, and therefore no harm has been done. It is much harder to find merit in the sentiment. If someone grumbles, "I am resentful for the cold wind and rain", it is hard to enter into the resentfulness. Such resentfulness is not something to encourage.

Rusk et al. (2016) discuss the upside of gratefulness. I imagine that there are inverse findings showing the downside of resentfulness (though I've not found much at Google Scholar). Smith writes: "Love is an agreeable, resentment a disagreeable passion" (TMS 15.5). Resentment is disagreeable to the one who suffers it and those who enter into his feeling. Just as gratefulness lifts one's spirits, resentfulness depresses one's spirits. Resentfulness is a downer.

What's more, actions prompted by resentment tend to be retaliatory, vengeful, or punitive—and hence directly destructive. In contrast, the action prompted by gratitude is constructive: a return of good offices. Destruction and construction are highly asymmetric in facility: It may take centuries for a culture to construct an exquisite building or monument, but an arsonist or terrorist can destroy it in a moment. There is good cause for stark asymmetry in our attitudes about resentful feelings and grateful feelings.

Furthermore, Smith explained that there is a parallel in the institution, as it were, of the self: We have built up habits, understandings, sensibilities, beliefs, affections—a life. And when our house burns down, our loved ones are lost, or our careers are destroyed, the pain is far more pungent and protracted than the fleeting felicity of any conceivable earthly blessing (TMS 44–5, 121.15). As has been often noted, Smith clearly saw psychological results now associated with prospect theory, loss aversion, and the endowment effect.

Finally, think of Shakespeare's Montagues and Capulets, the Hatfields and McCoys, or Israel and some of its neighbors. One man's punishment is another man's provocation, so acting on resentment can cause a cycle of violence. Interpretations of the good and the just are sometimes highly disjointed, even directly at odds.

Thus, the differences between gratefulness and resentfulness are at least four: *(a)* the disagreeableness of resentful feelings to the one feeling them and to his associates, as opposed to the agreeableness of grateful feelings; *(b)* the facility of destruction, compared with construction; *(c)* the depth and pungency of pain and suffering, as compared with the shallowness and transience of more than ordinary pleasure or felicity; and *(d)* the possible cycle of violence.

Given the fourfold difference, virtue would seem to lie in strict circumspection in any feelings of resentfulness and especially circumspection in letting such feelings flow into active resentment. Scruple in resentful feelings calls for four things:

- Name the malefactor;
- identify his malefaction; that is, what action did he take that was wrongful;
- explain the precepts that make it malefaction; and
- start with a presumption of innocence and show evidence of his violation of those precepts, and with a responsible understanding of the circumstances within which he acted.

Otherwise, keep a tight lid on resentfulness.

The modern world makes all this especially challenging. Today, generalized resentfulness is pervasive. It fuels delusive beliefs of malefaction. Delusive slogans are raised up—"anti-racism," "environmental justice"—and they arouse and feed contagions and rackets of resentfulness.

Hayek's atavism thesis

In a small simple setting, it is natural and proper for resentfulness to lead to a proper resentment. Take the case of a father of several teenage children. He awakens in the morning while everyone else is still asleep, and heads for the coffee. In the kitchen he finds the sink full of dirty dishes, a disagreeable sight and an inconvenience. He feels resentment at the disorder, but does not know who the malefactor is. Feelings of resentfulness spur investigation and may arrive at concrete resentment and action, such as chastising the slovenly one.

In the archetypical small simple setting of an extended and very familiar family, or cluster of families, in the upper-paleolithic band, 10,000 BC, a father awakens in the morning and finds that many of the band's 40 members are enjoying a hearty breakfast, whereas he, his mate, and his children are still famished from having scarcely eaten for days, and still without food. The inequality or disparity in wealth would, in the band, arouse feelings of resentfulness. This happens by instinct. We have instincts for equal portions around the campfire or dinner table. That is the way small simple societies maintained centric cohesion and cooperation, against the elements and against other bands.

In this case, the resentfulness is like the one for the dirty dishes. In the band of 10,000 BC, a small simple society, the leaders and fellows were all responsible for food distribution. There was, on their part, a malefaction in allowing some to eat well while others scarcely eat at all. The resentfulness prefigured a proper resentment. In small simple societies, those rude instincts made more sense. They were selected for, and they are still with us.

Another sort of experience would inspire great resentfulness in the small simple band of 10,000 BC: If some band members formed unto themselves a subgroup, which seemed separate from the central leadership of the band, that would arouse suspicion and resentfulness. Why are they acting independently of our leaders? What are they up to? Why don't they include me? Such formations spoiled the band's experiential and sentimental cohesion, its aspiration towards common knowledge, and its feeling of "effervescence," as Emile Durkheim (1915) called the heightened feeling of encompassment. Such exclusive formations threatened the centricity of the band itself; they were harmful to the band. Again, the resentfulness prefigured a proper resentment.

Thus, based on my reading of evolutionary researchers such as Christopher Boehm (2001; 2012) and David Sloan Wilson (2010), it seems fair to suppose that two of the primary sources of resentfulness and resentment were (a) inequality (or disparity) of wealth, and (b) non-inclusiveness. Those tendencies fit band life and survival, and are still in our genes. In the modern slogan "Diversity, equity, and inclusion," two of the three terms appeal to primeval instincts.

But we are not in the band anymore.

Now we have resentfulness that does not attend any proper resentment. Modern society is vastly complex. The nation state is an unknowable immensity, a social universe of unplumbable depths and disjointed experiences, interpretations, and intentions—and influenced in myriad ways by cultural forces beyond its borders.

Governors, like everyone else, are morally responsible for advancing the good of the whole. But opinions differ as to what constitutes the good of the whole and what advances that good. The perspective of Smithian liberalism was, in government policy, generally to make government stable, enlightened, and limited, and to affirm and sustain basic social grammars that would allow spontaneous forces to unfold in beneficial ways. "The fatal effects of bad government arise from nothing, but that it does not sufficiently guard against the mischiefs which human wickedness gives occasion to" (TMS 187.1).

Friedrich Hayek used "resent" in criticizing "social justice" and in advancing his atavism thesis about modern collectivist politics. The atavism thesis interprets modern collectivist politics as an appeal to, and reassertion of, band mentalities, instincts, penchants, and yearnings, now that the modern democratic polities are mythologized as super bands. Hayek wrote:

> Their demand for a just distribution in which organized power
> is to be used to allocate to each what he deserves, is thus strictly
> an *atavism*, based on primordial emotions. (1979, 165)

> But these habits had to be shed again to make the transition to
> the market economy and the open society possible. The steps of
> this transition were all breaches of that 'solidarity' which governed the small group and which are still resented. (1979, 162)

> It was this unavoidable attenuation of the content of our obligations, which necessarily accompanied their extension, that people with strongly ingrained moral emotions resented. (1978, 66)

Hayek said that "social justice" is "an attempt to satisfy a craving inherited from the traditions of the small group but which is meaningless in the Great Society of free men" (1976, 67). He suggested that "perhaps most people can conceive of abstract tradition only as a personal Will" (1988, p, 140). He then asked: "If so, will they not be inclined to find this will in 'society' in an age in which more overt supernaturalisms are ruled out as superstitions?"

Adam Smith advised us to keep a tight lid on resentful feelings:

> Resentment seems to have been given us by nature for defence, and for defence only. It is the safeguard of justice and the security of innocence. It prompts us to beat off the mischief which is attempted to be done to us, and to retaliate that which is already done, that the offender may be made to repent of his injustice, and that others, through fear of the like punishment, may be terrified from being guilty of the like offence. *It must be reserved, therefore, for these purposes, nor can the spectator ever go along with it when it is exerted for any other. But the mere want of the beneficent virtues, though it may disappoint us of the good which might reasonably be expected, neither does, nor attempts to do, any mischief from which we can have occasion to defend ourselves.* (TMS 79.4; italics added)

The good and the grateful

Elsewhere (Klein 2023, ch. 5), I have noted that Jonah Goldberg (2018), Donald Boudreaux (2019), and Bryan Caplan (2017) express a generalized gratefulness for the blessings of modern life and "the Miracle" of liberal civilization. Behind their sentiment there is no particular benefactor to point to. Such gratefulness is a healthy sentiment, and something to encourage. It builds on primeval instincts of sympathy and returning good offices. Again, it breeds serenity and pro-social conduct, as reviewed by Rusk et al.

Even though the gratefulness of Goldberg, Boudreaux, and Caplan is rooted in instincts that go back to the primeval band, I would not call their generalized gratefulness an atavism. "Atavism" usually suggests that the atavistic feature, which now re-emerges, is no longer suitable to modern conditions. The word "atavism," especially in sociology, tends to have a negative valence; it has defectiveness or badness built into it, like the word "bias". An atavism is a bad that stems from something that had been functional in former times under former conditions. It is a vestige that is no longer suitable. Virtue calls on us to overcome the tendency.

While generalized gratefulness is still beneficial and therefore is not an atavism, generalized resentfulness is not suited to human existence. It is a morphing of simple resentfulness—natural to the primeval band and the modern family household—into a pernicious ideology of generalized resentfulness. Based on the four differences mentioned above, we see that there is a propriety in holding very asymmetric attitudes about generalized gratefulness and generalized resentfulness: The first is good, the second is bad.

Our understanding helps us understand that anti-liberal purveyors of generalized resentfulness—from Rousseau to Marx to critical race theory—appeal to vestiges no longer suitable to modern life. Hayek's atavism theory provides a perspective about the ineluctable challenge that would come from the printing press, print culture, the nation state, and a modern form of politics that fashions the polity as a super band, a challenge profoundly explored and warned of by Alexis de Tocqueville.

Hayek's atavism theory also helps us understand that those most susceptible to generalized resentfulness are likely to be susceptible to related atavisms, such as a lack of compunction about proprieties, decencies, and decorum. In the band, such compunction was scant in the face of starvation, battle, and the competition for mates. Double standards, hypocrisy, and denial are band-man's unvirtuous response to the modern world.

We have in large part transcended the band and realized a somewhat liberal civilization, where we hope to continue to enjoy modern compunction. May *those* vestiges be retained and revitalized, and inspire gratefulness.

CHAPTER 12

Of Its Own Accord: Adam Smith on the Export-Import Bank

T his chapter assembles quotations by Adam Smith regarding bounties—subsidies paid to producers for their productions, usually for
export. Policies of export subsidization are still with us. One of
the agencies involved in export subsidization in the United States is the
Export-Import Bank ("Ex-Im"). The Smith quotations presented here suggest, perhaps, what Smith would say about Ex-Im. The export subsidies
that Smith treated were bounties paid directly to exporters, whereas those
of Ex-Im principally take the form of subsidized credit. But the form does
not much affect most of Smith's analysis of export subsidization.

In a 1780 letter, Smith (Corr., 251) writes of "the very violent attack I had
made upon the whole commercial system of Great Britain." In *The Wealth
of Nations*, Smith said that the "commercial" (or "mercantile" or, nowadays,
mercantilist) policy is notionally based on the idea that "wealth consisted
in gold and silver," possession of which would be augmented by the nation's
"exporting to a greater value than it imported." "Its two great engines for
enriching the country, therefore, were restraints upon importation, and
encouragements to exportation" (WN 450.35). The very idea that wealth
consists in gold and silver, Smith explained, is wrongheaded. Gold and silver are "utensils," like pots and pans: "it would be absurd to have more pots
and pans than were necessary for cooking the victuals usually consumed
[in a country]. [T]o attempt to increase the wealth of any country, either
by introducing or by detaining in it an unnecessary quantity of gold and
silver, is as absurd as it would be to attempt to increase the good cheer of
private families, by obliging them to keep an unnecessary number of kitch-
en utensils" (WN 439–440).

The good cheer of private families, or wealth of nations, Smith concludes, is ill served by mercantilist schemes. At the close of Book IV of *The
Wealth of Nations*, Smith concludes:

> It is thus that every system which endeavours, either, by extraor-
> dinary encouragements, to draw towards a particular species of
> industry a greater share of the capital of the society than what
> would naturally go to it; or, by extraordinary restraints, to force
> from a particular species of industry some share of the capital
> which would otherwise be employed in it; is in reality subver-
> sive of the great purpose which it means to promote. It retards,
> instead of accelerating, the progress of the society towards real
> wealth and greatness; and diminishes, instead of increasing, the
> real value of the annual produce of its land and labour.
>
> All systems either of preference or of restraint, therefore, being
> thus completely taken away, the obvious and simple system of
> natural liberty establishes itself of its own accord. Every man,
> as long as he does not violate the laws of justice, is left perfectly
> free to pursue his own interest his own way, and to bring both
> his industry and capital into competition with those of any oth-
> er man, or order of men. The sovereign is completely discharged
> from a duty, in the attempting to perform which he must always
> be exposed to innumerable delusions, and for the proper perfor-
> mance of which no human wisdom or knowledge could ever be
> sufficient; the duty of superintending the industry of private peo-
> ple, and of directing it towards the employments most suitable
> to the interest of the society. (WN 687.50–51)

Smith allowed exceptions to such maxims, but passages like the foregoing capture Smith's drift. In *The Wealth of Nations* he uses the expression "of
its own accord" (or "of their own accord") 28 times. Leaving private enterprise to proceed of its own accord was the position that Smith propound-

ed on the matter of bounties.[1] "Such are the liberal principles," said Dugald Stewart shortly after Smith's death, "which, according to Mr Smith, ought to direct the commercial policy of nations" (Stewart 1980, 317).

Smith explains why bounties are usually given only for exports:

> [I]t is not the interest of merchants and manufacturers, the great inventors of all these expedients, that the home market should be overstocked with their goods, an event which a bounty upon production might sometimes occasion. A bounty upon exportation, by enabling them to send abroad the surplus part, and to keep up the price of what remains in the home market, effectually prevents this. Of all the expedients of the mercantile system, accordingly, it is the one of which they are the fondest. (WN 517.25)

Smith suggests that Britain's export bounty on a good had the effect of shunting some portion of the supply of that good to foreign markets, driving up the price faced by the British consumer:

> The corn bounty, it is to be observed, as well as every other bounty upon exportation, imposes two different taxes upon the people; first, the tax which they are obliged to contribute, in order to pay the bounty; and secondly, the tax which arises from the advanced price of the commodity in the home market, and which, as the whole body of the people are purchasers of corn, must, in this particular commodity, be paid by the whole body of the people. (WN 508.8)

---

1. On the idea that certain interventions were justifiable because they favored British production of goods necessary for defense, Smith embraces the idea as justifying the Navigation Acts (WN 463–465.24–30), which favored British ships and crews, not by awarding them bounties but by obstructing and burdening non-British ships and crews. Smith raises the idea of export bounties for British sailcloth and gunpowder (WN 522–523.36–37), as well as internal bounties on the inland transport of coal (WN 874.12). Although Smith respectfully acknowledges the defense argument for specific bounties, he by no means says that such an argument provides sufficient justification, but rather seems, even in the cases of sailcloth, gunpowder, and inland transport of coal, to lean against bounties. So, in an age of sea power and perpetual conflict, Smith endorsed Britain's obstructing and burdening of non-British ships and crews, but his opposition to awarding bounties is really quite entire.

Some of Smith's analysis makes specific claims about effects and incidences of bounties, claims criticized by David Ricardo[2] and others. But Smith also argues with looser, more robust claims. Supposing that a bounty were necessary to make it worthwhile for a merchant to produce the goods subsidized, then, Smith says, "if the bounty did not repay to the merchant what he would otherwise lose upon the price of his goods, his own interest would soon oblige him to employ his stock in another way" (WN 505–506.3). "The effect of bounties, like that of all the other expedients of the mercantile system, can only be to force the trade of a country into a channel much less advantageous than that in which it would naturally run of its own accord" (WN 506.3).

In comparing alternative arrangements, Smith considered what Ronald Coase (1960, 44) calls "the total effect," including the political, moral, and cultural effects. He drew a contrast between, on the one hand, the endeavor to regulate the industry and commerce of a great country "upon the same model as the departments of a publick office," bestowing "upon certain branches of industry extraordinary privileges" and laying "others under as extraordinary restraints," and, on the other hand, "allowing every man to pursue his own interest his own way, upon the liberal plan of equality, liberty and justice" (WN 664.3). The broader background to *The Wealth of Nations* is *The Theory of Moral Sentiments*, which subtly illuminates moral and cultural advantages of the liberal plan.

Market failure was an integral part of Smith's political economy, but no less so was government failure. Smith treated the two impartially. Government privileges, such as bounties, require a conference between the government and the private parties who enjoy such privileges, for only the latter have some local knowledge of the local situation: "What is the species of domestick industry which his capital can employ, and of which the produce is likely to be of the greatest value, every individual, it is evident, can, in his local situation, judge much better than any statesman or lawgiver can do for him" (WN 456.10). Smith warned that creating and organizing interest groups, for example "to give such bounties to favourite manu-

---

2. See Ricardo's *Principles* chapter 22, "Bounties on Exportation, and Prohibitions of Importation" (Ricardo 2004/1817, esp. 307–318).

factures" (WN 523.37), works to create "a conspiracy against the public" (WN 145.27). "[T]hough the law cannot hinder people of the same trade from sometimes assembling together, it ought to do nothing to facilitate such assemblies; much less to render them necessary" (ibid.).

Smith held that "in the mercantile system, the interest of the consumer is almost constantly sacrificed to that of the producer" (WN 660.49). But he pointed out that "the producer" was really *certain privileged producers*: "In the mercantile regulations, ...the interest of our manufacturers have been most peculiarly attended to; and the interest...of some other sets of producers, has been sacrificed to it" (WN 662.54). He emphasized that intervention on behalf of "industry" is intervention on behalf of *particular complexes of industry*, a point that applies to the Export-Import Bank: "It is the industry which is carried on for the benefit of the rich and the powerful, that is principally encouraged by our mercantile system. That which is carried on for the benefit of the poor and the indigent, is too often neglected, or oppressed" (WN 644.4).

Intervention and privilege creates and empowers interest groups, but it also breeds a political culture of delusion and hubris:

> The statesman, who should attempt to direct private people in what manner they ought to employ their capitals, would not only load himself with a most unnecessary attention, but assume an authority which could safely be trusted, not only to no single person, but to no council or senate whatever, and which would nowhere be so dangerous as in the hands of a man who had folly and presumption enough to fancy himself fit to exercise it. (WN 456.10)

When social affairs are governmentalized, politics becomes central, and the players organize themselves into factions, as is plain in battles over the Export-Import Bank. The governmentalization of social affairs draws all players into factional politics, impelling each player to become a "party-man." This is a moral tragedy for society at large:

> A true party-man hates and despises candour; and, in reality,

there is no vice which could so effectually disqualify him for the trade of a party-man as that single virtue. The real, revered, and impartial spectator, therefore, is, upon no occasion, at a greater distance than amidst the violence and rage of contending parties. To them, it may be said, that such a spectator scarce exists any where in the universe. Even to the great Judge of the universe, they impute all their own prejudices, and often view that Divine Being as animated by all their own vindictive and implacable passions. Of all the corrupters of moral sentiments, therefore, faction and fanaticism have always been by far the greatest. (TMS 155–156.43)

Government privileges are inherently corrupting, for every member of society "has a principle of motion of its own, altogether different from that which the legislature might chuse to impress upon it" (TMS 234.17). "That bounties upon exportation have been abused to many fraudulent purposes, is very well known" (WN 517.25):

The bounties which are sometimes given upon the exportation of home produce and manufactures...have given occasion to many frauds, and to a species of smuggling more destructive of the publick revenue than any other. In order to obtain the bounty or drawback,[3] the goods, it is well known, are sometimes shipped and sent to sea; but soon afterwards clandestinely relanded in some other part of the country. The defalcation of the revenue of customs occasioned by bounties and drawbacks, of which a great part are obtained fraudulently, is very great. (WN 882.28)

Smith explained that certain kinds of fraudulence flatter foolish pride:

Heavy duties being imposed upon almost all goods imported, our merchant importers smuggle as much, and make entry of as

---

3. A drawback is repayment, in whole or only in part, of duties that the exporter had previously paid on inputs.

little as they can. Our merchant exporters, on the contrary, make entry of more than they export; sometimes out of vanity, and to pass for great dealers in goods which pay no duty; and sometimes to gain a bounty or a drawback. Our exports, in consequence of these different frauds, appear upon the customhouse books greatly to overbalance our imports; to the unspeakable comfort of those politicians who measure the national prosperity by what they call the balance of trade. (WN 883.29)

In 1778 Smith became a customs commissioner, enhancing his knowledge of the frauds and mischief, and leading to additions for the 1784 (third) edition of *The Wealth of Nations*. Among the additions were, as stated by Ian Simpson Ross, "analysis of the ill-advised attempt to promote the herring fishery through the bounty system" and "similar exposure of the bad effects of the corn bounty" (Ross 2010, 379). "It is difficult," Ross says, not "to see the message about the detrimental effect of most economic legislation intensified in the third edition" (ibid.). Amid the new material, Smith explained that bounties are not always paid according to amount produced: "the bounty to the white herring fishery is a tonnage bounty; and is proportioned to the burden of the ship, not to her diligence or success in the fishery; and it has, I am afraid, been too common for vessels to fit out for the sole purpose of catching, not the fish, but the bounty" (WN 520.32).

In his "Conclusion on the Mercantile System," Smith offers the following one-sentence paragraph: "It is unnecessary, I imagine, to observe, how contrary such regulations are to the boasted liberty of the subject, of which we affect to be so very jealous; but which, in this case, is so plainly sacrificed to the futile interests of our merchants and manufacturers" (WN 660.47).

Every intervention, such as an export bounty, Smith said, "introduces some degree of real disorder into the constitution of the state, which it will be difficult afterwards to cure without occasioning another disorder" (WN 472.44). "[I]n what manner the natural system of perfect liberty and justice ought gradually to be restored, we must leave to the wisdom of future statesmen and legislators to determine" (WN 606.44). Here Smith suggests a distinction between, on the one hand, enlightened political economy, "considered as a branch of the science of a statesman or legislator" (WN

428), which, in Smith's view, authorizes the maxims of the liberal plan, and, on the other hand, the art of enlightened politics, where the practicality and repercussions of a reform are often in doubt and one must take care not to make the best the enemy of the good. The art of judging particular reform tactics, Smith suggested, "does not, perhaps, belong so much to the science of a legislator, whose deliberations ought to be governed by general principles which are always the same, as to the skill of that insidious and crafty animal, vulgarly called a statesman or politician, whose councils are directed by the momentary fluctuation of affairs" (WN 468.39). Smith is not necessarily sneering at "that insidious and crafty animal," for he would, I believe, apply that appellation also to enlightened politicians, of which he knew many. Smith makes the distinction to clarify that his own discourse is concerned with the former realm of thought (the science of a legislator), not the latter (the art of enlightened politics). "Some general, and even systematical, idea of the perfection of policy and law, may no doubt be necessary for directing the views of the statesman. But to insist upon establishing, and upon establishing all at once, and in spite of all opposition, every thing which that idea may seem to require, must often be the highest degree of arrogance" (TMS 234.18).

However, in the discussion in *The Wealth of Nations*, Smith nonetheless proceeds to dip into the art of enlightened politics. He emphasizes (e.g., at 472.44) that since interventions create disorders that, thereafter, are very hard to correct or undo: do not fall into them in the first place! But, given that such disorders enmesh the statesman, Smith seems to suggest that the art of enlightened politics will, nonetheless, focus on quite radical liberalization (WN 468–472).

Moreover, on our subject of export subsidies, we have Smith's own private advice to an insidious and crafty animal of very great eminence,

William Eden.[4] In a letter dated 3 January 1780, amidst war with France and Spain and the American conflict, Smith advises Eden on "very obvious methods" by which Britain's fiscal situation can be improved "without laying any new burthen upon the people":

> The first is a repeal of all bounties upon exportation. These in Scotland and England together amount to about £300,000 a year; exclusive of the Bounty upon Corn which in some years has amounted to a sum equal to all the other bounties. It will probably amount to a very considerable sum this year. When we cannot find taxes to carry on a defensive war; our Merchants ought not to complain if we refuse to tax ourselves any longer in order to support a few feeble and languishing branches of their commerce. (Corr. 245)

Even in the realm of practical politics, Smith called for "repeal of all bounties upon exportation." Indeed, at the time of the letter Smith was a customs commissioner, and hence was himself a sort of statesman, an insidious and crafty animal.

Incidentally, in the letter to Eden, Smith says: "Prohibitions do not prevent the importation of the prohibited goods. They are bought everywhere, in the fair way of trade, by people who are not in the least aware that they are buying them." Smith then relates a personal discovery:

> About a week after I was made a Commissioner of the Customs, upon looking over the list of prohibited goods, (which is hung up in every Customhouse and which is well worth your considering)

---

4. Regarding Eden's political eminence, I quote from the biographical note provided by Ernest C. Mossner and Ian Simpson Ross, editors of Smith's correspondence: "William Eden (1744–1814), M.P. 1774–93; …Lord of Trade 1776–82; Commissioner for Conciliation with America 1778–9; Secretary to Lord Lieutenant of Ireland 1780–2; envoy to France on special commercial mission 1785–8; Ambassador to Spain 1788–9, and to the United Provinces 1789–93; President of the Board of Trade 1806–7; cr. Baron Auckland 1789. In France Eden negotiated a commercial treaty named after himself, whose provisions were based on the arguments advanced in WN IV.iii.c.12 that France would provide a better market than the American colonies. The chief beneficiaries, as Smith had predicted, proved to be British industry and the French vineyards" (Corr. 239 n.1).

and upon examining my own wearing apparel, I found, to my great astonishment, that I had scarce a stock, a cravat, a pair of ruffles, or a pocket handkerchief which was not prohibited to be worn or used in Great Britain. I wished to set an example and burnt them all. I will not advise you to examine either your own or Mrs. Edens apparel or household furniture, least you be brought into a scrape of the same kind. (Corr. 245–246)

Smith saw that effecting better policy required better politics, which required improvement in wisdom and virtue. All levels of the moral project find integration in his thought. "[W]hat civil policy can be so ruinous and destructive," he asked, "as the vices of men? The fatal effects of bad government arise from nothing, but that it does not sufficiently guard against the mischiefs which human wickedness gives occasion to" (TMS 187.1). Of such mischiefs, many of the most awful, Smith taught, find empowerment in departures from the liberal plan.

CHAPTER 13

The Divided Brain and Classical Liberalism

Foreword by Iain McGilchrist:

In a book called *The Master and His Emissary*, I described the way in which we each draw on two versions of the world, offered by the two hemispheres of the human brain. These "takes" on reality are apparently incompatible, yet each is necessary. In the left hemisphere's take, the world is like a map: populated by static, fixed, isolated, fragmentary, representational elements that can be manipulated easily, are decontextualized, abstracted, disembodied and mechanical. This world is useful for short-term purposes of manipulation, but is not a helpful guide to understanding the nature of the underlying reality. In the other (the right hemisphere version), as in the world that any map represents, things are almost infinitely more complex. All is flowing and changing, intrinsically uncertain, provisional, and complexly interconnected with everything else. Nothing is ever static, detached from our awareness of it, or disembodied; and everything needs to be understood in context, where, if it is not to be denatured, it must remain implicit. Here, wholes are different from the sum of the parts. This world is truer to what is, but is harder to express in language, and while less useful in the short term, is essential for a broader or longer-term understanding.

I never anticipated that the book's argument would be picked up by people in every walk of life—not just by psychologists, neurologists and philosophers, but by lawyers, economists, policy makers and business leaders. Yet if I am right, it should apply to *every* aspect of our lives. I am grateful to Dan Klein for so succinctly presenting my thesis as the ground of his discussion. While our political positions may differ, I believe his argument is

254 CENTRAL NOTIONS OF SMITHIAN LIBERALISM

well worth engaging with, and I hope it may offer a new light on the topic of classical liberalism.

Iain McGilchrist

Management is doing things right; leadership is doing the right things. (Covey 2004, 101)[1]

[V]ery little brain activity is in fact conscious (current estimates are certainly less than 5 per cent, and probably less than 1 per cent). (McGilchrist 2009, 187)

In 2018 I discovered the work of Iain McGilchrist, a British psychiatrist and literary scholar, a humane, charming, and brilliant man, and author of an important book: *The Master and His Emissary: The Divided Brain and the Making of the Western World* (2009). McGilchrist explains the divided brain—the division being between right and left hemispheres. Each hemisphere does different things. He cites a lot of science to back it up. I find him credible on the science.

When I discovered McGilchrist, it made sense to me. The distinction between the respective doings fit how I had thought about the brain's doings (Klein 2012, chs. 2, 7-10, and 271). But I didn't know to tag them "right" and "left." I take McGilchrist's word for it and hop on that train.

I offer a formulation, using a spiral. The spiral formulation is my way of explicating the divided brain. I hope people will comment on whether it's apt. I have had the good fortune to meet McGilchrist and try out the spiral formulation presented below. Although the conversation was brief, his reaction was kindly and favorable, and it heartened me to undertake the present essay.

McGilchrist suggests that our modern world drives us into left-hemisphere ruts, leaving our right hemisphere inert, losing contact with high-

---

1. Stephen R. Covey attributes the formulation to both Peter Drucker and Warren Bennis. Hat tip to Frederic Sautet.

er things, forsaking spiritual participation in higher things. Our doings lack upward vitality and come to feel empty and meaningless. McGilchrist speaks to policy and politics but mostly in vague terms. He warns against soulless bureaucracy, laments aspects of "capitalism" and "consumerism," and favors connectedness and tradition. I accept much of his treatment of modern society. I share McGilchrist's concern for right-hemisphere revitalization and upward vitality. But in my view McGilchrist's insights ought to move us to endorse classical liberalism, which maintains a presumption against the governmentalization of social affairs.

Left and right: Doing things right and doing the right thing

Suppose that during some weeks or months you've nursed a sense of inspiration, and now you feel resolved that some pursuit or goal or plan is worthy. So now you are decided.

To you it's a pretty big thing, so I use big letters and italics: *THING*.

As for your sense of its worthiness, maybe it flows from your immersion in a social problem, for example, youth gang violence, and you decide that doing *THING* would help. Or maybe it flows from a sense of what would actualize your own potential and sense of joy and fulfillment, maybe marriage or a career path. Your doing *THING* would make your life better. The two sources of worthiness are not so distinct and separate; both can be related to the betterment of the whole of humankind. You are part of that whole, so bettering your part betters the whole. Your efforts are usually more effective close to home, so you're justified in keeping the focus close to home.

Doing *THING* entails doing *things*. These are small in relation to *THING*, so I use small letters and again italics: *things*. But I introduce a subscript i to designate the relationship between the referent *THING* and the referent things: Thus, $things_i$ are the small things that constitute the steps or elements involved in effecting $THING_i$.

McGilchrist's 2009 book on the divided brain is titled *The Master and His Emissary*. The "master" is the right hemisphere that looks upward, that senses the vastness of the world, that comes to some understanding of its place in the larger cosmos, and resolves on $THING_i$. The master has an "emissary," an agent or executor—the left hemisphere—who does not decide the plan but sees to carrying it out.

The right hemisphere feels the world and decides $THING_i$. The left hemisphere ignores the larger world except to do $THING_i$ by tending to $things_i$. The right hemisphere looks up and arrives at $THING_i$. It then assigns to its "emissary," the left hemisphere, the business (busy-ness) of executing $THING_i$. The left hemisphere sees a $THING_i$-centered world and, from there, looks down to the business of $things_i$. The left hemisphere prides itself on its ability to manipulate $things_i$; the right hemisphere prides itself on its wisdom and worldliness.

The respective concerns are:

Right: Do the right $THING_i$.

Left: Do $things_i$ right.

That way of putting it fits the quotation at the head of this essay, a quotation I now adapt: "Management is doing $things_i$ right; leadership is doing the right $THING_i$." The left hemisphere is emissary/manager; the right hemisphere is master/leader.

The logic of our duality presupposes that the elements of $things_i$ are familiar and manipulable, at least as compared to $THING_i$. The left hemisphere has a set of best practices and accordingly applies treatments, rather mechanically. As for the right hemisphere, its way of arriving at $THING_i$ is less settled, less mechanistic.

To each corresponds certain sentiments. When the left hemisphere does $things_i$ right, the feeling is one of satisfaction or fulfillment. When it does not do $things_i$ right, the feeling is one of frustration and disappointment. The frustration may prompt an angry "God dammit!," as though joining with God in reprimanding a bungling subordinate. It is directed downward.

As for the right hemisphere, the positive feelings in doing $THING_i$ is, first, confidence and hopefulness, and retrospectively, affirmation. The negative feeling is, first, anguish or lack of confidence, and retrospectively, regret, remorse, or self-reproach. Looking upward, we sigh: "Oh Lord, what have I done?"[2]

TABLE 13.1: THE HEMISPHERES AND THEIR SENTIMENTS

	LEFT hemisphere: Sentiment in aiming to do *things*$_i$	RIGHT hemisphere: Sentiment in deciding on (or having decided on) *THING*$_i$
Positive	Satisfaction, fulfillment	In the moment: hopefulness, confidence
		Retrospectively: affirmation
Negative	Frustration, disappointment	In the moment: anguish
		Retrospectively: regret, self-reproach

The scheme informs other terminology. Kenneth Burke wrote: "If decisions were a choice between alternatives, *decisions* would come easy. Decision is the selection and formulation of alternatives" (Burke 1966, 215). We might associate decision with right hemisphere and *choice* with left. For problems, we might use error when there is a sense of regret over having decided on *THING*$_i$, and mistake for failure in executing *things*$_i$. The right hemisphere makes errors whereas the left makes mistakes.[3]

A spiral formulation of the divided brain

A friend greets Mary, "How's it going, Mary?" And Mary replies, "Not bad!"

Mary's sureness may reflect her good feeling about *THING*$_i$. But doing well is not a simple matter of *THING*$_i$. The essence of doing well is about something subtler. It is about *upward vitality*.

In the spiral figure below, we are looking into Mary's face, so her right hemisphere appears on the left, and left, right.

---

2. Such moment of regret or self-reproach may subsequently accede to sadness or melancholy in thinking back on the whole matter.

3. Such terminology does not always fit common usage, as when we speak of a baseball player making a fielding error, or when we speak of a typographical error. Still, I think there is merit to this distinction between error and mistake. It is elaborated in my book *Knowledge and Coordination* (Klein 2012, 101–106).

FIGURE 13.1: MARY'S RIGHT AND LEFT BRAIN

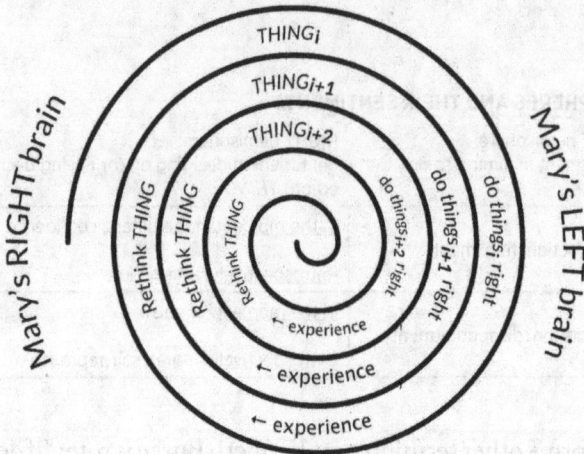

We pick up the story in loop i: Mary's right hemisphere comes to *THING$_i$*, which sets the left hemisphere to doing *things$_i$*. In doing *things$_i$*, Mary gains experience, perhaps fulfillment in the tasks; perhaps she becomes more adept in the elements of *things$_i$*. Perhaps she discovers ways to achieve *THING$_i$* more efficiently, to make tinkering improvements. Or, perhaps she experiences trouble, from mistakes or bad luck, generating frustration and disappointment.

Meanwhile, the right hemisphere, wondering at the heavens, also looks on at what's happening below, or receives reports. The sentiments of experience—whether satisfaction or frustration, whether affirmation or regret—inform and inspire the right hemisphere anew. The right hemisphere eventually rethinks *THING*, if only from the boredom that eventually sets in from standing pat with any particular *THING$_i$*. Moving forward, in the next loop, the right hemisphere decides *THING$_{i+1}$*, which sets the left about *things$_{i+1}$*.

It is now loop i+1. But there need be no major jump or discontinuity; the transition from loop i to loop i+1 might be more like a key change in a song. The new *THING$_{i+1}$* might be just a variant of *THING$_i$*. The concatenation *things$_{i+1}$* might closely resemble the concatenation *things$_i$*. There is a sense in which loop i+1 has nested within it the preceding loops, a wealth of experience.

Life is an experience of growth, a diachronic experience. Even if we find we must sometimes change course drastically or even double-back, we affirm a wholeness to the days of our life.

Looking at the spiral shown above, representing Mary, as we wind through the loops, our hope is that Mary is traveling *upward*. Imagine a third dimension, rising up from the page. The hope is that the spiral is winding upward in wisdom and virtue.

The joy of life consists, not in coming to some definite *THING* so right and good, but rather in a sense of upward vitality—that is, the upward movement found in deciding, doing, experiencing, learning, reinterpreting, and deciding anew. For example, Jordan Peterson exudes a sense of joy, giving him charisma. When I hear him speak, I sense his looking and reaching upward, not merely rehearsing some settled *THING*. He seems ever ready to reformulate his own formulations. Yet, even as he reformulates, there is usually a deeper cogency. We sense his upward vitality. To use Ralph Waldo Emerson's distinction, Peterson is *Man Thinking*, not mere thinking man.[4] That sense of upward vitality doesn't necessarily make Peterson a saint; there's a lot we don't know about his conduct in his world, and that's the way it is in the modern world (quite different from the ancestral band). But the sense of upward vitality is a good sign.

Spiral and upward vitality in McGilchrist's book

McGilchrist uses "spiral-like" to describe certain processes (145, 246) but does not use the word "spiral" extensively. Still, spiral clearly fits:

> [T]here is an important shape here which we will keep encountering: something that arises out of the world of the right hemisphere, is processed at the middle level by the left hemisphere and returns finally to the right hemisphere at the highest level. (126)

McGilchrist says that activities pass "from right hemisphere, to left

---

4. I borrow alluding to Emerson, who discusses Man Thinking in his 1837 address "The American Scholar," from Deirdre McCloskey, who also exemplifies it.

hemisphere, to the right hemisphere again," (178; Likewise 126, 131, 195, 203, 206, 207) "made truly new once again" (199). A simple circle lacks progression, but a spiral has distinct loops, each higher than its predecessor. The left hemisphere adds "enormously much" but "needs to return what it sees to the world that is grounded by the right hemisphere" in a process of analysis and reintegration (195):

> The values of clarity and fixity are added by the processing of the left hemisphere, which is what makes it possible for us to control, manipulate or use the world. For this, attention is directed and focussed; the wholeness is broken into parts; the implicit is unpacked; language becomes the instrument of serial analysis; things are categorised and become familiar. (195)

> There needs to be a process of reintegration, whereby we return to the experiential world again. The parts, once seen, are subsumed again in the whole, as the musician's painful, conscious, fragmentation of the piece in practice is lost once again in the (now improved) performance. The part that has been under the spotlight is seen as part of a broader picture; what had to be conscious for a while becomes unconscious again. (195)

> There is, in summary, then, a force for individuation (left hemisphere) and a force for coherence (right hemisphere)... [T]he 'givens' of the left hemisphere need to be once again 'given up' to be reunited through the operations of the right hemisphere. (203)

McGilchrist also expounds what I have termed *upward vitality*. He enlists from German *Aufhebung*: "The word...literally means a 'lifting up' of something" (203). He speaks of a "higher level" and "mounting the vertical axis," (204, 208) and explains the difference between the hemispheres in their orientations towards high and low: "The right hemisphere sees the lower values as deriving their power from the higher ones which they serve; the left hemisphere is reductionist, and accounts for higher values by reference to lower values" (160). In my terminology: The right hemisphere understands *things$_i$* as serving *THING$_i$*, whereas the left sees *THING$_i$* as nothing but *things$_i$*; perhaps it scarcely sees *THING$_i$* at all.

Friedrich Hayek warned against reductionism, the spurning of "metaphorical words" for understanding society; such spurning is a reductionist error in which "we deny the existence of what these terms are intended to describe," says Hayek ([1933], 29; see also 1955, 81-82). It is the right hemisphere that rediscovers the ghost in the machine, and the narrative in a sequence of events (191, see also 59). As McGilchrist says: "Metaphor (subserved by the right hemisphere) comes *before* denotation (subserved by the left)" (118).

McGilchrist writes of the left hemisphere extending its reach to grasp some particular thing and to make use of it, while the right hemisphere simply reaches out, without definite purpose (127). This reaching out is reaching *up*. The right reaches out for—longs for—something larger, a longer (hence higher) *THING*, and to belong (171-2, 308, 367, 390), to commune with the sublime. As McGilchrist says, "the sublime expands and extends, not dwarfs, the being of the beholder" (363).

Sympathy and moral experience are right hemisphere

The upward, integrative urge of the right hemisphere is an urge that is fundamentally social. Much like Adam Smith in *The Theory of Moral Sentiments*, and like Matthew D. Lieberman in his book *Social: Why Our Brains Are Wired to Connect* (2013), McGilchrist sees meaning, sociality, morality, and sympathy as a unified sphere, and the province chiefly of the right hemisphere (66, 86). Also, our sense of justice, as well as fresh understandings of metaphor and humor, spring from here (86; on metaphor see 115, 118; on humor see 59).

"Because of the right hemisphere's openness to the interconnectedness of things, it is interested in others as individuals" (57). Sympathy, or inhabiting the body of one like itself, is its way of understanding. "The right hemisphere is the locus of interpretation, not only of facial expression, but of prosody (vocal intonation) and gesture" (59). McGilchrist quotes Maurice Merleau-Ponty: "it is as if the other person's intentions inhabited my body and mine his" (148). If a being does not regard another as a being like itself, it does not relate; it is adrift. McGilchrist elaborates:

> When we put ourselves in others' shoes, we are using the right
> inferior parietal lobe, and the right lateral prefrontal cortex,
> which is involved in inhibiting the automatic tendency to espouse
> one's own point of view. In circumstances of right-hemisphere
> activation, subjects are more favourably disposed towards others
> and more readily convinced by arguments in favour of positions
> that they have not previously supported. (159)[5]

It is the right that experiences inspiration, God's breath (spirit) inside
us, and that propels us toward exemplars (329, 433), whom we emulate:
"we become who we are by imitating the models of people we admire or
respect" (121).

All this is quite different from the left hemisphere: "It is the left hemisphere alone that codes for non-living things"; "the left hemisphere is
unconcerned about others and their feelings" (55, 58).

Elusive ontology

The ontology of Mary is the nature of the being we call Mary. The reader
might ask: OK, so what about that ontology? What exactly *is* Mary?

McGilchrist dubs the right hemisphere "the master." He says the left
hemisphere is "parasitic" on the right (200). The reader might figure that
Mary's being is constituted by, or coextensive with, the right hemisphere's
activity, while the left is simply a part of the body, like the kidney.

But I don't think that's correct. First of all, McGilchrist says: "I do think
a hemisphere can have a will"—something I don't think he'd say about the
kidney. Maybe the right hemisphere is the "boss," but that boss is not the
totality within which such bossing occurs. Maybe Mary's ontology is more
like the whole organization, not just its boss.

Also, the word "hemisphere" can be misleading. In global geography,

---

5. Incidentally, McGilchrist touches on an important linkage between Adam Smith and Isaac Newton: "[T]his attractive power (in the literal sense of the word) is as mysterious and fundamental as the
attractive power of gravity in the physical universe" (159).

the hemispheres north and south make the whole. But in the brain the hemispheres right and left are not all. In between is the corpus callosum, which filters or inhibits connectivity between the two hemispheres, and presumably is not merely another "emissary" of the right hemisphere (on the corpus callosum: 198, 210-13). So the ontological Mary would subsume not only the "boss" (right hemisphere) but also other agents who inhibit the putative boss.

And "hemisphere" is again misleading, in that right and left are united in the body: "everything below the corpus callosum—the diencephalon, the cerebellum, the brainstem, the spinal cord, and all the rest—and all that the body communicates to them second by second, they continue to share" (211). Certain "umpire decisions" may come from "as far down as the brainstem" (216). The system seems to be somewhat Madisonian: Other wills check the "leader" (the right hemisphere).

And the hemisphere itself can be unpacked. McGilchrist suggests that the cortex of each hemisphere prevents inappropriate responses, and thus "exerts its influence more as 'free won't' than 'free will'" (198). "This negation is...hugely creative" (198).

"More than one will...does not mean more than one consciousness: so with one consciousness we can have more than one will, expressive of more than one aim" (225). Each of these wills, at any given moment, might be taken to be "Mary," just as a spokesperson can be taken to be the organization. But then there is Mary *the soul*, subsuming those wills, and that Mary, ontologically speaking, is elusive. McGilchrist writes:

> Just as an individual object is neither just a bundle of perceptual properties 'in here,' nor just something underlying them 'out there,' so the self is neither just a bundle of mental states or faculties, nor, on the other hand, something distinct underlying them. *(137)*

The ontological Mary, in reference to the spiral, is neither the right hemisphere, nor simply the spiral, nor some distinct thing hovering above the spiral. Rather, she is the spiral *and* something beyond.

The soul is elusive. I think of Adam Smith's "impartial spectator," always elusive upward: Perhaps we meet a spectator and feel sure that he applies a set of rules impartially. But is the set of rules itself impartial? Do we ever meet a spectator who is impartial *all the way up*? Likewise, do we ever have a complete and final conception of Mary's ontology? I think the answer is no.

Sometimes we have to content ourselves with knowing what Mary is *not*, as opposed to knowing what she is. Such knowledge, McGilchrist notes, is *apophatic* knowledge—of the soul, of the impartial spectator, of God—knowledge of what something is not, as opposed to knowledge of what it is (197).

The upshot is this: The terms "master," "leader," and "boss" are apt for the right hemisphere only as regards its relationship with the left hemisphere. And as we know, putative leaders and bosses can be inhibited by their subordinates, even enfeebled, maybe even usurped.

My 12,000-year narrative

Our genes have changed somewhat in the past 12,000 years—more lactose tolerance, more smarts—but basically we are still Upper Paleolithic. Imagine yourself in the ancestral band of 10,000 BC. Imagine how the right hemisphere was immersed in a definite, manifest social whole: the band of 50 people. The engulfing presence and vivid perception of that larger whole —the band's well-being—must have invigorated the right hemisphere, *vis-a-vis* the left. Every day it gripped the situation. Immediate encompassing experience made palpable the daily changes that required the band to stop attending to yesterday's "Doing *things* right" and rather to rethink THING, so as to "Do the right *THING*."

"Invention is kept alive"—said Adam Smith of simple "barbarous societies, as they are called"—"and the mind is not suffered to fall into that drowsy stupidity, which, in a civilized society, seems to benumb the understanding of almost all the inferior ranks of people. ... [Every man] is a warrior. Every man too is in some measure a statesman, and can form a tolerable judgment concerning the interest of the society, and the conduct of those who govern it" (WN 783).

In the ancestral band, experience continually prompted the rethinking of *THING*, and the conclusions of today's rethinking was visible to all, and validated in group action. Those better at "Doing the right *THING*" were more likely to survive and reproduce.

Then came agriculture. With settlement and traditional society, kings and clerics led and tended the higher things, and worked to sustain an engulfing, encompassing interpretation of the whole as understood by their people.

But in the 1400s came the printing press, and interpretation was busted wide open, followed by print culture and "the public," "the people," the nation-state. Commerce expanded, natural jurisprudence provided an operating system of lower things, and liberalism sprouted and delivered both guns and butter, and ever greater complexity. After more twists and turns, we come to today.

But meanwhile our genes haven't changed much since 10,000 BC, and *the right hemisphere has lost grip on any definite interpretation of the well-being of the larger whole*. It doesn't know what to *look up* toward. Each has his favored interpretations about the well-being of the larger whole and how to advance it, but those are broad and general, and there is little to be done in the way of *rethinking* them. The right hemisphere goes to sleep, or goes feeble from inactivation. Meanwhile the left hemisphere persists in *looking down* into the world it knows; it churns on with doing *things* right within that world. We become millionaires, celebrities, prize winners, vitae Vikings, feeble nonetheless in rethinking *THING*.

McGilchrist (2009) does not say anything about the ancestral band or the genes it bequeathed to us. What he does say, however, accords with my narrative. He suggests that from the year 1700 the right hemisphere has been losing its grip, leaving the left hemisphere to run amok. But before getting to socio-historical narrative, let's consider the tendencies of the left hemisphere.

The peril of usurpation by the left hemisphere

"I suppose it is tempting, if the only tool you have is a hammer, to treat everything as if it were a nail" (Maslow 1966, 15). Those words come from Abraham Maslow and the principle is known as the law of the instrument.

Here, *hammer* is a metaphor for one's system of instruments developed and wielded by the left hemisphere: "the left hemisphere has most syntax and most of the lexicon, which makes it very much the controller of the 'word' in general" (229). McGilchrist invites us to see people hammering away with their preferred systems. Commenting on McGilchrist, Brent Orrell sees as an example the push for ever more STEM education, even though what employers now say is chiefly lacking is "soft-skill" social competence—*character* (Orrell 2019).

Adam Smith noted that a man's dexterity improves the more he wields an instrument, and that a man "saunters a little in turning his hand from one sort of employment to another" (WN 17-18, 19). McGilchrist says that the left hemisphere exhibits "stickiness": "it only discovers more of what it already knows, and it only does more of what it is already doing" (86). With improved dexterity may come rewards, even pride and honor. The left hemisphere "builds systems," "piece by piece, brick on brick" (228).

The right hemisphere does not. Rather, it strives to rethink *THING*, to bring us to "an 'aha!' moment," and hopes to guide or influence the left hemisphere (228). But "it is hard for the right hemisphere to be heard at all: What it knows is too complex, hasn't the advantage of having been carved up into pieces that can be neatly strung together, and it hasn't got a voice anyway" (229).

The two hemispheres work on each other; the process pushes onward in the spiral. But the accumulation of experience grows so complex. We forget the discoveries and decisions that guided the steps on the path behind us, the reasons why. The world of things manipulated by the left hemisphere is a world that bears the legacy of the right hemisphere's active participation: It is world deep within the spiral.

Still, that world can become ossified, the legacy neglected, vitality lost. The right hemisphere may find it increasingly difficult to rethink the big picture and grows more passive or perhaps dreams in a subconscious realm. Activeness is increasingly that of the left hemisphere, busy within the grooves. As it presses on with its systems, they become its world. "[I]n the absence of such concerted action, the left hemisphere comes to believe its territory actually *is* the world" (219). The person may show great activity, but less inspiration, less upward vitality.

Such a person's left hemisphere "may come to think of itself as all in all," leading the person to grow dismissive of the larger searching of the right hemisphere (233). We come to a point in which the "emissary" usurps the "master." Here, says McGilchrist, the left hemisphere is prone to *ignore* the right hemisphere, and it may even "see the right hemisphere's world as undoing its work, challenging its supremacy" (219).

The left hemisphere is reinforced by the world it makes

McGilchrist's theorizing involves social context and incentives. He suggests that the articulate left hemisphere builds up systems that tend to exalt left-hemisphere virtuosos. He writes: "[P]assing on what the right hemisphere knows requires the other party already to have an understanding of it, which can be awakened in them; if they have no such knowledge, they will be easily seduced into thinking that the left hemisphere's kind of knowledge is a substitute" (229).

McGilchrist suggests a vicious social cycle: "[I]f a culture starts to mimic aspects of right hemisphere deficit, those individuals who have underlying propensity to *over*-rely on the left hemisphere will be *less prompted to redress* it, and moreover will find it harder to do so. The tendency will therefore be enhanced" (404, italics added). The system then "attracts to positions of influence individuals who will help it ever further down the same path. And the increasing domination of life by both technology and bureaucracy helps to erode the more integrative modes of attention…, much as they erode the social and cultural structures that would have facilitated other ways of being, so that in this way they aid their own replication" (408).

One thinks of the film *The Matrix*: "Once the system is set up it operates like a hall of mirrors in which we are reflexively imprisoned," "the left hemisphere has effectively closed off the escape routes" (229, 388). McGilchrist speaks of "the difficulty of escape from a self-enclosed system" (229).

What about Yoda-like right-hemispheric sages, individuals who avoid the traps and maintain upward vitality toward the larger whole? Adam Smith said that in modern society there might be wise men whose understandings are exceptionally "acute and comprehensive." "Unless those few, however, happen to be placed in some very particular situations, their great abilities, though honourable to themselves, may contribute very little to the good government or happiness of their society" (WN 783).[6] McGilchrist helps us understand Smith: If the sage has a sense that is five steps ahead, he will have difficulty imparting his wisdom to others, especially if the first step requires their left hemispheres to reverse some habits, to disavow some beliefs, and to let go of the pride associated with such habits and beliefs.

The societal peril as seen by McGilchrist

McGilchrist speaks of "the hubristic movement that came to be known as the Enlightenment" (329). I am not comfortable with that generalization. But there is something to what McGilchrist says about developments after 1700: The ways and tendencies of the left hemisphere advanced and gained prestige—in science, in political theory, in jurisprudence, in public administration, in commerce and industry. Without question there is a tendency in those fields to cut and divide things into pieces, to make those precise, to define any relation between things as yet another thing, to focus on such things in practical life, and thereby to hazard losing genuine contact with the larger whole. Cautioning us against that very hazard is one of the themes that looms large, however, in Hume, Smith, and Burke. Were they not Enlightenment thinkers? They admonished against left-hemisphere frenzy.

But I broadly go along with McGilchrist's societal concerns, and much of his characterization of the problem. Intense specialization and complexification, "in an almost unbelievably short period of time," have left people adrift as regards larger meaning, even unhinged (387).

Some might mention secularization. If people grow irreligious they might discard not only God but also any thought pattern associated with God. But our ethical thinking, I believe, follows the thought patterns of benevolent monotheism, so in discarding God they might leave the right hemisphere quite adrift. I would call myself an amiable agnostic, but I believe that growing irreligiosity is a significant part of the story of the right

---

6. Indeed, Smith often suggests that wisdom and virtue are lonely and largely unheeded; see also WN 265-267.8-10, 651.24; TMS 62.2, 77.8, 155.43, 162–63.1, 192.11, 253.30–31, 285.31, 335–36.23.

hemisphere's enfeeblement.

As for ideological tenor, McGilchrist sometimes sounds left-wing:

- "Capitalism and consumerism, ways of conceiving human relationships based on little more than utility, greed, and competition, came to supplant those based on felt connection and cultural continuity" (390).

- "Since the rise of capitalism in the eighteenth century, when according to Patricia Spacks boredom as such began, an 'appetite for the new and the different, for fresh experience and novel excitements' has lain at the heart of successful bourgeois society, with its need above all to be getting and spending money" (400).

- "But it is the Industrial Revolution which enabled the left hemisphere to make its most audacious assault yet on the world of the right hemisphere... It goes without saying that this move is of the profoundest consequence for the story of this book, and underwrites the defining characteristics of the modern world" (386).

- "Anthony Giddens describes the characteristic disruption of space and time required by globalisation, itself the necessary consequence of industrial capitalism, which destroys the sense of belonging, and ultimately of individual identity" (390).

- McGilchrist describes "an unprecedented assault on the natural world, not just through exploitation, despoliation and pollution, but also more subtly, through excessive 'management' of one kind or another, coupled with an increase in the virtuality of life, both in the nature of work undertaken, and in the omnipresence in leisure time of television and the internet, which between them have created a largely unsubstantial replica of 'life' as processed by the left hemisphere" (387).

At other times, however, McGilchrist associates usurpation by the left hemisphere with bureaucratic despotism, writing:

- "The essential elements of bureaucracy, as described by Peter Berger and his colleagues..., show that they would thrive in a world dominated by the left hemisphere" (429).

- "What de Tocqueville presciently saw was that the lack of what I would see as right-hemisphere values incorporated in the fabric of society would lead in time to a process in which we became, despite ourselves, subject to bureaucracy and servitude to the State" (346).

- McGilchrist quotes Tocqueville on the tutelary state trying to keep citizens in "perpetual childhood," under "a network of small complicated rules" (346).

- "The concept of the individual depends on uniqueness; but according to the left hemisphere's take on reality, individuals are simply interchangeable ('equal') parts of a mechanistic system, a system it needs to control in the interests of efficiency" (431).

- In a society dominated by the left hemisphere, "we would come to discard tacit forms of knowing altogether. There would be a remarkable difficulty in understanding non-explicit meaning, and a downgrading of non-verbal, non-explicit communication. Concomitant with this would be a rise in explicitness, backed up by ever increasing legislation, de Tocqueville's 'network of small complicated rules'" (433).

- "Cultural history and tradition, and what can be learnt from the past, would be confidently dismissed in preparation for the systematic society of the future, put together by human will" (434).

- "Such a government would seek total control—it is an essential feature of the left hemisphere's take on the world that it can grasp it and control it...but individual liberty would be curtailed" (431).

- "What if Fascism and Stalinism were...expressions of the deep structure of the left hemisphere's world?" (392).
- "Socialism and capitalism are both essentially materialist, just different ways of approaching the lifeless world of matter and deciding how to share the spoils" (401).

Much in McGilchrist suggests classical liberalism. Maybe the best way for the government to keep the right hemisphere vibrant is for it to withdraw from social affairs.

Governmentalization reduces upward vitality

By and large, classical liberalism favors reduction in the governmentalization of social affairs.

By "governmentalization," I mean not only government restrictions on individual liberty, but government-sector institutions as big players, living on taxation and privileged positions—that is, government not only as liberty violator but as benefactor, permission-granter, employer, landlord, customer, creditor, educator, transporter, access-granter, grant-maker, prestige conferrer, agenda-setter, organizer, law enforcer, prison keeper, recordkeeper, librarian, museum curator, park ranger, and owner of myriad, massive properties and resources within the polity.

McGilchrist emphasizes the need for correction mechanisms, and he argues that the right hemisphere especially impels correction by tending to larger things—by rethinking *THING* while looking upward. The right hemisphere generates *negative feedback*, critical to correction. The left hemisphere resists interference. And a social system dominated by the left hemisphere generates positive feedback, and tends to persist in error. McGilchrist writes: "blindly, the left hemisphere pushes on, always along the same track. Evidence of failure does not mean that we are going in the wrong direction, only that we have not gone far enough in the direction we are already headed." He speaks of a "zombie" persistence, and "[d]enial, a tendency to conformism, a willingness to disregard the evidence, a habit of ducking responsibility, a blindness to mere experience in the face of overwhelming evidence" (235, for other passages on correction and negative feedback, see 231, 194, 244, 390, 426).

Government and politics are by no means devoid of correction mechanisms. But if we candidly compare correction mechanisms in government to those in private enterprise (preferably free enterprise, and enjoying no privileges against competition), the contrast is enormous. In free enterprise, support and participation depends on voluntary decision-making. Private owners feel the consequence of error and dissatisfaction. Communication flows relatively freely, because participants do not wield coercive power over one another. Whatever it is that participants care about —including social connectedness and meaning—will affect their decision as to whether to participate. All this is so different from government institutions, which lack robust owners, which subsist chiefly on tax dollars or privileges, and which often stonewall, prevaricate, and intimidate critics and opponents. Governments are not good at admitting their errors, nor at correcting them. As for "zombie" organizations, or denial in the face of overwhelming evidence, consider the public school system. Government ownership and production doesn't deliver the goods, and it doesn't conduce to upward vitality. The governmentalization of social affairs tends to degrade morals and culture.

Governments regiment and rigidify with controls such as occupational licensing, labor restrictions, and so-called consumer protection restrictions. They protect and privilege certain practices and institutions, when what is needed is more openness to evolving interpretations and practices, a love of the adventure of life, including the adventure of earning one's keep. Free enterprise would best encourage the right/left symbiosis and balance that McGilchrist says is lacking. In a free market, private enterprise has to stay alert, nimble, creative. Where people are allowed to innovate and compete, rigidness is death. In a free market, participants in an operation depend on each other and have to work together as a team; they have to cooperate. If our attitudes would only allow it, if we would only appreciate the presumptive justness of pursuing honest income, we would better enjoy private enterprise as a beautiful scene of social connectedness. And if government restrictions were relaxed, work sites could more deftly expand non-wage attributes of the job into social life itself, including child care, schooling, housing, fitness, social activity, transportation, and basic health care services. It is governmentalization that enforces the cutting up and separation of social activities that otherwise would naturally exist together. Indeed, it is governmentalization—regulation, the tax code—that has artificially separated "for-profit" and "not-for-profit" private enterprise, a separation that has molded how people perceive "the economy," "business," and "the market." The separation did not exist in America in the 1830s when Tocqueville wrote of the glory of laissez-faire associative action (2000, II, 111-119; see also I, 68, 95). Alan Macfarlane has written about that glory as a legacy especially of Britain (Macfarlane 2014, 152). As the spirit of Mufasa told Simba in *The Lion King*: *Remember who you are. Remember.* (Re-member.)

Tocqueville's "small complicated rules" are troublesome especially to small businesses lacking expertise in compliance. Big businesses develop regulatory affairs divisions, achieving economies of scale in compliance, and small business cannot compete. If left-hemisphere lunacy characterizes big businesses, one driver is the tangle of small complicated rules imposed by government. And many of the restrictions are not so small; rather, they can shape whole industries, which are then beholden to rulers in government. Governmentalized social affairs are politicized social affairs.

McGilchrist writes of knowledge being flattened down to information, as exists within a uni-interpretational system managed by the left hemisphere. Again, such systems impose themselves on the social world. But that happens especially by governmentalization, for example by formal curricula, regulations, licensing requirements, and certifications required for employment in big-player government operations (e.g., teaching certification). Here is a lengthy quotation from McGilchrist that seems to describe a governmentalized world:

> Knowledge that came through experience, and the practical acquisition of embodied skill, would become suspect, appearing either a threat or simply incomprehensible. It would be replaced by tokens or representations, formal systems to be evidenced by paper credentials. The concepts of skill and judgment, once considered the summit of human achievement, but which come only slowly and silently with the business of living, would be discarded in favour of quantifiable and repeatable processes. Expertise, which is

what actually makes an expert (Latin *expertus*, 'one who is experienced'), would be replaced by 'expert' knowledge that would have in fact to be based on theory, and in general one would expect a tendency increasingly to replace the concrete with the theoretical or abstract, which would come to seem more convincing. (429)

The bleak picture painted by McGilchrist makes sense for social affairs regimented by governmental controls and suffocated by the groupthink of government personnel. But absent governmentalization, it does not. When free initiative (commercial or otherwise) governs social affairs, the voluntary participants *abstain* if the concrete good is forsaken for abstract falsity. Funding, support, participation are withdrawn. Also, participants exercise voice. Abstention and voice are channels of negative feedback. Owners and managers are impelled to change course. And that is the beauty of liberty: decisive authority and residual claimancy inhere in private ownership and voluntary agreement, and *signals*—both pecuniary profit-and-loss and non-pecuniary moral sentiments—flow from freedom.

McGilchrist notes that social connectedness "predicts lower rates of colds, heart attacks, strokes, cancer, depression, and premature deaths of all sorts" (436). What sort of government policy best conduces to meaningful social connectedness? I would suggest degovernmentalization and "allowing every man to pursue his own interest his own way," to quote Smith's capsule description of "the liberal plan of equality, liberty, and justice" (WN 664). The liberal plan allows people, moved by their right hemispheres, to reach out, to gain experience and relational knowledge, to create, discover, invent.[7]

McGilchrist emphasizes creativity—what I term upward vitality—as the allowing of things to emerge. But not all things. Improper or unjust things must be inhibited or negated, for otherwise our consciousness dissolves centrifugally and drowns in a welter of incoherence. The negating of multifarious things gives focus to the objects that survive the process of negation, and those objects give us coherence, meaning, and membership.

---

7. McGilchrist offers nice etymological remarks on "invention" at 230, explaining that it originally connoted dis-covering, or un-covering something that had already had existence.

"This negation is therefore hugely creative" (198).

McGilchrist points out that very little brain activity is conscious: "current estimates are certainly less than 5 percent, and probably less than 1 percent" (187). What emerges into consciousness is described as *things that have not been inhibited*, as what has been allowed to ramify, and only then pass into left-hemisphere codification and manipulation: "we can only either permit life, or not permit it" (230).

Classical liberalism places faith in the inhibitors *within the free person*, making for a social system of emergence and selection—an invisible hand. McGilchrist speaks of the right hemisphere as "the master." Classical liberalism is liberal, in an ancient, pre-political sense. It allows the individual to learn to *master* himself, to govern himself, to gain mastery of himself. The individual does so by observing propriety in social life and cultivating the man within the breast—the conscience—which seems to operate chiefly in the right hemisphere. Propriety involves rules, allegiance to which is the sense of duty, forged and enforced through self-command. In all of this, too, operates an invisible hand.

But when the inhibiting is supervened by the government, the individual is demeaned and the spontaneous mechanisms of propriety formation, conscience formation, and self-command are usurped, stunted, and misdirected. McGilchrist provides a simile apt for governmentalization: "like a cat pushing a dead mouse about the floor in order to see it move" (230). Smith wrote of the "man of system" moving pieces, presumed lifeless, on the chessboard of human society. The cat kills the mouse to play its game, and the man of system kills the piece's "principle of motion of its own" to gratify his conceit (TMS 234.17).[8] Not that anything works perfectly or that governmentalization is all bad—liberty *does* presuppose stable, functional authority[9]—but in our stable polity, by and large, we do not need preemptive governmental inhibiting of would-be actualizations. This classical liberal faith is an affirmation of the dignity and responsibility of the individual when allowed to pursue his own interest his own way. Allow

---

8. Incidentally, I fully accept that Smith's man of system critique is also intended as a critique of libertarian men of system.

9. Erik Matson and I endorse David Hume on liberty and authority in chapter 3 of this volume.

sin, to harvest virtue. Learning-by-doing applies to governing oneself. And pursuing life in one's "own way" of course includes voluntarily deferring to proprieties and enlisting the guidance of parents, friends, mentors, doctors, instructors, middlemen, agents, and so on. Manifold voluntary relationships of relational inferiority are all part of one's own way.

Smith said that passive sentiments tend to be "so sordid and so self-ish," while our active principles are often "so generous and so noble" (TMS 137.4). Smith's reasoning is as follows: Action is inherently sympathetic, sympathy is inherently social, social contact arouses the man within the breast, who calls to us to be generous and noble. Thus, when passive, los-ing our pinky finger looms larger than an earthquake in China, but when active the earthquake looms larger. All this conforms to McGilchrist. The right hemisphere is empathetic, social, and upward-looking, and it impels generosity and nobleness. But all of this depends on the situation being active. Governmentalization tends toward the opposite: It throws us into a passive situation, into accepting the situation. You can't fight city hall, or the mammoth school district, or the privileged labor union, and you can't influence an election. Paul Simon's words and music in "Mrs. Robinson" painted the truth:

> *Sitting on a sofa*
> *On a Sunday afternoon,*
> *Going to the candidates' debate,*
> *Laugh about it,*
> *Shout about it,*
> *When you've got to choose,*
> *Every way you look at this you lose.*

Sitting on a sofa, we tend toward sentiments sordid and selfish. Laugh about it, shout about it, and do nothing. Maybe now we take to Twitter. McGilchrist says that in a world dominated by the left hemisphere we see "fragmentation and passivisation, a loss of the self's unity and capacity for action" (396), "an increasing passivisation and suggestibility." "In relation to culture, we would expect people to become increasingly passive" (432-33). Passive spells sordid and selfish. Governmentalization makes us sordid and selfish. Governmentalization strips us of activeness and thereby retards our generosity and nobleness. Every way you look at this, you lose.

Governmentalization is not only regimentation by rules and restrictions, it is also the groupthink of the personnel of the big players. The following quotation from Friedrich Hayek fits McGilchrist's portrayal of a world dominated by the left hemisphere:

> The organizations we have created in these fields [labor, agriculture, housing, education, etc.] have grown so complex that it takes more or less the whole of a person's time to master them. The institutional expert...is [frequently] the only one who understands [the institution's] organization fully and who therefore is indispensable... [A]lmost invariably, this new kind of expert has one distinguishing characteristic: he is unhesitatingly in favor of the institutions on which he is expert. This is so not merely because only one who approves of the aims of the institution will have the interest and the patience to master the details, but even more because such an effort would hardly be worth the while of anybody else: the views of anybody who is not prepared to accept the principles of the existing institutions are not likely to be taken seriously and will carry no weight in the discussions determining current policy... [A]s a result of this development, in more and more fields of policy nearly all the recognized 'experts' are, almost by definition, persons who are in favor of the principles underlying the policy... The politician who, in recommending some further development of current policies, claims that 'all the experts favor it,' is often perfectly honest, because only those who favor the development have become experts in this institutional sense, and the uncommitted economists or lawyers who oppose are not counted as experts. Once the apparatus is established, its future development will be shaped by what those who have chosen to serve it regard as its needs. (Hayek 1960, 291)

Hayek here dovetails with McGilchrist. If McGilchrist gives classical liberalism a profound chance, maybe he'll find something enduring and worthy. He writes: "We have no longer a consistent coherent tradition in the culture, which might have passed on, in embodied and intuitive form, the fruits of experience in our forebears, what used to form the communal wisdom" (437). If we search for "a consistent coherent tradition," it will have to be elastic enough to accommodate the tremendous variation and change of cultural currents that characterize modernity. There's no putting that toothpaste back in the tube. But if not classical liberalism, then what? Big-government social democracy? Our right hemispheres should be recognizing the alternatives that truly matter, and in comparing one to another, awakening ourselves to the "total effect" of each, as Ronald Coase put it (Coase 1960, 43-44).

McGilchrist's theorizing could be extended to academia today, with its self-validating, self-replicating monoculture and its so-called progressive research programs. "The left hemisphere builds systems, where the right does not. It therefore allows elaboration of its own workings over time into systematic thought which gives it permanence and solidity, and I believe these have even become instantiated in the external world around us, inevitably giving it a massive advantage" (228). The campus grounds and buildings sure are pleasing.

McGilchrist makes some remarks favorable to religiosity, specifically Christianity (441). Our right hemisphere naturally seeks for meaning by relating to a larger enduring Other—God. Domination by the left hemisphere does not necessarily extinguish that longing. It might simply redirect it toward its own objects of worship: "When we decide not to worship divinity, we do not stop worshiping: we merely find something less worthy to worship" (441). Along the lines of Tocqueville, I would suggest that many today have sacralized ideological objects in lieu of the idea of a universal benevolent beholder. False ideological gods are indulged, and those gods are inculcated, propagated, and enforced by the governmentalization of social affairs. A new mindset feeds on the instinctual yearning for centricity and manifest social cues, features that afford terminus to the terrifying spiral of validation and interpretation. The mindset has been assembled piece by piece, brick by brick. Governmentalization becomes totem, altar, scripture, and clergy. It is the new centripetal force, promising cohesion and meaning, to fill the void. But it is a great idol dressed and propped up by the left hemisphere. Fouling the nest with denial (85, see also 84, 235), hypocrisy (234), complaining,[10] boredom (336, 400), and victimhood (432), the left hemisphere feeds the right a phony wholeness. Cowed and cornered, the right hemisphere fails to rethink *THING* suitably to the modern world. It is trapped in *The Matrix*, or perhaps asleep. "False notions of religion are almost the only causes which can occasion any very gross perversion of our natural sentiments" (TMS 176.12).

Home from market

Classical liberalism would unleash entrepreneurship and innovation in the market. Tradition and settled community are under constant challenge, much as Karl Polanyi expounded (1944). But classical liberalism also empowers personal retreat from the market, as James Buchanan has pointed ed out (1993). If growing potatoes on a farm in West Virginia is your thing, more power to you. McGilchrist could have cited Adam Smith where he writes: "increases in material well-being have little or nothing to do with human happiness" (434). Joy and the love of life depend on both movement and tranquility. In freedom, we are more apt to find our balance.

Classical liberalism invites us to rediscover what makes a *THING* worthy. Upwards vitality does not have to mean constant bustle. It can mean family, community, church involvement and support. McGilchrist tells us that the movement of life is not so much a linear journey from A to B, but a dance that "always ultimately returns to its origins" (447).

What dance shall we dance? What dance *can* we dance? Classical liberalism empowers a long, slow, tranquil path upward, if that is the way upward. Maybe some souls are more inclined to everyday tranquility, oth-

---

10. McGilchrist does not highlight complaining, griping, and protesting as a left-hemisphere speciality, but if one considers the negative sentiments I offer in the table above, it makes sense that frustration and disappointment would generate such noise-making, whereas anguish, regret, and self-reproach do not. While McGilchrist associates sadness and melancholy with the right hemisphere (2009, 54, 85), regret and remorse are mentioned only in relation to literature, not brain research (233, 301, 367). I speculate that it is difficult to evoke regret and remorse in brain research because those are phase sentiments, emerging when one realizes one's erring in life and then acceding to sadness and melancholy. So even if researchers evoke one's past erring, the sentiment now is sadness or melancholy, and no longer regret, remorse, or self-reproach.

ers to bustle. Under liberal institutions we can get along. It is governmentalization that perpetuates tensions, leaves failures uncorrected, and arouses the sordid and selfish sentiments that Smith associated with the passive situation.

There's no denying, however, that classical liberalism does not serve all human values. We're not in the band anymore. Classical liberalism would deny us a strong sense of shared purpose, shared action, shared experience, shared sentiment, encompassing the polity—a polity-wide solidarity. Classical liberalism says: *THING* is your responsibility. But with classical liberalism, chances are good that we are raised up to a personhood that finds ample resources to enjoy that responsibility and carry it off in becoming fashion, resources consisting not least of the healthy sympathies that flow in a free society.

In the meantime, shower the right hemisphere with the work of Iain McGilchrist.

CHAPTER 14
Liberalism and Allegory

Yours for $1.89

"We must look at the price system," wrote Friedrich Hayek (1945, 86), "as...a mechanism for communicating information if we want to understand its real function." Hayek's talk of communication enriched economic thinking. Indeed, the expression "price signal" came only after Hayek's 1945 article, as can be confirmed at Google's Ngram Viewer.

The talk of "price signals" and market communication is common among market-oriented economists. In their textbook, Tyler Cowen and Alex Tabarrok write: "[P]rice signals and the accompanying profits and losses tell entrepreneurs what areas of the economy consumers want expanded and what areas they want contracted" (85). Such talk is both illuminating and beautiful.

But the price of eggs communicates: "Yours for $1.89"—*And nothing more!*

If we are to be literal, we must mind the element of communion, or community, in communication. In its literal sense, communication is *a meeting of minds*. The knowledge communicated passes through us as commonly experienced ideas, images, or notions.

For the entrepreneur computing her profit or loss, there really is no communication in the literal sense, no meeting of minds—Whose mind would she meet? In no literal sense do prices and other market phenomena tell entrepreneurs what to do. We want to talk of prices as "signals," but they are not signals in a literal sense.

The prudent shipmaster and the invisible hand

Adam Smith illuminated the marvels of markets by using simile and metaphor. He sketches an aspect of social coordination: "It is the interest of the people that their daily, weekly, and monthly consumption should be proportioned as exactly as possible to the supply of the season." The grain dealer adjusts his prices and quantities in ways that conduce to such coordination:

> Without intending the interest of the people, he is necessarily led, by a regard to his own interest, to treat them, even in years of scarcity, *pretty much in the same manner as the prudent master of a vessel is sometimes obliged to treat his crew.* When he foresees that provisions are likely to run short, he puts them upon short allowance. Though from excess of caution he should sometimes do this without any real necessity, yet all the inconveniences which his crew can thereby suffer are inconsiderable in comparison of the danger, misery, and ruin to which they might sometimes be exposed by a less provident conduct. (WN 525, italics added)

The simile of the prudent shipmaster—which may have been inspired by a passage in Hume *History* (II, 177)—is a miniature of the metaphor of the being whose hand is invisible:

> [The individual] generally, indeed, neither intends to promote the public interest, nor knows how much he is promoting it. ... [A]nd by directing that industry in such a manner as its produce may be of the greatest value, he intends only his own gain, and he is in this, as in many other cases, *led by an invisible hand* to promote an end which was no part of his intention. (WN 456, italics added)

Sometimes a metaphor uses an animal or a spirit to represent human existence, or as a foil to human existence. Charles John Smith (1871, 319) writes that *allegory* "differs both from fable and parable, in that the properties of persons are fictitiously represented as attached to things, to which they are as it were transferred."

Allegories of Joy

Figures such as metaphors and allegories involve a target, to be illuminated, and a figure, that illuminates. For economic allegory, the target is the economy, while the allegory is, for example, the figure whose hand is invisible, that sends signals, and so on. An example of a figure is Smith's prudent shipmaster; the target is the grain market in the real economy. Smith's shipmaster story illuminates the grain market.

After Smith's time, thinkers denounced allegory. They fell into touting fact and logic, accuracy and precision. It was the occasional figure who made open use of allegory, such as Edwin Cannan—an ardent Smithian and editor of *The Wealth of Nations*. He wrote:

> The reasons why it pays to do the right thing—to do nearly what
> *an omniscient and omnipotent benevolent Inca would order to be done*
> —are to be looked for in the laws of value. (Cannan 1902, 461;
> italics added)

The free-enterprise system, Cannan suggests, leads to patterns of activities somewhat like those pleasing to a benevolent being in an allegory. An Inca who orders affairs is the figure, offered by Cannan to illuminate the target, which Cannan calls "the laws of value."

The allegory is that a super being—let's call her Joy—has super knowledge, encompassing what Knud Haakonssen (1981, 79) distinguishes as system knowledge and contextual knowledge. Joy has system knowledge and contextual knowledge for every individual. The allegory is that Joy issues instructions, or requests, cooperatively, to each market participant spelling out "the right thing" to be done. Joy is benevolent toward all those she surveys.

In the allegory, Joy tells Bridget the baker that perhaps she should buy new ovens, look out for better deals in flour, and advertise her confections. In the allegory, Joy communicates these instructions. In the allegory there is a meeting of Joy's and Bridget's minds regarding these actions. In the allegory, Bridget is sensible to Joy's benevolence and ethical wisdom, and feels entrusted to advance what Joy finds beautiful. Bridget follows, not market signals, but Joy's communications, which are embraced *voluntarily* by Bridget from what Smith would call her sense of duty—she "enters, if I may say so, into the sentiments of that divine Being" (Smith, TMS 276). *In the allegory*, those communications tell Bridget to take actions rather like those that she is led to take in the actual world, from market signals. Cannan suggests that the market conduces to socially beneficial actions much as a benevolent system of superior knowledge, communication, and cooperation would.

Liberal allegorizing for the economy with and without philosophical agents

In authoring an economic allegory of Joy, we do not necessarily assume that the target is populated by philosophical agents who hear the allegory or think along the lines of the allegory. It might be only we philosophers who ever hear anything of the allegory. The agents in the target may be quite non-philosophical. Even if the agents in the actual economy are rather random as in Armen Alchian's buckshot metaphor (1950), who, like one of the pellets of the shotgun cartridge, happens to hit an opportunity and gets adopted by the environment, the Joy allegorizing works: The point is that we *analysts or philosophers* see a similitude between the actual economy and the allegory. There is merit in allegorizing even if agents in the economy know nothing of the allegory.

Now, let's suppose instead that agents in the economy are philosophical. It is really here that the Joy figure graduates from metaphor to allegory, because now agents in the economy, imagining a Joy, find a sort of connection with Joy and through Joy. In this case of philosophical agents, those agents continue, in their economic life, to respond to prices, profit and loss, and so on. And let's say, further, that they do so in just the same way as they would if they were not philosophical agents, in terms of how many loaves of bread they bake or how much tin they buy. However, they can now make sense of their own activity in a new light, which may indeed bring them more satisfaction and joy (Joy!) in their life and work.

The Joy figure is useful then, both in helping we philosophers realize the desirability of freedom and in making people within the economy find more meaning and peace and joy in life and work. It helps us persuade people to favor freedom, and, irrespective of what we wind up being stuck with in terms of government policy, it makes life in that society better.

Insights gained by allegory

How does allegorizing help us persuade people to favor freedom?

The allegorical talk of communication equips us to formulate questions about rules and institutions, questions that prove fruitful:

1. What arrangements generate the "signals" that best "communicate" what to do? Such talk gets us to focus on what the relevant signals are. It gets us to focus on how well they conduce to the general interest. It helps us appreciate how "communications" adjust when practices go wrong.

2. If the signals start "telling" people to go in the wrong direction, will the system correct itself? Will it tend to correct errors? Indeed, it is allegory that gives cogency to the idea of "market error" or "social error."

3. Will the system tend to keep up with changes? How readily and reliably will it "communicate" instructions to adjust to changes?

4. Will it dig up new opportunity, new matters for "communication"? What are the system's tendencies to discover and adopt new opportunities for advancing the good of the whole?

5. How do the "communicative" properties of the system fare when the system is laden with governmental restrictions and government-privileged big players?

6. What "signals" operate in politics and government? Are they more reliable than those of voluntary affairs, such as private markets? Are they less reliable?

The allegory of Joy communicating instructions enables one to reason in reference to the perspective of one who has superior knowledge and purposes that we go along with—even while we emphasize that we mere mortals do not have such knowledge. We discuss what Joy feels about what she sees, but do not pretend to see what she sees.

Moreover, we do not pretend to feel what she feels. She feels universal benevolence. We cannot and do not. Shedding the faux benevolence does not mean callousness; it means accepting our true station.

One's pursuit of wisdom and virtue is not so much the aspiration to become like Joy as it is to become more like those who, it seems, excel in advancing what she finds beautiful. Emulating such exemplars, learning to feel as *they* feel, we do our duty to advance universal benevolence.

The private enterprise system as a system of cooperation

Many have suggested that the economy was a system of cooperation, including Jeremy Bentham, Thomas Hodgskin (1827, 25), Richard Whately (1832, 98, 99), Frederic Bastiat, William Graham Sumner, Henry George, and Philip Wicksteed. We find such talk in Milton and Rose Friedman's *Free to Choose*. To bring the tradition down to today, let's turn again to Cowen and Tabarrok: "To bring just one product to your table requires the cooperative effort of millions. Moreover, *this immense cooperation* is voluntary and undirected."

But Karl Marx emphasized that the system, in its immensity, was not cooperation—and condemned it for that: "[A]ll labour in which many individuals cooperate necessarily requires a commanding will to coordinate and unify the process…much as that of an orchestra conductor" (Marx 1998, 382). We dispute that genuine cooperation depends on a "commanding" will: When you and I cooperate in making lunch, we scarcely need regard anyone's will as "commanding." But cooperation does entail some sense of direction of a common enterprise, to which we mutually contribute.

Hayek would seem to concur: "Cooperation, like solidarity, presupposes a large measure of agreement on ends as well as on methods employed in their pursuit. It makes sense in a small group whose members share particular habits, knowledge and beliefs about possibilities" (1988, 19).

It is true that the economy in all its immensity entails myriad *instanc-*

es of cooperation, but it also entails myriad instances of non-cooperation. It entails myriad instances of abstention, of deciding *not to cooperate* with certain parties. It entails myriad instances of competition and rivalry. It entails myriad instances of rather impersonal exchange that, as cooperative moments, are tiny and often ambivalent. It entails myriad instances of ethically ambiguous moments of *not sharing* intelligence. It entails many instances of deception and misrepresentation. It entails a lot of things, not just instances of cooperation.

Above and beyond that, here is the key point: The immensity can scarcely be said to constitute a common enterprise that the actors share a mutual sense of. Unlike genuine cooperation, the actors do not have any mutual sense of mutually advancing some shared goal or enterprise.

Face it: In a literal sense, it is wrong to say that you have cooperated with the myriad people who contributed to the production of the pencil or the woolen coat.

But does that mean we should surrender the useful and agreeable talk of communication and cooperation?

No, we should embrace the useful and agreeable talk. But we should recognize that it is not literal. It is allegorical.

We can affirm the cooperation talk: *In an allegory*, individuals communicate with Joy and voluntarily follow her guidance, to produce a pleasing concatenation of activities. In the allegory, Joy is like a quarterback with whom everyone communicates. And *in the allegory* the members of society have common knowledge that each communes with Joy and so there is a mutual sense of advancing the coordination of a vast concatenation of their actions, just as the members of a football squad have common knowledge that each communicates with the quarterback and there is a mutual sense of advancing the coordination of a concatenation of their actions. *In the allegory*, there is leadership. *In the allegory*, there is an immense cooperation.

Then, when we turn to the real-life system and we say that the immense system is "a system of cooperation," we mean—and understand that we mean—that it functions *somewhat like our imagined allegorical system of cooperation* functions.

The tragedy of allegophobia

Adam Smith's *The Theory of Moral Sentiments* is a profoundly allegorical work, involving such formulations as "the man within the breast," "the impartial spectator," "the wisdom of nature," and "universal benevolence." The moral and political judgments of TMS were openly aesthetic and lacking in theoretical foundations.

Smith died in 1790, and things went downhill, or even dropped off a cliff. TMS was steadily criticized. The critics recognized that TMS lacks foundations. The critics said: Science, real knowledge, calls for foundations, not allegory; it calls for precision and accuracy, not aesthetic judgment. Not long after Smith's death the work fell into oblivion, and reemerged only beginning around 1980, once enough people had stopped holding its non-foundationalism against it.

During that long oblivion, liberalism was led principally by allego-phobes. Like any phobia, allegophobia is deficient in self-awareness and self-understanding. While touting foundations and a grammar-like scientific status, liberals in fact wanted poetry, too. Not only were they poets who didn't know it, they were poets who *denied it*. The contrarieties made their so-called science vulnerable, even ridiculous, and liberalism faltered terribly. From about 1885 onwards, liberalism collapsed among the young and rising generations.

I shall refrain from cataloging criticisms of TMS (35 critics are presented are in Klein 2021). But I share some samples of the continuing willy-nilly urge to poetry and allegory.

Consider the man who called natural rights "nonsense upon stilts," Jeremy Bentham: "The work of Adam Smith is a treatise upon *universal benevolence*...that nations are associates and not rivals in *the grand social enterprise*" (1843). But "universal benevolence" is itself allegorical, as it refers to pleasing the benevolent beholder of the immense whole. The immense whole is a "grand social enterprise" allegorically speaking only.

Frédéric Bastiat exemplified the tendency to depict the free market system as a system of harmony and cooperation. In *Economic Harmonies*, he used "co-operation" recklessly, and celebrated the immense market system as "a marvelous association" (1850, 68). Another free-trade champion, Henry George, said that under liberty "competition...becomes the most simple, most extensive, most elastic, and most refined system of co-operation" (1886, 307). Philip Wicksteed spoke of "a vast system of co-operation" and "one huge mutual benefit society" (1910, 183). H.C. Macpherson wrote that Smith's division of labor unconsciously transforms "the selfish solitary worker into a member of a huge co-operative organization" (1899, 69). Milton and Rose Friedman take similar poetic license: "Cooperation is worldwide, just as in the economic system" (1980:17).

Science anxieties

William Graham Sumner exhibits certain science anxieties that developed especially from the early nineteenth century and have beset us ever since: "Science is investigation of facts by sound methods, and deduction of inferences by sound processes…[O]f the highest importance is the subjection of societal phenomena to scientific investigation, together with the elimination of metaphysics from this entire domain" (1913, 75). Also marked for elimination was "sentimentalism," which Sumner defines as believing that which one finds agreeable and denying facts that happen to be disagreeable (1914, 31). During the long oblivion of Adam Smith book on moral *sentiments*, sentiment came to connote "sentimental"—surely contrary to science!

And yet, Sumner expounds on how one's dinner comes from "thousands…all over the globe…All these thousands and millions of people, therefore, have co-operated with each other for the common good of all" (1913, 284). Somehow Sumner's "investigation of facts by sound methods" told him that millions have cooperated for the common good.

In work coauthored with Albert G. Keller, Sumner writes:

> There is every justification and call for studies of society which shall be purely scientific; coldly scientific; so austerely unmindful of contemporary 'problems' as deliberately to seek distance and detachment from them. Under some Darwin of the future, such studies can result in the apprehension of societal laws; then the [human] race can make a farsighted and accurately planned campaign against the problems…(Sumner and Keller 1927, 2247)

Here, Sumner and Keller are wrongheaded, and their wrongheadedness stems from science anxieties. The "purely scientific" "societal laws" in fact emerge fully within a moral universe of social problems and lived interpretations, interpretations that depend on allegories, if only tacitly. Just three pages hence Sumner and Keller write: "The presence of pepper on a New England table unites its user in the coöperative relation with some Malay whom he will never see, as well as with the long chain of men who handle the product...This concept of the solidarity of mankind is part of the insight derivable from even a slight knowledge of the facts" (2250). Sumner and Keller see the New Englander and the Malay in a cooperative relationship—a truth dependent on allegory! Sumner and Keller are poets but don't even know it. Their science paints a picture of "the solidarity of mankind."

Like Hayek, I see cooperation as entailing a mutual consciousness among the cooperators. Yet some economists tried to expound a cooperation *without* such feature. Edward Gibbon Wakefield distinguished between "simple co-operation," as among workers in a factory or members of a sports team, and "complex co-operation," a system of spontaneous concatenate coordination.[1] John Stuart Mill (1871, 118f) followed and elaborated Wakefield's distinction. Max Hirsch (1901, 278, 282–283) made a parallel distinction: *conscious* and *unconscious* cooperation.

Unconscious cooperation? Sounds like unconscious square-dancing, or unconscious pass completion in American football.

Or unconscious communication. If a loved one complains that you're not listening, explain that you *are*, just not consciously. —And duck!

If classical liberals wish to praise the free enterprise system as a system of cooperation, they had better be prepared to explain how two people who have no mutual consciousness, who know nothing of each other, can be said to be cooperating.

1. Wakefield is quoted at length by Mill (1871/1909: 116–118). The citation given is "Wakefield's edition of Adam Smith, vol. I, 26." Wakefield's distinction also appears in Scott (1900: 237).

Sages of allegory

Smith well knew that the immense system is one of cooperation allegorically only. Smith is self-consciously figurative when he invokes the metaphor of the prudent shipmaster. He is equally conscious that his invocation of "an invisible hand" is metaphorical or theological.

After expounding on the far-flung efforts that make the woolen coat, Smith notes that we are then sensible of our dependence on "the assistance and co-operation of many thousands" (23). But he then says that one's "whole life is scarce sufficient to gain the friendship of a few persons" (26). In a shift of mood, he says that, instead, we rely on *exchange*, which is painted as something other than friendship and cooperation. The shift is reminiscent of a juxtaposition in *The Theory of Moral Sentiments*, of the warm society of beneficence to the cold one of merely commutative justice (85–86). Smith is well aware that the world's immense system is one of cooperation allegorically only. His book *The Wealth of Nations* is an annex to *The Theory of Moral Sentiments*, the ethics of which are developed in terms of the great beholder. Meanwhile, Smith's writings on science are ironic about the interpretations we pragmatically adopt to muddle along (Matson 2017).

Smith had profound awareness of the role of allegory and interpretation, and an ironic attitude about foundationalist postures in moral philosophy. David Hume is genius in similar ways. I think also of the liberal statesman Edmund Burke, as well as Alexis de Tocqueville and the great Swedish liberal Erik Gustaf Geijer, quoted below. I see them as *above* such figures as Jean-Baptiste Say, Bastiat, Mill, Herbert Spencer, and Sumner. Hayek is remarkable for overcoming attitudes of his day and leading us back up to higher awareness.

Allegorical communication

In talking of the price system as a system of communication, and prices as a form of communication, or "signals," Hayek (1945, 1976) was highly original (again, check out "price signals" at the Google's Ngram Viewer). He was also boldly allegorical, even if he did not confess it. Hayek's most confessional moment seems to have come in 1933, in his lecture at the London School of Economics, "The Trend of Economic Thinking":

Unfortunately, this oldest and most general result of the theory of social phenomena [viz., the spontaneous coordination of individual efforts] has never been given a title which would secure it an adequate and permanent place in our thinking. The limitations of language make it almost impossible to state it without using misleading metaphorical words. The only intelligible form of explanation for what I am trying to state would be to say—as we say in German—that there is *sense [Sinn]* in the phenomena; that they perform a necessary *function*. (Hayek 1933, 27)

Hayek then notes a danger in allegory:

But as soon as we take such phrases in a literal sense, they become untrue. It is an animistic, anthropomorphic interpretation of phenomena, the main characteristic of which is that they are not willed by any mind. (Hayek 1933, 27)

But then he adds what I consider to be the important point for us at present:

And as soon as we recognize this, we tend to fall into an opposite error, which is, however, very similar in kind: we deny the existence of what these terms are intended to describe. (Hayek 1933, 27, italics added)

If we expel the ghost from the machine, our talk of the machine will be barren. Thus, we must work in a zone between embrace and rejection of allegory. We do that by recognizing allegories to be allegories. We embrace allegories as ways of interpreting the world, but—we hope!—reject them where they would mislead. The best way to manage the fruits and the dangers is to recognize allegory in our thought and discourse.

During the remainder of his career, Hayek wrote only fleetingly of a "social mind" in his own theorizing. It may be that, launching as he did so fully into attacking collectivist thought, he underplayed the allegory behind his own text. James Buchanan is notable for wavering between embracing and rejecting the allegory—mostly rejecting but not always convincingly (see e.g., 1999; 193–196).

Other benefits of confessing allegory

Earlier in this chapter I enumerated six sets of questions about "signals," questions that help us see the benefits of employing allegorical talk of communication and cooperation. Now, also: There are benefits to *confessing* the allegorical nature of such talk. It is good to declare the allegory. By doing so we confess the limits of our understanding, and confess its regions of looseness—for example, in the aesthetic beauty or health of the whole. But if we hide the allegorical nature of our talk, we talk tentatively and confusedly, not really recognizing and admitting what we do, wavering incoherently between rejection and unartful embrace.

By declaring allegory, we tell skeptics that the communication and cooperation are not literal. We must declare allegory to handle their challenges to our talk of communication and cooperation (and more, such as social error and correction). Without allegory those useful and agreeable teachings make no sense. We then appear foolish.

The allegorical being Joy, in her universal benevolence, represents an idea of the social. If we deny allegory, we play into the hands of those who paint us as unattuned to the social. So another benefit of declaring allegory is that it helps ensure that we are attuned to the social, and it makes our tunefulness plain to others.

Many fear allegory and an ethic of universal benevolence because they think they put us on a path to statism. There is something to the fear, but again the best solution is declaring allegory. Cannan makes the being an Inca to make sure that his readers do not start looking around for a benevolent, omniscient, omnipotent being. Making the allegory explicit makes it clear that it is a fiction. There is no being telling Bridget to replace her ovens. And to the extent that moral norms exist within living society, they do not make a social organism. If Joy were a god, she would not have any powers over the individual except perhaps that of conveying her approbation or disapprobation, sensed imperfectly within one's own breast. The more the allegory is spelled out—in particular, as Joy being universally benevolent and having super knowledge and capabilities of direct personal communication—the less it seems to correspond to any external being or institution, *and perhaps least of all to government.* The coercive nature and overwhelming power of government, in fact, makes it especially incapable of candid, intimate communication. The more we make the allegory explicit, the more we make it innocuous.

If we deny allegory, we relinquish it to others, notably those who take it in anti-liberal directions. Liberals should counter anti-liberal allegory, not with denials of allegory, but with liberal allegory.

Indeed, allegory is necessary to the idea of law above government law: A higher law of universal benevolence, an allegorical law upon which to judge government law.

Liberal allegory may not teach us where to look for life's higher things, but it may teach us where *not* to look. That leaves things wide open—the pursuit of happiness is really up to you, and your responsibility—but it at least can guide people away from certain self-deceptive and hypocritical ways of being, ways that make the whole less beautiful.

But perhaps allegory can help to answer, in an enlightened way, the yearning for meaning and connection, "the solidarity of humankind," to paraphrase Sumner and Keller. Liberal allegory might afford spiritual comfort to the individual as she plays her part in the "immense cooperation," in the more impersonal contributions she makes to universal benevolence. In an article titled "An Economic Dream," published in 1847 just two months before his death, Sweden's celebrated poet, composer and historian Erik Gustaf Geijer wrote:

> This *liberty* is tantamount with *disorder,* a thousand voices shout.
> On the contrary, she is a new, self-evolving order; so do others
> comfort themselves, the more industrious, the wiser. That liberty,
> even if she brings disorder for a passing while, follows her own
> rules and develops from within, implanted in her by the Creator,
> her own *law*: that is the full faith of *liberalism* and it leads to salvation…

> What is the *new order of things*? With each day, its *law* evolves more

clearly; its *substance* is already so apparent that one can thereof judge its nature and the spirit of progress. This substance is the *day-by-day, constantly evolving, all-encompassing fellowship and interaction of human powers and needs*. This new, but actually ancient law of labour is that of *intelligence*, which works in expanding circles. From there comes the dependency, from there the interaction in all occupations, equally familiar and acknowledged, and which, to the extent of this increasingly ardent acknowledgement, communicates ever more directly with its own essence and from this new, greater powers emerge, day-by-day and without surcease. Therefore, every seeming defeat is a true victory for it. It needs hardly touch the earth to feel at home and rise again with renewed vigour. (Geijer [1847], 443, 444)

Have we ended up somewhere else?

In *The Theory of Moral Sentiments*, Adam Smith developed a remarkable allegory of a universal impartial spectator who is super knowing and universally benevolent. We never get to the impartial spectator, but, as Haakonssen (1981) puts it, we "search for a common standpoint"—noting that it may be only the search "that is common, not necessarily the standpoint" (58).

After Smith there were a few liberals, like the Swede Geijer, who embraced allegory knowingly. But many liberals foolishly sought to spurn allegory, thus retarding their moral theory. There was little regard for allegory in classical economics and neoclassical economics.

After liberalism turned away from allegory, the world turned away from liberalism. Many liberals fell into emotional depression: Their science anxieties left them crushed. An outlook embracing allegory would have allowed them to remain more cheerful and vibrant—come what may.

Yogi Berra once said: "If you don't know where you are going, you could end up somewhere else."

References

Adler, M. and N. Fagley, N. 2005. Appreciation: Individual Differences in Finding Value and Meaning as a Unique Predictor of Subjective Well-being. *Journal of Personality* 73(1): 79–114.

Alchian, Armen A. 1950. Uncertain, Evolution, and Economic Theory. *Journal of Political Economy* 58: 211–221.

Alden, Joseph. 1886. *The Science of Government*. New York: Sheldon and Company.

Ardal, Pall. 1977. Convention and Value. In David Hume: *Bicentenary Papers*, edited by G.P. Morice, 51–68. Austin: University of Texas Press.

Asher, K. H. 2021. Moderation and the Liberal state: David Hume's History of England. *Journal of Economic Behavior & Organization* 184: 850–859.

Bacon, Francis. 2002 [1605]. *The Advancement of Learning*. In *Francis Bacon: The Major Works*, edited by Brian Vickers. Oxford: Oxford University Press: 120–313.

Baier, Annette C. 1991. *A Progress of Sentiments: Reflections on Hume's Treatise*. Cambridge: Harvard University Press.

Baier, Annette. 1988. Hume's Account of Social Artifice—Its Origins and Its Originality. *Ethics* 98(4): 757–78.

Baier, Annette. 1991. *A Progress of Sentiments: Reflections on Hume's Treatise*. Cambridge: Harvard University Press.

Barrington, Donal. 1954. Edmund Burke as an Economist. *Economica* 21(83): 252–258. Republished in *Econ Journal Watch* 16(1), 2019: 146–154.

Barry, Brian. 2010. David Hume as a Social Theorist. *Utilitas* 22 (4): 369–92.

Bastiat, Frédéric. 1996 [1850]. *Economic Harmonies*. Translated by W. Hayden Boyers. Edited by George B. de Huszar. Irvington-on-Hudson, N.Y.: The Foundation for Economic Education, Inc.,

Bax, Ernest Belfort. 1891. *Outlooks from the New Standpoint*. London: Swan Sonnenschein and Co.

Bentham, Jeremy. 1843. *The Works of Jeremy Bentham, Vol. 1*. Edited by J. Bowring. Edinburgh: William Tait.

Berlin, Isaiah. 1969. *Two Concepts of Liberty*. In Berlin's Four Essays on Liberty. New York: Oxford University Press: 118–72.

Berry, Christopher J. 1982. *Hume, Hegel and Human Nature*. The Hague: Martinus Nijhoff Publishers.

Binmore, Ken. 1998. *Game Theory and the Social Contract: Just Playing*. Cambridge: MIT Press.

Binmore, Ken. 2005. *Natural Justice*. New York: Oxford University Press.

Black's Law Dictionary. 1983. Abridged 5th ed. St. Paul, Minnesota: West Publishing.

Block, Walter. 2008 [1976]. *Defending the Undefendable*. Auburn: Ludwig von Mises Institute.

Boehm, C. 2001. *Hierarchy in the Forest: The Evolution of Egalitarian Behavior* (revised ed.). Cambridge: Harvard University Press.

Boehm, Christopher. 2012. *Moral Origins: The Evolution of Virtue, Altruism, and Shame*. New York: Basic Books.

Bonica, Mark. 2013. *Adam Smith on Liberty and Reputation: Is Reputation Property? Are Defamation Laws Coercive?* Doctoral dissertation, Department of Economics, George Mason University, Fairfax, Virginia.

Boudreaux, D. 2019. Looking Back—With Enormous Gratitude—Over the Past 61 Years. Cafe Hayek, 10 September.

Bourke, Richard. 2015. *Empire and Revolution: The Political Life of Edmund Burke.* Princeton: Princeton University Press.

Brewer, Anthony. 2008. *Adam Smith's Stages of History.* University of Bristol Discussion Papers: University of Bristol, UK.

Brown, Vivienne. 1994. *Adam Smith's Discourse: Canonicity, Commerce and Conscience.* London: Routledge.

Buchanan, James M. 1979. The Justice of Natural Liberty. In *Adam Smith and Modern Political Economy: Bicentennial Essays on The Wealth of Nations.* Edited by G.P. O'Driscoll. Ames: Iowa State University Press: 117–131.

Buchanan, James. 1993. *Property as a Guarantor of Liberty.* Cheltenham: Edward Elgar.

Buchanan, James M. 1999. *The Logical Foundations of Constitutional Liberty.* Indianapolis: Liberty Fund.

Buckle, Stephen. 1991. *Natural Law and the Theory of Property: Grotius to Hume.* Oxford: Clarendon Press.

Burke, Edmund [Anonymously]. 1759. Review of The Theory of Moral Sentiments, by Adam Smith. *Annual Register* 2: 484–489.

Burke, Edmund. 1904 [1777]. Letter to the Sheriffs of Bristol. Edited by J.H. Moffatt. Philadelphia: Hinds, Noble & Eldredge.

Burke, Edmund. 1961. *The Correspondence of Edmund Burke,* Vol. III. Edited by G.H. Guttridge. Chicago: University of Chicago Press.

Burke, Edmund. 1992. *Further Reflections on the Revolution in France.* Edited by D.E. Ritchie. Indianapolis: Liberty Fund.

Burke, Edmund. 1999a [1790]. *Reflections on the Revolution in France.* Edited by E.J. Payne and F. Canavan. Indianapolis: Liberty Fund.

Burke, Edmund. 1999b. *Letters on a Regicide Peace.* Edited by E.J. Payne and F. Canavan. Indianapolis: Liberty Fund.

Burke, Edmund. 1999c. *Miscellaneous Writings.* Edited by F. Canavan. Indianapolis: Liberty Fund.

Burke, Edmund. 2015. *The Writings and Speeches of Edmund Burke, Vol. IV.* Edited by P.J. Marshall and D.C. Bryant. Oxford: Clarendon Press.

Burke, Edmund. 2019 [1800]. Thoughts and Details on Scarcity. *Econ Journal Watch* 16(1): 155–179.

Burke, Kenneth, 1966 [1932]. *Towards a Better Life.* Berkeley: University of California Press.

Burke, William, and Edmund Burke [both anonymously]. 1757. *Account of the European Settlements in America. In Six Parts.* 2 vols. London: R. and J. Dodsley.

Campbell, T.D. 1971. *Adam Smith's Science of Morals.* London: George Allen & Unwin.

Canavan, Francis. 1995. *The Political Economy of Edmund Burke.* New York: Fordham University Press.

Cannan, Edwin. 1902. The Practical Utility of *Economic Science.* Economic Journal 12(48): 459–471.

Capaldi, Nicholas. 1990. The Preservation of Liberty. In *Liberty in Hume's History of England.* Edited by Capaldi and Donald Livingston. Dordrecht: Kluwer: 195–224.

Caplan, B. 2017. The Consumer Gratitude Heuristic. EconLog, 1 May.

Caplan, Bryan. 2007. *The Myth of the Rational Voter: Why Democracies Choose Bad Policies.* Princeton: Princeton University Press.

Caplan, Bryan. 2009a. Joe Sacco's Palestine: Some Unanswered Questions. EconLog, April 4.

Caplan, Bryan. 2009b. EconLog Book Club: For a New Liberty, Chapter 12. EconLog, April 14.

Caplan, Bryan. 2020. Moral Approximates.

EconLog, February 19.

Carmichael, Gershom. 2002 [1724]. *Natural Rights on the Threshold of the Scottish Enlightenment: The Writings of Gershom Carmichael*. Edited by J. Moore and M. Silverthorne. Translated by M. Silverthorne. Indianapolis: Liberty Fund.

Carter-Ruck, Peter F. 1972. *Libel and Slander*. London: Archon Books.

Charron, William C. 1980. Games of Strategy, and Hume's Philosophy of Law and Government. *American Philosophical Quarterly* 17(4): 327–34.

Clark, Michael J. 2010. *The Virtuous Discourse of Adam Smith: The Political Economist's Measured Words on Public Policy*. PhD dissertation, George Mason University Department of Economics.

Clark, Michael J. 2021. Adam Smith as Solon: Accommodating on the Edges of Liberty, Not Abandoning It. *Journal of Economic Behavior and Organization* 184: 739–747.

Clarkson, Thomas. 1808. *The History of the Rise, Progress, & Accomplishment of the Abolition of the African Slave-trade, by the British Parliament, 2 volumes*. London: Longman, Hurst, Rees, and Orme.

Coase, Ronald H. 1960. The Problem of Social Cost. *Journal of Law and Economics* 3:1–44.

Collins, Gregory M. 2017. Edmund Burke on the Question of Commercial Intercourse in the Eighteenth Century. *Review of Politics* 79: 565–595.

Collins, Gregory M. 2019a. Edmund Burke on Slavery and the Slave Trade. *Slavery and Abolition* 40(3): 494–521.

Collins, Gregory M. 2019b. The Limits of Mercantile Administration: Adam Smith and Edmund Burke on Britain's East India Company. *Journal of the History of Economic Thought* 41(3): 369–392.

Collins, Gregory M. 2019c. Burke's Political Economy Reconsidered. *Law & Liberty*. November 21.

Collins, Gregory M. 2020a. The Limits of the Invisible Hand and Doux Commerce:

What Edmund Burke Could Teach Adam Smith and All Classical Liberals about Market Economies. Unpublished ms. presented at George Mason University 8 February 2020.

Collins, Gregory M. 2020b. *Commerce and Manners in Edmund Burke's Political Economy*. New York: Cambridge University Press.

Covey, Stephen R. 2004. *Seven Habits of Highly Effective People: Powerful Lessons in Person Change*. New York: Free Press.

Cowen, Tyler and Alex Tabarrok. 2010. *Modern Principles: Microeconomics*. New York: Worth Publishers.

Cowen, Tyler. 2007. The Importance of Defining the Feasible Set. *Economics and Philosophy* 23(1): 1–14.

Cronk, Lee. 1999. *That Complex Whole: Culture and the Evolution of Human Behavior*. Boulder: Westview Press.

Cropsey, Joseph. 2001. *Polity and Economy: With Further Thoughts on the Principles of Adam Smith*. South Bend, Indiana: St. Augustine's Press.

Davis, David Brion. 1975. *The Problem of Slavery in the Age of Revolution: 1770–1823*. Ithaca: Cornell University Press.

de Waal, Frans. 2009. *The Age of Empathy: Nature's Lessons for a Kinder Society*. New York: Three Rivers Press.

DelliSanti, Dylan. 2018. Innovation, Discovery, and the Tumult of Liberalism: An Esoteric Interpretation of Adam Smith. Unpublished ms., George Mason University.

Diesel, Jonathon. 2020. Two Superiors, Two Jural Relationships in Adam Smith. In *Adam Smith Review*. Routledge: 103–116.

Diesel, Jonathon. 2021. Adam Smith on Usury: An Esoteric reading. *Journal of Economic Behavior & Organization* 184:727–738.

Diesel, Jonathon, and Daniel B. Klein. 2021. A Call to Embrace Jural Dualism. *Economic Affairs* 41(3): 442–457.

Drylie, Scott. 2021. Adam Smith on Schooling: A Classical Liberal Rereading. *Journal of Economic Behavior & Organization* 184: 748–770.

Dunn, William Clyde. 1941. Adam Smith and Edmund Burke: Complementary Contemporaries. *Southern Economic Journal* 7(3): 330–346.

Durkheim, E. 1915. *The Elementary Forms of Religious Life.* Translated by J. Swain. George Allen & Unwin.

Emerson, Roger. L. 2008. The Scottish Contexts for *David Hume's Political-Economic Thinking.* In David Hume's Political Economy, edited by Carl Wennerlind and Margaret Schabas. London: Routledge: 10–30.

Emerson, R.W. 2008. The American Scholar. In *Handbook of Research on Teacher Education.* Routledge: 69–78.

Epstein, Richard A. 2011. Bundle-of-Rights Theory as a Bulwark Against Statist Conceptions of Private Property. *Econ Journal Watch* 8(3): 223–235.

Fleischacker, Samuel. 2004. *On Adam Smith's Wealth of Nations.* Princeton: Princeton University Press.

Forbes, Duncan. 1975. *Hume's Philosophical Politics.* London: Cambridge University Press.

Forman-Barzilai, Fonna. 2010. *Adam Smith and the Circles of Sympathy: Cosmopolitanism and Moral Theory.* Cambridge: Cambridge University Press.

Franklin, Benjamin. 1914. *Poor Richard's Almanack.* Waterloo, Iowa: U.S.C. Publishing Co.

Friedman, David D. 1994. A Positive Account of Property Rights. *Social Philosophy and Policy* 11(2): 1–16.

Friedman, Jeffrey. 2007. A 'Weapon in the Hands of the People': The Rhetorical Presidency in Historical and Conceptual Context. *Critical Review* 19(2): 197–240.

Friedman, Milton, and Rose D. Friedman. 1980. *Free to Choose: A Personal Statement.* New York: Harcourt Brace Jovanovich.

Fuller, Lon. 1969. *The Morality of Law.* New Haven: Yale University Press.

Gauthier, David. 1979. David Hume, Contractarian. *Philosophical Review* 88 (1): 3–38.

Geijer, Erik Gustaf. 2017. *Freedom in Sweden: Selected Works of Erik Gustaf Geijer.* Edited by Björn Hasselgren; translated by P.C. Hogg. Stockholm: Timbro Förlag.

George, Henry. 1886. *Protection or Free Trade.* New York: Robert Schalkenbach Foundation, undated reprint.

Gissurarson, Hannes. 1987. *Hayek's Conservative Liberalism.* New York: Garland.

Goldberg, Jonah. 2018. *Suicide of the West: How the Rebirth of Tribalism, Populism, Nationalism, and Identity Politics Is Destroying American Democracy.* New York: Crown Forum.

Gregg, Samuel. 2009. Metaphysics and Modernity: Natural Law and Natural Rights in Gershom Carmichael and Francis Hutcheson. *Journal of Scottish Philosophy* 7(1): 87–102.

Gregg, Samuel. 2019. Note to Conservatives: Burke Believed in Trade Liberalization. Law and Liberty, August 26.

Greig, J. Y. T. 1932. *The Letters of David Hume.* Oxford: Clarendon Press.

Griswold, Charles L. 1999. *Adam Smith and the Virtues of Enlightenment.* New York: Cambridge University Press.

Griswold, Charles L. 2006. On the Incompleteness of Adam Smith's System. *Adam Smith Review* 2: 181–186.

Grotius, Hugo. 2005 [1877]. *The Rights of War and Peace.* Edited and with an Introduction by Richard Tuck, from the edition by Jean Barbeyrac. Indianapolis: Liberty Fund.

Haakonssen, Knud, 2010. *Natural Law and Personhood: Samuel Pufendorf on Social Explanation.* Max Weber Lecture Series, European University Institute.

Haakonssen, Knud. 1981. *The Science of a Legislator: The Natural Jurisprudence of David Hume and Adam Smith.* Cambridge: Cambridge University Press.

Haakonssen, Knud. 1996. *Natural Law and Moral Philosophy: From Grotius to the Scottish Enlightenment*. Cambridge: Cambridge University Press.

Haakonssen, Knud. 2016. The Lectures on Jurisprudence. In *Adam Smith: His Life, Thought, and Legacy* Edited by R.P. Hanley. Princeton: Princeton University Press: 48–66.

Habermas, Jurgen. 1976. *Legitimation Crisis*. London: Heinemann Educational.

Haidt, Jonathan. 2012. *The Righteous Mind: Why Good People Are Divided by Politics and Religion*. New York: Pantheon.

Hall, Jacob, and Daniel B. Klein. 2020. Jural Pluralism and Jural Integration in David Hume's *History of England*: A Compendium of 142 Quotations. GMU Working Paper in Economics No. 20–36. Available at SSRN.

Hall, Jacob, and Marcus Shera. 2020. Classical Liberals on 'Social Justice.' *Economic Affairs* 40 (3): 467–83.

Hardin, Russell. 1990. Contractarianism-Wistful Thinking. Constitutional Political Economy 1(2): 35-52.

Hardin, Russell. 1999. *Liberalism, Constitutionalism, and Democracy*. New York: Oxford University Press.

Hardin, Russell. 2007. *David Hume: Moral and Political Theorist*. Oxford: Oxford University Press.

Hart, David M. (ed.). 2018. The Place of Liberty in David Hume's Project. Liberty Matters, Liberty Fund, January.

Hart, H. L. A. 2012 [1961]. *The Concept of Law*. 3rd ed. Oxford: Oxford University Press.

Harwood, George. 1882. *The Coming Democracy*. London: Macmillan and Co.

Hayek, Friedrich A. 1955. *Counter-Revolution of Science: Studies in the Abuse of Reason*. New York: Free Press.

Hayek, Friedrich A. 1945. The Use of Knowledge in Society. *American Economic Review* 35(4): 519–530.

Hayek, Friedrich A. 1948. *Individualism and Economic Order*. Chicago: University of Chicago Press.

Hayek, Friedrich A. 1960. *The Constitution of Liberty*. Chicago: University of Chicago Press.

Hayek, Friedrich A. 1967. *Studies in Politics, Philosophy, and Economics*. Chicago: University of Chicago Press.

Hayek, Friedrich A. 1973, 1976, 1979. *Law, Legislation and Liberty* (3 vols.) Chicago: University of Chicago Press.

Hayek, Friedrich A. 1976. *Law, Legislation and Liberty. Volume 2: The Mirage of Social Justice*. Chicago: University of Chicago Press.

Hayek, Friedrich A. 1978 [1974]. The Pretence of Knowledge (Nobel lecture). In Hayek's *New Studies in Philosophy, Politics, Economics and the History of Ideas*. Chicago: University of Chicago Press: 23–34.

Hayek, Friedrich A. 1978. The Atavism of Social Justice. In *New Studies in Philosophy, Politics, Economics and the History of Ideas*, 57–68. Chicago: University of Chicago Press.

Hayek, Friedrich A. 1979. The Three Sources of Human Values. In *Law, Legislation and Liberty: Volume 3, The Political Order of a Free People*. Chicago: University of Chicago Press: 153–176.

Hayek, Friedrich A. 1988. *The Fatal Conceit: The Errors of Socialism*. London: Routledge.

Hayek, Friedrich A. 1991 [1933]. The Trend of Economic Thinking. *Economica* 40: 121–137. Reprinted in *The Trend of Economic Thinking: Essays on Political Economists and Economic History*, edited by W.W. Bartley III and S. Kresge. Chicago: University of Chicago Press: 17–34.

Himmelfarb, Gertrude. 1986. *Marriage and Morals among the Victorians*. New York: Knopf.

Himmelfarb, Gertrude. 2004. *Roads to Modernity: The British, French, and American Enlightenments*. New York: Knopf.

Hirsch, Fred. 1977. *Social Limits to Growth*. London: Routledge & Regan Paul.

Hirsch, Max. 1901. *Democracy versus Socialism*: London: Macmillan.

Hirschman, Albert O. 1977. *The Passions and the Interests: Political Arguments for Capitalism before Its Triumph*. Princeton: Princeton University Press.

Hirschman, Albert O. 1982. Rival Interpretations of Market Society—Civilizing, Destructive or Feeble. *Journal of Economic Literature* 20:1463–84.

Hobhouse, L.T. 1910. Contending Forces. *English Review* VI: 359–71.

Hobhouse, Leonard T. 1994 [1911]. *Liberalism and other Essays*. Cambridge: Cambridge University Press.

Hobson, John Atkinson. 1974 [1909]. *The Crisis of Liberalism*. New York: Harper & Row Publishers.

Hodgskin, Thomas. 1966 [1827]. *Popular Political Economy*. Reprinted: New York: Augustus M. Kelley.

Hoffman, Frank Sargent.1894. *The Sphere of the State*. New York: G. P. Putnam's Sons..

Hohfeld, Wesley Newcomb. 1913. Some Fundamental Legal Conceptions as Applied in Judicial Reasoning. *Yale Law Journal* 23(1): 16–59.

Hohfeld, Wesley Newcomb. 1917. Fundamental Legal Conceptions as Applied in Judicial Reasoning. *Yale Law Journal* 26(8): 710–770.

Hollander, Samuel. 1973. *The Economics of Adam Smith*. Toronto: University of Toronto Press.

Hont, Istvan, and Michael Ignatieff. 1983. Needs and Justice in *The Wealth of Nations: An Introductory Essay*. In *Wealth and Virtue: The Shaping of Political Economy in the Scottish Enlightenment*, edited by Hont and Ignatieff. Cambridge: Cambridge University Press: 1–44.

Huemer, Michael. 2013. *The Problem of Political Authority: An Examination of the Right to Coerce and the Duty to Obey*. London: Palgrave Macmillan.

Huemer, Michael. 2021. *Justice before the Law*. London: Palgrave Macmillan.

Hume, David, 2007a [1739–40]. *A Treatise of Human Nature*. Edited by David F. Norton and Mary J. Norton. Oxford: Clarendon Press.

Hume, David. 2000 [1748]. *An Enquiry Concerning Human Understanding*. Edited by Tom L. Beauchamp. Oxford: Clarendon Press.

Hume, David, 1998 [1751]. *An Enquiry Concerning the Principles of Morals*. Edited by Tom L. Beauchamp. Oxford: Clarendon Press.

Hume, David. 2007b [1757]. *A Dissertation on the Passions*. Edited by Tom L. Beauchamp. Oxford: Oxford University Press.

Hume, David. 1983. *The History of England from the Invasion of Julius Caesar to the Revolution in 1688*. Edited by W.B. Todd. 6 vols. Indianapolis: Liberty Fund.

Hume, David. 1987. *Essays, Moral, Political, Literary*. Edited by Eugene F. Miller. Indianapolis: Liberty Fund.

Huntington, Samuel. 1957. Conservatism as an Ideology. *American Political Science Review* 51(2): 454–473.

Hutcheson, Francis, 2007 [1747]. *A Short Introduction to Moral Philosophy* (Philosophiae Moralis Institutio Compendiaria. Edited by L. Turco. Indianapolis: Liberty Fund.

Hutcheson, Francis. 1755. *A System of Moral Philosophy*. 2 volumes. London: A. Millar.

Hutcheson, Francis. 2008 [1725]. *An Inquiry into the Original of Our Ideas of Beauty and Virtue in Two Treatises*. Edited by Wolfgang Leidhold. Indianapolis: Liberty Fund.

Jasay, Anthony de. 2010. Ordered Anarchy and Contractarianism. *Philosophy* 85(333): 399–403.

Johnson, Samuel. 1798. *Doctor Johnson's Table Talk*. London: C. Dilly.

Kahneman, Daniel. 2011. *Thinking, Fast and Slow*. New York: Farrar, Straus and Giroux.

Kemp Smith, Norman. 2005. *The Philosophy of*

David Hume: A Critical Study of Its Origins and Central Doctrines. 2nd ed. New York: Palgrave Macmillan.

Kennedy, Gavin. 2013. Adam Smith on Religion. In *The Oxford Handbook of Adam Smith*, edited by C. J. Berry, M. P. Paganelli, and C. Smith. Oxford: Oxford University Press: 464–484.

Kirk, Russell. 1960. *The Conservative Mind.* Third ed. Chicago: Regnery.

Kirk, Russell. 1997. *Edmund Burke: A Genius Reconsidered.* Wilmington: Intercollegiate Studies Institute.

Klein, Daniel B. 1997. Convention, Order, and the Two Coordinations. *Constitutional Political Economy* 8: 319–35.

Klein, Daniel B. 2012. *Knowledge and Coordination: A Liberal Interpretation.* New York: Oxford University Press.

Klein, Daniel B. 2016. Adam Smith's Nonfoundationalism. *Society* 53(3): 278–286.

Klein, Daniel B. 2019. Liberalism 1.0. (A PowerPoint file and video presentation as part of a debate with Helen Rosenblatt at Timbro, Stockholm, May 2019).

Klein, Daniel B. 2021. TMS's Appeal Has Moved with Openness to Nonfoundationalism: 35 Critics, 1765–1949. GMU Working Paper in Economics No. 21–19. Online at SSRN.

Klein, Daniel B. 2023. *Smithian Morals.* CL Press.

Klein, Daniel B., and Michael J. Clark. 2010. Direct and Overall Liberty: Areas and Extent of Disagreement. *Reason Papers* 32(Fall): 41–66.

Klein, Daniel B. and Michael J. Clark. 2012. Direct and Overall Liberty: Replies to Walter Block and Claudia Williamson. *Reason Papers* 34(2): 133–143.

Klein, Daniel B. and Stewart Dompe. 2007. Reasons for Supporting the Minimum Wage: Asking Signatories of the 'Raise the Minimum Wage' Statement. *Econ Journal Watch* 4(1): 125–167.

Klein, Daniel B., and Michael J. Clark. 2010. Direct and Overall Liberty: Areas and Extent of Disagreement. *Reason Papers*

32: 41–66.

Klein, Daniel B. 2011. Against Overlordship. *Independent Review* 16(2):165-171.

Kliemt, Hartmut. 2021. Two Concepts of Libertarianism—Buchanan v Jasay. EconLib (blog). July 19, 2021.

Koppl, Roger. 2010. The Social Construction of Expertise. Society 47(3): 220–226.

Kramnick, Isaac. 1977. *The Rage of Edmund Burke: Portrait of an Ambivalent Conservative.* New York: Basic Books.

La Rochefoucauld, François de. 1959. *The Maxims of La Rochefoucauld*, translated by L. Kronenberger. New York: Random House/Modern Library paperback.

Latsis, John. 2009. Hume and the Concept of Convention. In *L'invention Philosophique Humienne* Edited by Philippe Saltel. Grenoble: Université Pierre Mendes France: 217–34.

Lerner, Ralph. 1994. *Revolutions Revisited: Two Faces of the Politics of Enlightenment.* Chapel Hill: University of North Carolina Press.

Levin, Yuval. 2014. *The Great Debate: Edmund Burke, Thomas Paine, and the Birth of Right and Left.* New York: Basic Books.

Levin, Yuval. 2019. Burke and the Nation. Law and Liberty, July 19.

Lewis, David. 1969. *Convention: A Philosophical Study.* Cambridge: Harvard University Press.

Lieberman, Matthew. 2013. *Social: Why Our Brains Are Wired to Connect.* New York: Crown Publishers.

Livingston, Donald W. 1991. Hayek as Humean. *Critical Review* 5(2): 159–77.

Livingston, Donald W. 1998. *Philosophical Melancholy and Delirium: Hume's Pathology of Philosophy.* Chicago: University of Chicago Press.

Livingston, Donald. 1984. *Hume's Philosophy of Common Life.* Chicago: University of Chicago Press.

Livingston, Donald. 1995. On Hume's Conservatism. *Hume Studies* 21(2): 151–164.

Locke, John. [1764]. *Two Treatises of Govern-*

ment, Edited by Thomas Hollis. London: A. Millar et al. http://oll.libertyfund.org/titles/222.

Lucas, Brandon M. 2010. *Adam Smith's Congruence with the Hayekian Narrative:The Influence of Adam Smith: The Invisible Hand, Hayekian Narrative, and Honest Profit*. PhD diss., George Mason University.

Macdonald, James Ramsay. 1900. *The People in Power in Ethical Democracy*. Edited by Stanton Coit. London: Grant Richards: 60–80.

Macfarlane, Alan. 2014. *The Invention of the Modern World*. Les Brouzils: Odd Volumes.

Mackie, J. L. 1980. *Hume's Moral Theory*. London and New York: Routledge.

Macpherson, Hector C. 1899. *Adam Smith*. Edinburgh: Oliphant, Anderson & Ferrier.

Martin, Christopher. 2011. Adam Smith and Liberal Economics: Reading the Minimum Wage Debate of 1795–96. *Econ Journal Watch* 8(2): 110–125.

Martin, Christopher. 2015. Equity, Besides: Adam Smith and the Utility of Poverty. *Journal of the History of Economic Thought* 37(4): 559–81.

Martin, Christopher. 2021. Adam Smith and the Poor: A Textual Analysis. *Journal of Economic Behavior and Organization* 184: 837–49.

Marx, Karl. 1998. Capital. Vol. III. Vol. 37 of *Karl Marx-Frederick Engels Collected Works*. London: Lawrence B. Wishart.

Maslow, Abraham. 1966. *The Psychology of Science*. New York: Harper & Row.

Matson, E. W. 2018. Adam Smith's Humean Attitude towards Science: Illustrated by *The History of Astronomy*. In *Adam Smith Review*. Routledge. 265-280.

Matson, Erik W. 2017a. The Dual Account of Reason and the Spirit of Philosophy in Hume's Treatise. GMU Working Paper in Economics No. 17–49.

Matson, Erik W. 2017b. Hume's Way of Reasonableness in Epistemology, in Politics, and in Political Economy. GMU Working Paper in Economics No. 17–50.

Matson, Erik W. 2019. Reason and Political Economy in Hume. *Erasmus Journal for Philosophy and Economics* 12 (1): 26–51.

Matson, Erik W. 2021. Satisfaction in Action: Hume's Endogenous Theory of Preferences and the Virtues of Commerce. *Journal of Economic Behavior and Organization* 183: 849–60.

Matson, Erik W. A Dialectical Reading of Adam Smith on Wealth and Happiness. *Journal of Economic Behavior & Organization* 184 (2021): 826–836.

Matson, Erik W., and Colin Doran. 2017. The Elevated Imagination: Contemplation and Action in David Hume and Adam Smith. *The Journal of Scottish Philosophy* 15(1): 27–45.

Matson, Erik W., Colin Doran, and Daniel B. Klein. 2019. Hume and Smith on Utility, Agreeable, Propriety, and Moral Approval. *History of European Ideas* 45(5): 675–704.

McAleer, S. 2012. Propositional Gratitude. *American Philosophical Quarterly* 49(1), 55–66.

McBride, Ian. 2012. Burke on Ireland. In *The Cambridge Companion to Edmund Burke*. Edited by D. Dwan and C.J. Insole. Cambridge: Cambridge University Press: 181–194.

McCloskey, Deirdre N. 2006. *Bourgeois Virtues: Ethics for an Age of Commerce*. Chicago: University of Chicago Press.

McCloskey, Deirdre N. 2016. *Bourgeois Equality: How Ideas, Not Capital or Institutions, Enriched the World*. Chicago: University of Chicago Press.

McCloskey, Deirdre N. 2020. Free Will Entails Free Markets. Ms. written for a conference at the University of Virginia.

McGilchrist, Iain. 2009. *The Master and His Emissary: The Divided Brain and the Making of the Western World*. Yale University Press.

McGilchrist, Iain. 2019. How Our Brains Make the World. *AEI Paper & Studies*: 1–10.

Melzer, Arthur M. 2014. *Philosophy Between the Lines: The Lost History of Esoteric Writing.* Princeton: Princeton University Press.

Merrill, Thomas W. 2015. *Hume and the Politics of Enlightenment.* New York: Cambridge University Press.

Merrill, Thomas W. 2018. *Hume's Revolution: Puritanism, Divine Right Monarchy, and the Origins of Liberalism.* Unpub. ms.

Mill, John Stuart. 1909 [1871]. *Principles of Political Economy.* Edited by William James Ashley. London: Longmans, Green and Co.

Miller, David. 1980. Hume and Possessive Individualism. *History of Political Thought* 1(2): 261–78.

Miller, David. 1981. *Philosophy and Ideology in Hume's Political Thought.* Oxford: Clarendon.

Miller, William Galbraith. 1884. *Lectures on the Philosophy of Law.* London: Charles Griffin and Co.

Millican, Peter. 1998. Hume on Reason and Induction: Epistemology or Cognitive Science? *Hume Studies* 24(1): 141–59.

Minowitz, Peter. 1993. *Profits, Priests, and Princes: Adam Smith's Emancipation of Economics from Politics and Religion.* Stanford: Stanford University Press.

Mitchell, Harvey. 1987. 'The Mysterious Veil of Self-Delusion' in Adam Smith's Theory of Moral Sentiments. *Eighteenth Century Studies* 20(4): 405–421.

Mitchell, Wesley Clair. 2013 [1949]. *Lecture Notes on Types of Economic Theory.* Hassell Street Press.

Montaigne, Michel de. 1960. *The Complete Essays of Montaigne.* Edited by D. Frame. Stanford University Press.

Mossner, Ernest. C., and Ian S. Ross (Eds.), 1986. *The Correspondence of Adam Smith.* Indianapolis: Liberty Fund.

Mueller, Paul D. 2021. Adam Smith on Moral Judgment: Why People Tend to Make Better Judgments within Liberal Institutions. *Journal of Economic Behavior and Organization* 184: 813–25.

Munger, Michael C. 2018. Can Libertarianism Be a Governing Philosophy? Law & Liberty, March 1.

Murphy, Robert P. 2010. Coordination: A Critique of Daniel Klein. *Journal of Private Enterprise.* 25(2): 117–27.

Nicholson, J. S. A Plea for Orthodox Political Economy. 1885. *National Review* 6(34): 553–63.

Noell, Edd S., Stephen L. Smith, and Bruce G. Webb. 2013. *Economic Growth: Unleashing the Potential of Human Flourishing.* Washington, D.C.: American Enterprise Institute.

Norton, Rictor. 2014. Burke Proposes Abolition of the Pillory, 1780. *Homosexuality in Eighteenth-Century England: A Sourcebook.*

O'Brien, Conor Cruise. 1992. *The Great Melody: A Thematic Biograph of Edmund Burke.* Chicago: University of Chicago Press.

Orrell, Brent. 2019, January 31. Crossing the STEM Divide. *American Enterprise Institute,* Washington, D.C.

Otteson, James. 2016. Adam Smith and the Right. In *Adam Smith: His Life, Thought, and Legacy.* Edited by R.P. Hanley: 494–511. Princeton: Princeton University Press.

Passmore, John. 1951. *Hume's Intentions.* Third ed. London: Duckworth.

Peltonen, Markku. 2003. *The Duel in Early Modern Europe: Civility, Politeness, and Honour.* Cambridge: Cambridge University Press.

Pennington, Mark. 2011. *Robust Political Economy: Classical Liberalism and the Future of Public Policy.* Cheltenham: Edward Elgar Publishing.

Plumb, J. H. 1967. *The Growth of Political Stability in England, 1675-1725.* London: Macmillan.

Pocock, J. G. A. 1983. Cambridge Paradigms and Scotch Philosophers: A Study of the Relations between the Civic Humanist and the Civil Jurisprudential Interpretation of Eighteenth-century Social Thought. In *Wealth and Virtue: The Shaping of Political Economy in the Scottish Enlightenment*, edited by I. Hont and M. Ignatieff: 235–52. Cambridge: Cambridge University Press.

Pocock, J. G. A. 1985. *Virtue, Commerce, and History: Essays on Political Thought and History, Chiefly in the Eighteenth Century*. Cambridge: Cambridge University Press.

Polanyi, Karl. 1944. *The Great Transformation*. New York: Farrar & Rinehart.

Price, John Valdimir. 1966. Hume's Concept of Liberty and 'The History of England.' *Studies in Romanticism* 5(3): 139–57.

Pufendorf, S. 1931 [1672]. *Two Books of the Elements of Universal Jurisprudence*. Edited by T. Behme and translated by W. A. Oldfather. Indianapolis: Liberty Fund.

Pufendorf, Samuel von. 2003 [1673]. *The Whole Duty of Man According to the Law of Nature*. Edited by Ian Hunter and David Saunders. Translated by Andrew Tooke. Indianapolis: Liberty Fund.

Pufendorf, Samuel. 1729. *Of the Law of Nature and Nations*. Fourth edition. Translated by B. Kennett, with notes of J. Barbeyrac. London: Printed for Walthoe et al.

Pufendorf, Samuel. 2007 [1696]. *The Present State of Germany*. Edited by M. J. Seidler. Translated by E. Bohun. Indianapolis: Liberty Fund.

Pufendorf, Samuel. 2009. *Two Books of the Elements of Universal Jurisprudence*. Translated by W. A. Oldfather, revised and edited by T. Behme. Indianapolis: Liberty Fund.

Rae, John. 1895. *Life of Adam Smith*. London: Macmillan.

Raphael, D .D. 2001. *Concepts of Justice*. Oxford: Oxford University Press.

Reeder, John, ed. 1997. *On Moral Sentiments: Contemporary Responses to Adam Smith*. Bristol: Thoemmes Press.

Ricardo, David. 2004 [1817]. *On the Principles of Political Economy and Taxation*. Edited by Piero Sraffa. Indianapolis: Liberty Fund.

Robinson, John. 2016. *Property and Exclusion: Ownership in the Scottish Enlightenment, Adam Smith, and English Literature*. George Mason University, Economics, PhD dissertation.

Robinson, John. 2017. In-rem Property in Adam Smith's Lectures on Jurisprudence. *Journal of Scottish Philosophy* 15(1): 75–100.

Ross, I. S. 1995. *The Life of Adam Smith*. New York: Oxford University Press.

Ross, Ian Simpson. 2010. *The Life of Adam Smith*. 2nd ed.. Oxford: Oxford University Press.

Rothbard, Murray N. 1998. *The Ethics of Liberty*. New York: New York University Press.

Rothbard, Murray N. 2006 [1978]. *For a New Liberty: The Libertarian Manifesto*. 2nd ed. Alabama: Ludwig von Mises Institute.

Rothschild, Emma. 2001. *Economic Sentiments: Adam Smith, Condorcet, and the Enlightenment*. Cambridg: Harvard University Press.

Rothschild, Emma. 2004. Dignity or Meanness. *Adam Smith Review* 1: 150–62.

Rousseau, Jean-Jacques. 1997. *Rousseau: The Discourses and Other Early Political Writings*. Edited by V. Gourevitch. Cambridge: Cambridge University Press.

Rubin, Paul H. 2002. *Darwinian Politics: The Evolutionary Origins of Freedom*. New Brunswick, NJ: Rutgers University Press.

Rubin, Paul. 2003. Folk Economics. *Southern Journal of Economics* 7(1): 157–171.

Rusk, R., D. Vella-Brodrick, and L. Waters2016. Gratitude or Gratefulness? A Conceptual Review and Proposal for the System of Appreciative Functioning. *Journal of Happiness Studies* 17: 2191–2212.

Sabl, Andrew. 2012. *Hume's Politics: Coor-*

dination and Crisis in Hume's History of England. Princeton: Princeton University Press.

Salter, John. 1994. Adam Smith on Justice and Distribution in Commercial Societies. *Scottish Journal of Political Economy* 41(3): 299–313.

Salter, John. 2012. Hume and Mutual Advantage. *Politics, Philosophy, & Economics* 11(3): 302–21.

Schelling, Thomas C. 1960. *The Strategy of Conflict.* Cambridge,: Harvard University Press.

Schneider, Robert. 2004. Duel. Europe, 1450 to 1789. *Encyclopedia of the Early Modern World.* Encyclopedia.com.

Schotter, Andrew. 1981. *The Economic Theory of Social Institutions.* New York: Cambridge University Press.

Scott, William R. 1900. *Francis Hutcheson: His Life, Teaching and Position in the History of Philosophy.* Cambridge: Cambridge University Press.

Scott, William R. 1923. Adam Smith and the City of Glasgow. *Proceedings of the Royal Philosophical Society of Glasgow* 52: 138–148.

Selby-Bigge, L.A. 1975. Editor's Introduction. In *Enquiries Concerning Human Understanding and Concerning the Principles of Morals,* by David Hume, edited by L.A. Selby-Bigge, 2nd ed. Oxford: Clarendon Press.

Siedentop, Larry. 2014. *Inventing the Individual: The Origins of Western Liberalism.* London: Allen Lane.

Smith, Adam. 1976 [1790]. *The Theory of Moral Sentiments.* Edited by D. Raphael & A. Macfie. Clarendon Press.

Smith, Adam. 1976 [1776]. *An Inquiry into the Nature and Causes of the Wealth of Nations,* edited by R. H. Campbell, A. S. Skinner, and W. B. Todd. Oxford: Oxford University Press. Reprint: Indianapolis: Liberty Fund, 1981.

Smith, Adam. 1976 [1790]. *The Theory of Moral Sentiments,* edited by D. D. Raphael and A. L. Macfie. Oxford: Oxford Uni-

versity Press.

Smith, Adam. 1980. *Essays on Philosophical Subjects.* Edited by W. P. D. Wightman and J. C. Bryce. New York: Oxford University Press. Reprint: Indianapolis: Liberty Fund, 1982.

Smith, Adam. 1982. *Lectures on Jurisprudence.* Edited by R.L. Meek, D. D. Raphael, and P. G. Stein. Oxford: Oxford University Press.

Smith, Adam. 1987. *The Correspondence of Adam Smith.* Edited by E.C. Mossner and I.S. Ross. Oxford: Oxford University Press.

Smith, Charles John. 1871. *Synonyms Discriminated.* London: Bell & Daldy.

Smith, Craig. 2013. Adam Smith: Left or Right? *Political Studies* 61(4): 784–798.

Sober, Elliott, and David Sloan Wilson. 1998. *Unto Others: The Evolution and Psychology of Unselfish Behavior.* Cambridge: Harvard University Press.

Solomon, R. 1977. *The Passions: The Myth and Nature of Human Emotion.* Anchor Press.

Stewart, Dugald. 1854. Dissertation: Exhibiting the Progress of Metaphysical, Ethical, and Political Philosophy, Since the Revival of Letters in Europe. In *The Collected Works of Dugald Stewart,* Vol. 1, edited by William Hamilton. Edinburgh: Thomas Constable and Co.

Stewart, Dugald. 1980 [1793]. Account of the Life and Writings of Adam Smith. Edited by Ian Simpson Ross. In Adam Smith, *Essays on Philosophical Subjects.* Edited by W. P. D. Wightman and J. C. Bryce. New York: Oxford University Press: 269–351.

Stewart, John B. 1992. *Opinion and Reform in Hume's Political Philosophy.* Princeton: Princeton University Press.

Strauss, L., 1952. *Persecution and the Art of Writing.* Chicago: University of Chicago Press.

Sugden, Robert. 2005 [1986]. *The Economics of Rights, Co-Operation, and Welfare.* 2nd ed. New York: Palgrave Macmillan.

Sugden, Robert. 2009. Can a Humean Be a

Contractarian? In *Perspectives in Moral Science: Contributions from Philosophy, Economics, and Politics in Honour of Hartmut Kliemt*. Edited by M. Baurman and B. Lahno. Frankfurt: Frankfurt School Verlag: 11–24.

Sugden, Robert. 2011. Salience, Inductive Reasoning, and the Emergence of Conventions. *Journal of Economic Behavior & Organization* 79: 35–47.

Sugden, Robert. 2013. Contractarianism as a Broad Church. *Rationality, Markets, and Morals* 4:61–66.

Sugden, Robert. 2018. *The Community of Advantage: A Behavioural Economist's Defense of the Market*. Oxford: Oxford University Press.

Sumner, William Graham and Albert G. Keller. 1927. *The Science of Society, Vol. III*. New Haven: Yale University Press.

Sumner, William Graham. 1913. *Earth-Hunger and Other Essays*. Edited by A. G. Keller. New Haven: Yale University Press.

Taylor, Jacqueline A. 2015. *Reflecting Subjects: Passion, Sympathy, and Society in Hume's Philosophy*. New York: Oxford University Press.

Tocqueville, Alexis de. 1955. *The Old Regime and the French Revolution*. Translated by S. Gilbert. New York: Anchor.

Tocqueville, Alexis de. 2000 [1835/1840]. *Democracy in America*. Edited by H. C. Mansfield and D. Winthrop. Chicago: University of Chicago Press.

Tuck, Richard. 1979. *Natural Rights Theories*. Cambridge: Cambridge University Press.

Turco, Luigi. 2007. Introduction. In *A Short Introduction to Moral Philosophy*, by Francis Hutcheson, edited by Luigi Turco. Indianapolis: Liberty Fund: ix–xxii.

Tuschman, Avi. 2013. *Our Political Nature: The Evolutionary Origins of What Divides Us*. Amherst: Prometheus Books.

Vanderschraaf, Peter. 1998. The Informal Game Theory in Hume's Account of Convention. *Economics and Philosophy* 14: 215–47.

Viner, Jacob. 1927. Adam Smith and Laissez-Faire. *Journal of Political Economy* 35(2): 198–232.

Vinogradoff, Paul. 1914. *Common-Sense in Law*. New York: Henry Holt.

Walker, A. 1980. Gratefulness and Gratitude. *Proceedings of the Aristotelian Society* 81: 39–55.

Weinstein, Jack Russell. 2001. *On Adam Smith*. Belmont, Calif.:Wadsworth.

Whately, Richard. 1966 [1832]. *Introductory Lectures on Political Economy*. New York: Augustus M. Kelley.

Whatmore, Richard. 2012. Burke on Political Economy. In *The Cambridge Companion to Edmund Burke*. Edited by D. Dwan and C. J. Insole Cambridge: Cambridge University Press.: 80–91.

Whelan, Frederick G. 1985. *Order and Artifice in Hume's Political Philosophy*. Princeton: Princeton University Press.

Whelan, Frederick G. 1994. Hume and Contractarianism. *Polity* 27(2): 201–24.

Whewell, William. 1845. *Elements of Morality, including Polity*. 2 volumes. New York: Harper & Brothers.

Whewell, William. 1853. *Grotius on the Rights of War and Peace: An Abridged Translation*. Cambridge: Cambridge University Press.

Wicksteed, Philip H. 1967 [1910]. *The Common Sense of Political Economy*. Reprint: New York: Augustus M. Kelley.

Wilson, Bart J. 2020. *The Property Species: Mine, Yours, and the Human Mind*. New York: Oxford University Press.

Wilson, D. 2010. *Darwin's Cathedral: Evolution, Religion, and the Nature of Society*. Chicago: Chicago University Press.

Winch, Donald. 1978. *Adam Smith's Politics: An Essay in Historiographic Revision*. Cambridge: Cambridge University Press.

Winch, Donald. 1992. Adam Smith: Scottish Moral Philosopher as Political Economist. *Historical Journal* 35(1): 91–113.

Winch, Donald. 1996. *Riches and Poverty: An*

Intellectual History of Political Economy in Britain, 1750-1834. Cambridge: University of Cambridge Press.

Winters, Barbara. 1979. Hume on Reason. *Hume Studies* 5(1): 20–35.

Wittman, Donald. 1995. *The Myth of Democratic Failure: Why Political Institutions Are Efficient.* Chicago: University of Chicago Press.

Witztum, Amos. 1997. Distributive Considerations in Smith's Conception of Economic Justice. *Economics and Philosophy* 13(2): 241–259.

Young, Jeffrey T. 2005. Unintended Order and Intervention: Adam Smith's Theory of the Role of the State. In *The Role of Government in the History of Economic Thought,*. Edited by S.G. Medema and P. Boettke. Durham: Duke University Press: 91–119.

Young, Jeffrey T., and Barry Gordon. 1996. Distributive Justice as a Normative Criterion in Adam Smith's Political Economy. *History of Political Economy* 28(1): 1–25.

Zuckert, Michael P. (1994) *Natural Rights and the New Republicanism.* Princeton: Princeton University Press.

Zurbuchen, Simone. 2019. Dignity and Equality in Pufendorf's Natural Law Theory. In *Philosophy, Rights and Natural Law: Essays in Honour of Knud Haakonssen.* Edited by I. Hunter and R. Whatmore. Edinburgh: University of Edinburgh Press: 147–168.

Index

and Burke as representing liberalism, 116; on allegory, 261, 281, 291–92; on experts and governmentalization, 277; on cooperation, 286

hemispheres of the brain, right and left, 253–80; spiral diagram of, 258; sentiments of, 257

higher things, 67, 255, 265, 294

highwayman extorts a promise, 118n5

Himmelfarb, Gertrude, liberal descent, 130

historicity, 19, 21, 33, 63; despite it and by virtue of it liberty is pinned down thanks to jural logic of one's own, 64–65, 67

Hobbes, Thomas, 108; legal positivism of, 46,

Hobhouse, Leonard T., on overlordship, 207

Hobson, John Atkinson, the public as a corporation, 206

Hodgskin, Thomas, 286,

Hoffman, Frank Sargent, natural right a State right, 206

Hohfeld, Wesley N., on jural, 20n5, 191, 197

Hollander, Samuel, on Smith presumption, 44

homosexuality, Burke on, 131

honest income, honest dealings, honest profits, justice of, 217–30; defined, 229; provides focal points, 220–21; when the pursuit of it is unbecoming, 229–30

Hotel USA, 204

human ontology, elusive, 262–64; against infinitesimalizing, 115

Hume, David, see esp. chs. 3, 4, & 5 (51–139); on reputation, 154–55, 175, 177; good on allegory, 291

Huntington, Samuel, on Burke, 130

Hutcheson, Francis, Humean convention forerunner only faintly, 86, 99, 110–11; moral authorizer of honest income, 67; on reputation and simple/intensive esteem, 141, 142n1, 153–55, 159, 166, 173, 177; and "superior," 196; on law as involving precept and sanction, and laid down by superior, 213

impartial spectator, 26; and distributive justice, 165; cool, 180; elusive, 263–64; allegorical, 288, 295. See God/Joy.

imperfect right, 146n3, 153, 154, 166, 184,

182n4

inclusiveness, 232, 238

information, as opposed to knowledge, 273

ingratitude, 234

initiation of coercion, overt the hallmark of a jural superior, 64, 119, 201; and the jural logic of one's own, 119, 175; the precept of commutative justice is against, 216

innovation, finds approval, 67

insidious and crafty animal, 250, 251

instinct from band past, for "the people," 199; for equal portions, 238; for encompassment, 200; for manifest social cues, 278; for centricity, 278; for inclusiveness, 238; for complete circuitry of rights and of duties, and for coincidence of commutative and distributive justice, 228, 240; for finding a person to feel resentful at or grateful to, 240; for static and common interpretation, 183; for jural monism, 79, 200. See circuitry.

intelligence, allegorical, 295

intensive esteem/reputation, 19, 142, 147–51, 154

interest rates, status-quo ceiling on endorsed by Smith, 40, 44, 81n15, 125

interpretation, a facet of knowledge, 30; and right hemisphere, 261; and left hemisphere, 273; busted open by printing press, 265, and are expansive and people disagree so don't governmentalize, please, 188–89

invisible hand, 282, 223, 227, 291

invisible parable, 223

Jasay, Anthony de, on Hume and Sugden, 107n22

Johnson, Samuel, money innocent, 222, 223

Joy (a God-light allegorical benevolent beholder of the whole), communicates to Bridget the baker, 283. See God, allegory.

judgment, a facet of knowledge, 30; an object for estimation, 24, 30

jural dualism, a call to embrace it, 191–210; 65–67; refers to a difference species of object than does jural pluralism, 123

jural integration, 52, 67, 68, 122, 123

jural logic of one's own, 118–121, 21, 64, 175

price signals, 225–27; evocation 227

primogeniture, Burke on, 132

printing, printing press, 241, 265

proffering coolly, 180–81, 185, 189

promises due, part of one's own, 158, 160, 179; promise need not be behind convention, 84, 92

propertization, 61, 193, 199

property, in one's person, ownership extended from natural property, 61, 193. *See* one's own.

propriety, 28, 33, 41, 162, 223, 275,

prudent shipmaster, 224, probably originated with Hume, 282

pulling together, allegorically, 227

quarterback, God/Joy as, for Team Society, 183–84, 287; and Burke, 119

quasi-contract, adapted to political theory, 110–111

rationing, how best to do, 226

reason, contrariety in Hume, 51

recreation, and the good of the whole, 220

regularity, and Lewisian convention, 88–90, 93–95; a would-be regularity other than the one that is convention, 88

religion. *See* God, church establishment.

replication of itself, a left-hemisphere tendency, 267

representative of the impartial spectator, 214

reputation, whether covered by commutative justice, 24, 117n2, 141–69; as part of one's own in the distributive justice sense of one's own, 33; and defamation laws, 169–77. *See* intensive esteem.

resentfulness, 235–241; just resentfulness calls for four things, 237

resentment, counterpart to gratitude, 234–35; and violations of justice, 235; can be virtuous, 235; a disagreeable passion, 236

retaliation, feuding, 236

Ricardo, David, 246,

rights. *See* natural rights, circuitry.

Robertson, William, good in languages, 183

Robinson, John, elaborates exclusion in Hume's idea of property, 60n10

Ross, Ian Simpson, says Smith could repeat the Calvinist Catechism, 147; on Smith

on bounties, 249

Rothbard, Murray, 81; on reputation and commutative justice, 141, 145, 146; as jural monist, 200–202, 209; parses commutative justice/liberty like Smith does, 207

Rothschild, Emma, on Dugald Stewart on Smith, 124n11; on Burke and Smith, 128–29

Rousseau, Jean-Jacques, footnote on distributive justice, 39n15; use of "convention," 111

rule of law, in readings of Hume, 54–55, 66

rules, seven sets of, 212; four nonconflicting sets of, 212; and law, 213

rules for writing, parallel to rules for conduct, 27-28

Rusk, Reuben, on gratefulness, 232

S-i, superior-inferior jural relationship, 20. *See* jural relationships.

Sabl, Andrew, on liberty in Hume, 54, 55, 74n13, 106, 122; on focal-point ideas and convention in Hume, 61, 85n3, 92, 95, 103n18, 106; on barons becoming gentlemen, 66

Sabrina (movie), 224

sacred, the word in TMS, 172–73

sadness, and regret, 257n2

sanction, distinguished from precept, 212–16; disapproval as a sanction, 214

Say, Jean-Bapiste, 291

Schelling, Thomas, focal, 61, 84, 86, 96, 103

science anxieties, and allegophobia, 289

science of a legislator, 113, 249–50

Scott, William R., quoted on polity fabric, 116

secularization, and left-hemisphere running amok, 268

Selden, John, warm regard to liberty, 78

self, the, as an institution, 236

self-interests, narrow are focal, 220; virtues lost in, 221

self-ownership, 57–58, 62, 99, 101n15, 102, 117, 155

self-reproach, 257, 279n10

semantics, carry presumptions, 200

sentimentalism, defined by Sumner, 289

signals, other than price also imperfect, 225;

lousy under governmentalization, 274. *See* correction.

Simba, 273

Simon, Paul, "Mrs. Robinson," 276

simple esteem, 19, 142, 147–51, 154

slander, 141, 148n4, 151, 152, 167–68, 173

slave trade, slavery, Burke on, 131; and simple reputation, 152; Smith called loudly against, 180

small business, hosed by big government, 273

Smith, Adam, set an example, 252

Smith, Charles John, on allegory, 282

Smith, Craig, on Smith's presumption, 45

Smith, Norman Kemp, on Hume, 51

social connectedness, 274

social contract, 39, 60, 98n13, 105–107

social grammar. *See* grammar.

social justice, 217; as an atavism, 232, 239

solidarity, 239, 294

Solon, 48–49

soul, the, 277

Spencer, Herbert, 291

spiral, 30; presentation of divided brain, 257–60, 263, 266

stable polity, 52. *See* jural integration, jural pluralism.

Stalinism, as left-hemisphere tyranny, 271

staples of commutative justice, 143

statesman, everyone was once, 264; insidious and crafty, 250, 251

status quo, presumption of, 82, 124, 202

Stewart, Dugald, 111, 116, 124, 182n4, 245

Stewart, John B., on liberty in Hume, 54

stuff, of commutative justice, 25; of distributive justice, 25. *See* reputation, promises due.

sublime, 261

substratum, to conceive the collectivist configuration of ownership, 52. *See* configuration of ownership.

Sugden, Robert, on convention in Hume, 91; suggests Hume contractarian, 106, 107n22

suicide, 58, 125n12, 132

Sumner, William Graham, as poet, 289–90, 294; science anxieties, 289–291

superior, ontological, 214

superior-inferior jural relationship (abbreviated in ch. 1 as S-i), 20. *See* jural relationships.

suum (one's own), 18n4, 62, 117, 123, 193, 195n2; should not include reputation, 163

sympathy, and right hemisphere, 261, 276

Tabarrok, Alexander, on economic allegorical signals, 281; "immense cooperation," 286

tacit convention, 109–111

take the liberty, 183

taxation, neither theft nor voluntary payment, 193

Team Society, God/Joy as quarterback of, 183, 208, 231, 239, 241

the people's romance, 199

those we live with, 170

Tocqueville, Alexis de, on England, 139; his warning, 192, 241; and McGilchrist's warning of left-hemisphere tyranny, 270, 273; allegorical, 291

total effect, the, 246, 278

Trenchard, John, and "convention," 109

truth, duties to, in Smith, 187

two-worlds hypothesis, 192. *See* atavism.

ungratefulness, 234

uniformity amidst variety, 99

upward vitality, 257; McGilchrist calls *Aufhebung*, 260

usury laws, Smith on, 40, 44, 81n15, 125

Vanderschraaf, Peter, 91

Vella-Brodrick, Dianne, on gratefulness, 232

Viner, Jacob, on Smith's presumption, 44

Vinogradoff, Paul, ownership as *in personam*, 207

virtue is lonely, 162n11

Wakefield, Edward Gibbon, "simple" vs. "complex" cooperation, 290

Walker, A. D. M., on gratefulness 233

warrior, everyone was once, 264

Waters, Lea, on gratefulness, 232

Wentworth, Peter, "harangue" 76; warm regard to liberty, 78

whale of estimative justice, we are within, 46

Whately, Richard, 286

Whelan, Frederick sees mere-liberty in Hume, 53

Searchable PDF of some or all of this book,
with colors in figures, open access, free:
https://clpress.net/

CL Press

A Fraser Institute Project

https://clpress.net/

Professor Daniel Klein (George Mason University, Economics and Mercatus Center) and Dr. Erik Matson (Mercatus Center), directors of the Adam Smith Program at George Mason University, are the editors and directors of CL Press. CL stands at once for classical liberal and conservative liberal.

CL Press is a project of the Fraser Institute (Vancouver, Canada).

People:

Dan Klein and **Erik Matson** are the co-editors and executives of the imprint.

Jane Shaw Stroup is Editorial Advisor, doing especially copy-editing and text preparation.

Zachary Yost is Production Manager of CL Reprints.

Advisory Board:

Craig Smith, *Univ. of Glasgow*
Emily Skarbek, *Brown Univ.*
David Walsh, *Catholic Univ. of America*
Richard Whatmore, *Univ. of St. Andrews*
Barry Weingast, *Stanford Univ.*
Lawrence H. White, *George Mason Univ.*
Amy Willis, *Liberty Fund*
Bart Wilson, *Chapman Univ.*
Todd Zywicki, *George Mason Univ.*

Why start CL Press?

CL Press publishes good, low-priced work in intellectual history, political theory, political economy, and moral philosophy. More specifically, CL Press explores and advance discourse in the following areas:

- The intellectual history and meaning of liberalism.

- The relationship between liberalism and conservatism.

- The role of religion in disseminating liberal understandings and institutions including: humankind's ethical universalism, the moral equality of souls, the rule of law, religious liberty, the meaning and virtues of economic life.

- The relationship between religion and economic philosophy.

- The political, social, and economic philosophy of the Scottish Enlightenment, especially Adam Smith.

- The state of classically liberal ideas and policies across the world today.

www.ingramcontent.com/pod-product-compliance
Lightning Source LLC
Chambersburg PA
CBHW011833020426
42335CB00024B/2842